# Headwinds

A Memoir by
## Edna Bell-Pearson

*Dedicated to
Dianna Booth Byrd*

Meadowlark (an imprint of Chasing Tigers Press)
meadowlark-books.com
PO Box 333, Emporia, KS 66801

This book is a work of non-fiction; it is an accurate account of the events of
four years taken from newspaper articles and a weekly "Flying Column" written
by the author for *The Marysville Advocate* and *The Marshall County
News*. Conversations and details are taken from the author's memories and from
the author's perspective. Some names have been fictionalized, as the author felt
appropriate.

ISBN: 978-1-7322410-6-0

Library of Congress Control Number: 2019904950

# *Headwinds*

## A Memoir by
## Edna Bell-Pearson

**A MEADOWLARK BOOK**

# Chapters

# Introduction

When World War II ended in 1945, hundreds of military-trained pilots returned home and opened flying services. Many of them leased or bought cow pastures, alfalfa fields, meadows, or sand-swept desert flats on which to launch airports adjacent to towns, large and small, throughout the United States.

As hundreds of these flying schools were getting underway, many a citizen, whose previous acquaintance with an airplane was watching it fly overhead, flocked to the newly-established local airport to get a close-up look at the planes and the people who flew them, and the thrill of going for their first airplane ride.

My husband, Carl Ungerer, who had flown B-24s and B-29s during the war, was one of these pilots.

In the sixty-two-month period between July 1940 and August 1945, nearly 300,000 aircraft—mostly military—were produced in the United States. Post World War II there was a rapid growth in civil aviation and manufacturers turned to domestic aircraft.

Never before in history had an industry developed so rapidly; in this, the postwar "Air Age," the United States became the largest aviation manufacturing country in the world. During these years small planes, designed for flight training and private ownership, with innovations never before dreamed of, rolled off the production lines of Cessna, Taylorcraft, Piper, Beech, and others.

The GI Bill of Rights made it possible for veterans to take flight training at government expense. As time passed thousands of them, who had washed out or just missed out on flying during the war, became pilots.

The growth in general aviation also included the training of mechanics and technicians needed to service the aircraft; the development, production, and storage of fuel required for these planes;

and countless other socioeconomic factors which were directly related to this growth.

*Headwinds* is the story of one family's experiences set against those exciting and exuberant early days of the "Air Age."

Edna Bell-Pearson
December 8, 2018

# World War II

World War II was in full swing when I did what I considered my patriotic duty and joined the Kansas Civil Air Patrol. We wore crisp, khaki uniforms and jaunty caps, piped in red, and drilled on the athletic field north of the high school before most folks were out of bed in the morning.

Not one to do things halfway, I enrolled in a private pilot course and started taking flying lessons in a 1939 bright yellow, 65 horsepower, Piper J-3 Cub.

I'd dreamed of flying ever since I saw my first airplane—at the age of six—when one flew over our house in Plains, Kansas, so I paid for the complete course, even though I'd never before been near one of the "contraptions" (Granddaddy's name for the device that had been instrumental in the death of his idol, Will Rogers).

I reported to Bonnie Thompson, proprietor of the grass-topped, two-runway airport southeast of town on a sunny, spring morning in 1944. Bonnie and I walked slowly around the plane as he explained the various features with which I should become acquainted. He then buckled me into my seat, spun the prop, got in, taxied to the end of the runway. And we were off!

My most vivid memory of that early stage in my flying career was struggling to compensate for the relentless southwest wind, which invariably blew me off course, as I resolutely practiced pylon turns and lazy eights, rectangles, spirals, wing-overs and stalls, first with Bonnie, and then solo.

I'd only logged two or three hours solo when I took off one morning into a strong southwest wind, leveled off at 500 feet and found myself, literally, flying backward—at full throttle. Instead of being southwest of the field—the direction I was headed—I was directly over it! I nervously pointed the nose ground-ward and slowly eased back on the throttle. When I leveled off, I was virtually at the same point from which I'd taken off. I was too scared to worry about bounces, but the landing went more smoothly than I expected. Once safely on the ground, I taxied to the hangar, cut the motor and climbed out of the plane, a little more shaken than I cared to admit.

Bonnie was waiting to meet me. He assured me that finding oneself flying backward was not unusual when flying a 65 horse-power, fabric-covered plane into a seventy mile per hour wind. Together, we hangared the plane, and I made an appointment for the following day.

I arrived at the field the next morning, relieved to see the windsock hanging limply on its pole atop the hangar. From then on, everything went smoothly. I practiced faithfully, sharpening my skills as I worked toward accumulating the hours necessary to qualify for a private pilot license.

I was about halfway through the course when the air base came to Liberal, Kansas.

Piper J3 Cub
(Photo by "Armchair Aviator" D. Miller, Flickr - Used per Creative Commons Lic. 2.0)

# The Air Base

Once the war began, most of the young people left town—the boys for one branch of the service or another and the girls for places they could get jobs to help in the war effort. Since I had a good job at Arganbright's Photography Studio—a job I loved—I opted to stay in Liberal. This also allowed me to continue my flying lessons uninterrupted.

After the initial excitement wore off, we drifted into a sort of humdrum routine. There weren't many young people around, but otherwise the war hadn't changed Liberal all that much.

Businessmen took care of their businesses, and farmers raised their crops. With the demand for food to feed the troops being what it was, prices were good, so we were better fixed financially. Having just gone through the Great Depression followed by the "Dirty Thirties," that was a welcome relief.

When folks ran into each other at the post office or at Harry's Coffee Shop, the talk was usually about the war and who had received a letter from this young'un or that. When the boys came home on leave, they'd get together downtown on Saturday afternoon and saunter up and down the street so everybody could see how good they looked in their uniforms.

When we started hearing rumors that the government might build an air base near Liberal, it sounded pretty far-fetched. I ran into George Davis at the post office one morning and asked him what he knew about it. George had been mayor three times and usually knew what was going on.

"No more'n you do, I reckon," he said. "Seems to me that this is a logical location for one though. We sure as hell got room for it."

The implications were so great, folks spent a lot of time mulling that one over. Not many of the townsfolk had even been up in one of Bonnie's Piper J-3 Cubs.

When the newspaper reported that the government actually *was* going to build a base near Liberal, we figured it would probably change things some. Hopefully, it would bring a little more money into the area.

No one dreamed just how much it would change us and our town.

Once the decision was made, the government didn't waste any time. Within weeks, we were standing on the corner of Main and Second Street watching cars, trucks, and construction equipment rumbling in from every direction—all headed for the west edge of town.

What with the magnitude of the prairie surrounding us, we'd always considered ourselves sort of isolated out here. Now it appeared that a broad ocean and a half continent between us and the enemy—both east and west—no longer safeguarded us from the far-reaching tentacles of war.

Construction of the airbase began on January 9, 1943. In the weeks that followed, our lives were virtually turned upside down and inside out. Everything happened so fast we were overwhelmed, but we somehow managed to cope as hundreds of construction workers and their families poured into town.

The wide streets we'd always been so proud of were soon congested with trucks and automobiles. Hotels, motels, and apartments filled up overnight, and folks began renting out spare rooms and converting garages, basements, and attics into sleeping rooms and apartments. When they were full, people began spilling over into nearby towns.

The Office of Price Administration opened a new office to supply ration cards for meat and sugar, gas, and shoes. Everyone who was able-bodied went to work to help fill the needs of this sudden influx of people who demanded, not only food, but clothing, toilet articles, cigarettes, and beer. Everyone seemed in a rush, and wherever lines formed—at restaurants, stores, and theaters—people joked about "waiting to hurry up."

Impatient construction workers, in khakis and jeans, overalls and denim shirts, crowded into restaurants for breakfast each morning before dawn. While they ate, waitresses rushed around, filling their battered lunch pails with sandwiches, pie, and coffee. When the workday ended, they returned for dinner. At night, beer flowed freely in taverns, and music and laughter echoed from smoke-filled "private" dining clubs, so-called to circumvent Kansas's prohibition laws.

Liberal was no longer a struggling, depression-scarred, dust-bowl town. As we watched it grow and expand, we were proud to be a part of it; proud to be doing something besides raise grain to help win the war. As money passed from hand to hand, it was more than most of us had seen in a lifetime.

Meanwhile, west of town, long-legged jackrabbits and wary coyotes loped off across the prairie as their natural habitat was destroyed by monstrous construction equipment. Almost overnight, land that once produced corn and wheat, prairie grass and tumbleweeds was transformed into runways of solid cement.

Then, around it all, they built a high steel fence.

Gigantic steel hangars and row upon row of long, narrow barracks, mess halls, and office buildings appeared as if by magic on the once-barren landscape. Five months after construction began, crews and equipment moved on and hundreds of young soldiers, some children only yesterday, arrived to take charge and assume the roles necessary to take care of the needs of the expected student pilots.

On June 20, the huge, hulking B-24 Liberators[1] began arriving, and on July 1, the first class was introduced to the bomber.

Overnight, it seemed, young soldiers poured in to fill the roles of pilots and co-pilots, navigators, tail-gunners, bombardiers, maintenance crew, and operating personnel. Each training cycle covered a period of nine weeks. A new class began halfway through the cycle, so that a class graduated every four and a half months.

In the coming months, the skies over the Great Plains roared and groaned and shrieked as the four-engine instruments of peace and destruction thundered in to lay claim to the concrete manifestation.

As the Air Force song echoed from taverns and barracks and from automobiles congesting the streets, "Off we go into the wild blue yonder" became more familiar to us than "Home, home on the range."

The war, which had been a distant two-headed monster we read about in newspapers and letters from loved ones just months ago, had come to Liberal, bringing with it the regimentation, the excitement, the insidious fear—and the prosperity it engendered.

As we became accustomed to bombers rumbling overhead, echoing across the prairie, we learned to determine by sound if it was one or three or a squadron. We also learned the difference between the thrumming sound of the B-17 and the lumbering sound of the B-24—the Liberator—and, later, the roar of the B-29 which would ultimately bear the instrument of destruction and free our country from war. With the passing of time, we lost interest in rushing outside, our eyes upward, gazing in awe at their presence.

We no longer had time to stand around at the post office, or on street corners, exchanging small talk about "how the war was going." We knew first hand because we were a part of it. It monopolized our thoughts and our dreams. All our activities—everything we did—was planned around "The War."

---

[1] The B-24 Liberator, a four-engine heavy bomber designed by Consolidated Aircraft of San Diego, California, was used extensively in World War II. It served in every branch of the American armed forces, as well as several Allied air forces and navies in every theater of operations. Over 19,000 units were manufactured, over 8,000 by Ford Motor Company in the "Long Hangar" a Willow Run, Michigan assembly plant. The world's largest building, it turned out a plane every 55 minutes. The B-24 holds records as the world's most produced bomber, heavy bomber, multi engine aircraft, and American military aircraft in history.

World War II B-24 Liberator Bomber
(US Air Force archived photograph, Public Domain)

# War Days

Southwest Kansas was just recovering from the Dust Bowl days and business was slow when I asked Mr. Arganbright, photographer and proprietor of Arganbright Studio, for a job. I didn't expect him to hire me, but surprisingly, he did. This was the best job I'd had since graduating from high school.

At first, our three or four sittings a week hardly met the bills. It was certainly not enough to warrant—or support—an apprentice; it kept him hustling to find enough to keep me busy. I wondered why he'd hired me, but I vacuumed, dusted, and polished until everything in the studio shone. As time passed, Mr. Arganbright taught me how to keep the books, how to take portraits; develop, print and retouch film, and how to tint and mount the finished pictures in brown and gray cardboard folders.

Not having many customers, we took photos of each other and worked with them. I learned quickly and, with plenty of time to practice, plus a great deal of patience on Mr. Arganbright's part, got pretty good at my job.

"You learn fast, kid," he said, patting me on the back. "You're going to make a great photographer."

After the air base came to town, Mr. Arganbright's benevolence began to pay off. Business boomed. In the past year, I'd received three salary increases and had been awarded the title of "Assistant Photographer."

It was one of those hot, windy, mid-summer afternoons that plains people dread, but have learned to endure, when I left the studio, after lunch, for a photo shoot southwest of town. Tossed by a twenty-five mile an hour wind, the weather-worn "Arganbright Studio" sign shrieked with a rhythmic screech of metal on metal as I loaded the camera and equipment into the car.

Though such weather is not unusual in July, even those born and raised in Southwest Kansas had never really become accustomed to temperatures in excess of one-hundred degrees for days on end, relentless southwest winds, blowing sand, parched throats, burning eyes, chaffed skin, and a perpetual, unquenchable thirst.

In the early days, the region was called The Great American Desert, but folks didn't like to think about that.

Pulling out onto Main Street, I drove south out of town, then turned west on the unpaved road bordering the southern boundary of the air base—the road which, on a more pleasant day, would be lined with carloads of townspeople watching the B-24s take off and land.

Driving as fast as the narrow, rutted road allowed, I kept my eyes glued to the road, jerking the steering wheel to the right, then to the left, to avoid the potholes. Clouds of sand, churned up by the car, obscured the road behind while dancing dust devils tossed tumbleweeds into the grill. Billowing dust rolled through the open windows, clogging my nostrils, powdering my hair, coating my skin and teeth with a fine layer of grit.

Photographing a family reunion on such a hot afternoon wasn't an assignment to look forward to, but the job had to be done, so I had volunteered.

Twenty minutes from town, just past a battered, galvanized mailbox bearing the name Larson, I pulled into a driveway.

The rooms were small and overflowing with people. I despaired. How could I possibly pose thirty people for a family portrait in this small space?

"We *must* find a way," said Grandma Larson. "All our children were born and raised in this house and today is our Golden Wedding Anniversary."

Faces were shining with perspiration; hair and clothing were damp and disheveled. However, spirits remained high, the seemingly impossible was accomplished and, eventually, the family portrait was safe on film.

As I loaded the equipment back into the car, perspiration dripped from my forehead stinging my eyes, leaving a salty taste on my lips. My hair clung to my neck, and my underclothing felt as though it was fused to my body.

As I drove back to town, the sun, a white, luminescent orb, hung low in the dust-laden, western sky. The wind had lost some of its fury, but a brisk breeze blew through my damp clothing, cooling my body.

Now after five, stores and shops had closed for the day, and Main Street was deserted except for a few parked cars. The street gutters were cluttered with trash and debris, and waves of golden sand drifted across the sidewalks.

The only sign of life was a man running, head down into the wind, to his automobile.

I turned off Main and parked in the alley. Everyone had left for the day. The workroom, which had been bustling with activity when I left, seemed eerily silent.

I decided to wait until morning to process the film. If I came in at four, I could be finished before the studio opened at eight.

Right now, I needed an ice-cold drink, followed by a light supper, a cool bath, and bed—in that order.

Although portraits such as those I had taken today had once been a photographer's mainstay, the major portion of our business now came from the young airmen stationed at the air base. We could expect a surge in business every four and a half weeks when, at the end of a training period, fledgling bomber pilots received promotions in rank. To record this significant occasion, they came to have portraits made to mail home to wives, sweethearts, and mothers.

As they posed—stiffly and self-consciously, so the camera would capture the highly polished wings and the bars newly-pinned to their uniforms—I always felt a little sad. Soon they would leave for duty overseas, a new detail of bright young faces would appear, and the cycle would be repeated.

I had a recurring dream of young flyers in tropical tans, undulating in the wind like waves of golden wheat.

When I reached the street door, Mr. Arganbright, who ate early to avoid the crowds, was just entering, the ever-present pipe drooping from the corner of his mouth, eye glasses smudged, hair disheveled.

He looked tired.

"Hi, kid!" he said. "How did it go out at the Larson's?"

"Hot, as you can imagine, but I got some great shots. I'm sure we'll get a big order out of it."

He grinned broadly and patted my shoulder.

"I don't know what I'd do without you, kid," he said.

"You just wouldn't make so much money," I teased.

He shoved me playfully toward the door.

"Go on—get yourself some dinner before they run out of meat," he said.

"How's the food today?"

Wartime shortages and a population triple what it was before the construction of the air base strained the resources of the town's restaurants and cafes. The Grill, three doors north, was the best café in town. However, with the shortage of many food items, inconsistencies in quality, and a dearth of qualified employees, meals were not always as good as they might be.

"Not bad," he replied. "So-so."

"I need a cold drink more than I need food," I said, stalling for time.

If I knew Mr. A, he would head for the darkroom as soon as I walked out the door, and work until midnight developing film.

What he should do was rest.

"Judging by that stack of plates in the darkroom, you had a pretty busy day too," I said.

"Sixteen sittings!" he said proudly.

"If you'll wait until morning, I'll help process the film. I'm coming in around four to do mine anyway."

"That would be great, kid!" he said, brightening up.

We seldom found time to work together now. I knew he enjoyed the camaraderie. It eased his loneliness. His son and daughter had moved to the West Coast after his wife died, and he seldom heard from them, unless they wanted money—which he always wired post-haste, no questions asked, glad to be needed.

I'd always suspected that it was his need for companionship that had prompted him to hire me.

"I'll just run a few prints so they can be drying overnight then hit the hay," he said, waving me out.

When I opened the door, a strong blast of wind, now from the southeast, almost blew me off my feet. As I ran toward The Grill, it plastered my skirt to my bottom, propelling me forward, and sharp particles of sand from miniature whirlwinds stung at my ankles.

My cousin, Marie, running toward the studio, head bent into the wind, was almost even before she saw me.

"Hi!" she exclaimed, grappling with her billowing skirt and nego-tiating a prancing skip to right herself in the wind as she changed directions. "I was just coming to see what you planned to do about dinner."

"I'm on my way to The Grill. Come on; let's get out of this wind."

"Thank God, we beat the dinner crowd," I said, once we were inside.

We headed for our favorite booth.

"Ah, just what I need," I said as the hostess set tall glasses of ice water before us.

"So. It was a rough day?" Marie said.

"Exhausting! And hot. After I eat, I'm going home, take a nice cool bath and go to bed."

"Heck, I was hoping we'd go dancing."

"Not tonight, Ree. I promised Mr. A I'd be at the studio at four. The film in that darkroom is stacked this high." I indicated a point several inches above my head.

"You're working too hard, and too many hours," she complained.

A flurry of activity drew our attention to the front of the restaurant. Diners were crowding into the café; seating space was filling rapidly. Two lines had formed—the first businessmen, farmers, and laborers; the second commissioned and non-commissioned Air Corps personnel.

For some, the wait would be long.

"A lot of them will have to settle for the vegetable plate tonight," Marie observed.

"I wonder who the VIPs are?" I said, nodding toward two airmen standing to one side, appraising the waiting lines.

Dressed in formal tropical tans, the pilot's wings and first lieutenant bars polished to a sheen, they stood out, even from other Air Corps personnel.

Both were tall and strikingly handsome—one lean and rangy with dark hair and eyes; the other, a bit heavier, more athletic in build, the color of his blond hair blending with that of his uniform.

"I've seen the dark guy somewhere," Marie mused. "Oh, I remember—he was at The Tavern Saturday night with Betty Jarvis. His name is Ted—Somebody. I've never seen the other one though; he's sure good looking, isn't he?"

My eyes on the handsome blond airman, I didn't reply.

At that moment, Ted "Somebody" spied Marie. After a short conference, he and his companion eased toward our booth.

"Oh, God—they're coming over! I look terrible! I'm leaving!" I exclaimed.

"Sit still. You look fine," Marie ordered, then smiled up at the handsome airman who had paused at her side.

"Hi, again!" Ted said.

"Hi!" Marie replied. "You two are awfully dressed up for such a hot afternoon. What are you celebrating?"

"My birthday. Mind if we join you?"

"Not at all," Marie smiled flirtatiously, moving over.

Avoiding his eyes, I made room for his friend.

*Darn, I would have to meet this guy when I'm sweaty and smelly and look my worst,* I thought.

"I'm Ted Holmes and this is Carl Ungerer," Ted said. "Carl, this is Marie Roth and—"

Now smiling into a pair of teasing blue eyes, I wasn't listening.

"Sorry, I've got to get some sleep," I said when they suggested we go to the officer's club. "It's been a rough day and I have to be at the studio at 4:00 AM."

After several minutes of coaxing, I finally gave in. "You can come down to the house for a couple of drinks, but I *am* going to get eight hours sleep tonight.

I didn't get eight hours sleep. I got five.

After I bathed and dressed, we had a few drinks and sat around and talked until almost midnight. I got to know Carl Ungerer pretty well. Surprisingly, I didn't feel as dead on my feet the next morning as I thought I would.

A little diversion is good for the soul, I told myself and promptly resolved to take more time off.

Carl Ungerer

# After Training

The airbase was the biggest thing our lackadaisical prairie town had ever seen. Whereas conversations once consisted of discussions about the weather, wheat crops, and how the coyotes were playing havoc with the livestock, they now included "airplane talk" and news about the war. All any of us knew about the B-24 Liberator was that it was doing a wonderful job in this war in which we were involved.

Carl was only one of approximately seven thousand members of the United States Air Corps stationed at the Liberal Air Base. When we met he was into week three of his nine-week training period. Knowing that our time together would be short, we began seeing each other on a regular basis, spending every minute together that our schedules allowed.

Between late nights out and long workdays, the next few weeks were a veritable whirlwind, and my hours flying with Bonnie dropped off drastically.

I'm sure my work at the studio suffered as well, but Mr. Arganbright didn't complain. On the contrary, he seemed to enjoy hearing about my new social life.

Marie and Ted were also dating. As a foursome, we attended parties, dances at the officers' club, went on picnics, and participated in Carl's favorite outdoor recreations—fishing and hunting.

In the same class, Carl and Ted would complete their training the last of October. Men and planes were badly needed in combat areas, so there was no doubt they would be assigned to overseas duty.

I dreaded to see him go. I'd grown quite fond of my tall, handsome airman. We'd had a lot of fun together.

When the day for orders to be issued arrived, I left the studio early to make dinner for the boys one last time.

After straightening up the house, I took a bath and dressed, then started preparing the chicken we'd been lucky to buy from a farmer on our last hunting trip.

I was feeling depressed when Carl arrived, a little before five. He looked awfully cheerful, I thought, for a man about to head overseas for combat duty.

"I looked for you down at the studio," he said. "I left Ted at Marie's office." He sauntered into the kitchen, mixed two drinks, handed me one and raised his glass. "To the future," he toasted.

"Oh?" I said in the way he always teased me about.

He set his drink down on the counter and took a sheet of paper from his shirt pocket.

"See this?"

I nodded. His orders. I couldn't speak.

"Want to know what it says?"

Without waiting for me to reply, he continued.

"It says here—*ahem*—that Carl Ungerer is hereby assigned to permanent duty at the Liberal, Kansas Air Base as B-24 Flight Instructor!"

He looked up and laughed. It must have been the expression on my face because he leaned over and kissed me.

"Ted, too!" he said.

I put the chicken back in the refrigerator, changed into my best dress, and we went down town to meet Ted and Marie for a real celebration.

Carl decided that as long as he was going to be in Liberal for a while, he should have an airplane of his own. The government was auctioning single engine, war-surplus planes; he thought he could pick one up for around a thousand dollars. He and Ted flew to Wichita to look over the planes being offered. He placed a bid and, in less than a month, was the proud owner of a silver, blue, and red Taylorcraft.

The day after he and Ted flew to Wichita to bring the plane back to Liberal, he made another important announcement: As long as he was going to be around for a while, he and I might as well get married!

It wasn't exactly the kind of proposal I'd hoped for, but my acceptance was a foregone conclusion. I'd known for some time that Carl Ungerer never did things in a conventional manner, so when I said "all right" that was good enough as far as he was concerned.

To celebrate our engagement, Carl took me for a ride in his new airplane.

"It's a 1942 Army liaison plane," he explained. "It's called an L-2."

A Taylorcraft DC065, it boasted a 65 horsepower Continental engine, was stick controlled, two-passenger, tandem seating, and was built for service—not comfort. The cockpit was enclosed by a Plexiglas bubble.

Thus enclosed, it was well air-conditioned from cracks where the windows and doors didn't quite fit, and it was as noisy on the inside as it was on the out. One could see in all directions, and—although the view was somewhat distorted by waves in the Plexiglas, that had obviously not been a problem for the navigator, who rode in the back seat and faced the rear during reconnaissance—his equipment was laid out on the built-in table before him. The space beneath the table was used to store supplies.

In civilian life, the seat faced forward, and the table made a handy place to deposit purses, cushions, and maps. Unless traveling some distance, the baggage compartment remained unoccupied.

Unlike many of the current models at that time, the pilot could fly solo from the front seat without throwing the airplane out of balance, a distinct advantage for the simple reason that, from the front seat, it was easier to see where you were going.

Accompanied by Marie and Ted, we drove to Garden City one clear, crisp January day, and Carl and I exchanged vows before a Justice of the Peace.

Newlyweds Edna and Carl Ungerer

# The Old Man

"Well," Carl announced a few days later, "guess I'd better call The Old Man and bring him up to date on all the news."

His father was jubilant about his new assignment and, when told that he'd purchased a plane responded, "Good thinking."

"Best news of all, Dad—I got married!"

This announcement was met with silence.

"Hello? Dad? Did you hear what I said? I'm married!"

Standing close by, I heard a croaking sound on the line.

"You *what?*" the voice choked.

"Got married, Dad."

He later told me that his father's marriage to Carl's mother had ended unpleasantly and, though he was now happily married to a woman about Carl's age, he had told all three of his boys that, if he had it to do over, he would never marry.

"Live with them if you want, but don't get hitched up," was his salty advice.

He'd considered his advice well-taken when Carl reached the age of twenty-eight without "getting hooked by some designing female."

"Listen, Son," he said now in a calm, reassuring voice. "If you're in trouble, we'll get you out of it. I'll send you money to buy her off. There's ways these things can be handled. If necessary, I'll come out there—"

"No, Dad—wait a minute! You don't understand. I *want* to be married. She's a wonderful girl."

Another silence.

"Dad?"

"You're sure?" his father asked.

"Yes, Dad, I'm sure."

"She's not knocked up, is she?"

"No, Dad. Not yet anyway. I'd like to wait till I get out of this war before starting a family."

"Okay, Son. Let me know if there's anything I can do to help." Carl's father didn't hide his skepticism.

"If you'd really like to help," Carl said, ending the conversation, "you can pay for this phone call. It's going to cost a fortune."

"Sure, Son."

"I'm going to bring her up to meet you as soon as I can get away, Dad—you'll love her."

Carl's next step was to apply for a leave.

What could be more fitting, he reasoned, than to fly his new bride, in his new airplane, home to Marysville—in northeast Kansas—and show them off simultaneously to family and friends?

Needless to say, I didn't share Carl's enthusiasm. After hearing his father's reaction to our marriage, I looked forward to meeting him with apprehension.

What if he didn't like me?

"We got the leave!" he shouted a few evenings later, racing into the house.

"When?"

"Week from Friday. Four days—that'll give us a day to fly there, two days to visit, and a day to fly back. Now all we have to do is pray for good weather."

He nervously monitored the weather bureau. If adverse weather conditions prevented our flying, heaven only knew when he could get another leave.

On Wednesday afternoon, he called.

"Good news!" he said. "First, the weather is going to be perfect and, second, I think I can get away from the base about three tomorrow. If we leave then and stop midway for the night, we'll get there by noon Friday and have more time at home. Can you be ready?"

"Sure. I'll pack tonight."

"Good! See you pretty soon, sweet."

At four o'clock Thursday afternoon, we were off. The L-2 climbed smoothly into a bright, clear sky and, as we flew east, the late afternoon sun cast an iridescent glow on the silver wings. The air was smooth and a light west wind, blowing across the plains, rippling the green wheat fields below, provided a welcome tailwind.

Carl climbed to three thousand feet and leveled off while I settled back in the rear seat and watched patterned fields slip by beneath the wings.

The sun was setting when we touched down on a grassy runway at a small airport in central Kansas.

"Well, we're halfway there," Carl said lifting me out of the plane.

I stretched my stiff limbs and watched while he helped the airport operator, who introduced himself as Mike, tie the plane down for the night.

"Wait until I close up here, and I'll give you a lift into town," Mike said.

A few minutes later, we crowded into the front seat of an ancient jalopy. Mike let us off at the door of a small hotel.

"You can get a good meal up the street there," he said, pointing to a café halfway up the block. "It ain't very fancy, but the food is pretty tasty."

"Thanks," Carl said, reaching for the bags.

"I'll pick you up about seven in the morning," Mike said before he drove off.

We registered at the hotel, then walked up the street to the restaurant. It felt good to stretch our limbs. As Mike had said, the food was tasty.

Back in our room, Carl watched with amusement as I washed and carefully rolled my hair and manicured my nails, last minute chores I hadn't got to because of the earlier than expected departure.

"You're going to a lot of trouble for plain, ordinary folks," he teased.

"They're *your folks*," I retorted, "and I want to look nice when I meet them. I'm almost scared to meet your dad anyway. I *do* want him to like me."

"He's gonna love you to death—just like I do."

"Silly," I said. "Nevertheless, I want to look my best."

We woke at sunrise and hurried to dress and be on our way.

"Darn!" I said. "My hair isn't dry. Well—I guess I can leave the curlers in and comb it out before we get there."

I tied a scarf around my head, deciding to wait until we were airborne to apply my make-up as well. I wanted to look my best for that all-important meeting with my in-laws.

"A perfect day for flying," Carl exclaimed as we walked out into the fresh morning air. The grass was moist with dew and a slight breeze rustled the trees.

"We'll have a tailwind again today," he said as we ate breakfast. "If we take off by seven-thirty, we should be there by around ten o'clock."

Mike picked us up promptly at seven.

"Put my makeup case on the table so I can reach it," I cautioned as Carl stowed the bags in the plane.

We took off at seven-thirty. It was a beautiful morning. The plane sailed smoothly through the air and I felt a mounting excitement as I surveyed the rapidly changing landscape below. The rolling green hills and tree-lined streams were immensely different from the expanse of square fields and the wide prairie of southwest Kansas.

I leaned forward, raising my voice so Carl could hear me above the roaring engine.

"I had no idea there was any place in Kansas like this!"

He turned slightly.

"Just wait until you see Marysville—you'll love it!"

Two hours into the flight, I reached for my cosmetic case and was just balancing it on my knees then Carl tapped me on the arm and pointed ahead. Beyond the whirling propeller, surrounded by green fields, was a beautiful, tree-studded town.

"That's Marysville!" he announced proudly above the roar of the engine. "We'll be landing in a few minutes."

"But it isn't time yet!" I said frantically. "I don't even have my hair combed!"

"We had a strong tailwind," he shouted.

I fumbled with the catch on my cosmetic case.

"Don't bother with that, hon," Carl said. "We'll land in a few minutes and you can fix up when we get to the house."

"But I want to look nice when I meet your folks," I wailed. "Can't we fly around—just long enough for me to put on my makeup and comb my hair?"

"You look fine," he said, reaching back and patting my knee.

I looked at him helplessly.

"You're beautiful just as you are," he consoled. Then the clincher: "Besides, The Old Man likes his women to look natural."

Although not totally convinced, I did as he suggested, put my cosmetic case back on the shelf and peered out the windows, first left, then right, the better to see the town that would be my future home.

There were trees, green gardens, and colorful flowers everywhere.

Carl pointed out Main Street and the court house. As we flew over, people on the streets stopped to look up. Others emerged from doorways to look and wave. Carl responded by dipping the wings of the plane from side to side as we flew on beyond the town.

He flew a short distance east of town and pointed to a square of pasture land.

"That's my Uncle George's pasture," he said as he eased back on the throttle and glided down so that we were barely skimming the ground.

"It'll do!" he announced, pushing the throttle forward. Climbing sharply into the air, we headed back toward town, flying just over the tops of the trees.

At the edge of town, he pointed to a two-story frame house surrounded by trees and flowering bushes.

"There it is!" he said proudly. "That's home! Now we'll buzz The Old Man and tell him where to pick us up."

Flying low over the house, he eased the throttle forward, then back, then forward again.

"We'll make another pass!" he shouted. Pushing the throttle full forward, he made a sharp, climbing turn then glided down to fly low over the house again.

As we passed over, I did a double-take. In the backyard, a broad grin on his face, stood a middle-aged man, dressed only in a suit of baggy, white flannel underwear, waving both arms wildly.

Carl opened the window and cut the throttle. The only sound was the wind whistling through the wing struts.

"George's pasture!" he shouted.

The man nodded his head and waved his arms again. As Carl shoved forward on the throttle, I couldn't resist a backward glance at the baggy white drawers disappearing into the house.

Carl landed the plane smoothly and taxied toward the road, skillfully dodging rocks and prairie dog holes. I saw a car drive up.

"They certainly got here fast," I said.

By the time he'd turned the plane into the wind and cut the motor, two more cars had arrived.

"Looks like we've got a welcoming committee," he said, indicating others speeding toward us in a cloud of dust.

"Not the way I look!" I wailed.

By the time we were out of the plane, cars lined both sides of the road and more were approaching from both directions.

"Looks like you're a celebrity, Honey," Carl said.

As people swarmed into the pasture, he began shaking hands. I forced back tears of frustration and managed to smile and nod as he introduced me to friends and relatives, all the while wishing I could crawl into one of those prairie dog holes. This was one of the most important events of my life, and I had never before appeared in public looking so unsightly!

I seethed, inwardly wishing I hadn't listened to Carl.

Blissfully unaware of how I felt, he was having the time of his life.

To make matters even worse, a photographer and a reporter arrived insisting we pose for pictures one of which was later published in *The Marshall County News* over the caption:

THE FIRST BRIDE EVER BROUGHT TO HER
NEW HOME IN MARYSVILLE IN AN AIRPLANE!
(Local Air Corps Lieutenant Flies Here With Bride In Own Plane)

It was a masterpiece. There wasn't a shadow or a blur. It captured every wrinkle in my pant suit; each curler came out in sharp detail, and my bare face shown rosily. My embarrassment was obvious.

The reporter, a very attractive girl about my age, was interviewing Carl when his father arrived.

He had donned overalls and a blue denim shirt. A battered felt hat, cocked forward over his eyes, revealed shocks of unruly grey hair sprouting from the crown of his head. He chomped furiously on a well-used cigar as he shook hands with Carl then, tears streaming down his cheeks, he turned and folded the newspaper girl in his arms!

Carl set him right, and I received a very wet, affectionate kiss. The smile felt frozen on my face as Dad, his arms around both of us, chomped on his cigar and wept.

I was next introduced to Dad's wife, Lillian, an attractive slender, blond woman.

When, at last, everyone began drifting toward their cars, Carl tied down the plane and retrieved our bags, and we led a procession back to town. When we arrived, other people were crowding into the house.

I'm afraid I made a very poor first impression. I felt dazed, unable to believe that I, looking as tacky as I did, was actually attending a party held in my honor. What must they be thinking? I could think of only one thing—getting away to make myself presentable.

It seemed hours before I could ask Lillian to show me to our bedroom so I could freshen up. Once there, I dropped onto the bed and sat very still for a long time, listening to the buzz of voices beyond the wall.

Finally, I roused myself. Moving slowly, deliberately, I applied my makeup, combed my hair and changed into a dress. Then I sat down again on the edge of the bed. Although I had regained my composure somewhat, I still felt overwhelmed. I wished I could just sit there and rest. However, after a critical appraisal of myself in the mirror, I took a deep breath and opened the door.

The odor of home-cooked food permeated the air and the house literally swarmed with people. Gathered in groups, everyone seemed to be talking at once. Other than an occasional smile and a nod, no one seemed to notice me as I worked my way through the crowded room. In the dining room, a sideboard was laden with bottles of every kind of spirit imaginable.

I discovered Carl in the living room surrounded by a group of men. He didn't see me when I paused at the door, so I followed the sounds and the odor of food to the kitchen where the chatter of women's voices intermingled with the clatter of pots and pans.

It was as crowded as the rest of the house. Women maneuvered around each other, stirring things, dishing up food. A plump-faced, white-haired lady looked up from the turkey she was basting and smiled at me. Someone was frosting a cake and others were tossing salads, dishing up vegetables, rolls, pickles, and jams. They rushed back and forth from kitchen to dining room, carrying containers of food, arranging platters on a long table and a buffet already laden with fruit salads, pies, cakes, cookies, and preserves.

Lillian rushed by on her way to the dining room with a dish of food.

"What can I do to help?" I asked.

"Well—hello there!" she said. "Not a thing, Honey. You just relax and enjoy yourself. Dinner's almost ready."

A blond-haired lady was dishing up bowls of food.

"Here," I said. "Let me help."

"No—I've got it," she said cheerfully.

I watched for a while, feeling more out of place than I'd ever felt in my life. Occasionally, someone looked up and smiled or patted me on the shoulder as they hurried back and forth, shaking their head if I made a move to help.

I was moving constantly to keep out of the way, so I left the kitchen and went back toward the living room. My head was beginning to ache.

I had decided to slip back into the bedroom and lie down for a bit when Carl's dad looked up and saw me.

He stopped talking, mid-sentence, and came and put his arm around me. Without speaking, weaving in and out among the bustling women, he led me to the kitchen, opened the refrigerator and took out a Coke.

"Don't you mind all this," he said in a conspiratorial whisper as he opened the bottle. "Everybody's just having a good time. You'll get used to it—you'll see."

He poured a third of the Coke down the drain, led the way back to the dining room and filled the bottle with whiskey.

"Drink this," he ordered. "You'll feel better in no time."

He put his arm around me again and we stood in the door to the living room watching the men, laughing and joking. Carl looked up and winked.

Dad was right. I felt much better. The spiked soda helped, but knowing that Dad was going to be my friend helped most. Among all these people, he alone had understood my dilemma.

"Dinner's ready!" Lillian announced.

Carl came to where we were standing and patted Dad on the shoulder. Then he took my other arm and the three of us led the way to the table.

THE FIRST BRIDE EVER BROUGHT TO HER NEW HOME

IN MARYSVILLE IN AN AIRPLANE!

Local Air Corps Lieutenant Flies Here With Bride In Own Plane

# The B-29

Now that Carl was an instructor, we had nothing to worry about. He would, likely as not, sit out the war in Liberal. Or so we thought until, nine months later, our bubble burst.

I was making dinner when he arrived home from the base. His kiss was the same, as was his smile, but I sensed immediately that something was different.

I turned my back on the stove.

"What is it?" I said.

He turned away.

"We're being transferred—to train for overseas duty."

I felt the blood drain from my face. My heart started pounding so hard I was sure he could hear it across the room. The old fears returned.

"They're bringing combat pilots back to the states to do our job, and those of us who haven't served overseas will check out in the B-29 for our share of combat duty. We'll get our crews and training at Barksdale Air Force Base—just out of Shreveport, Louisiana."

"When?" I asked.

"Immediately," he replied. "When the Air Corps says 'go,' you go. We have only a week to report to Barksdale."

"What about me?" I asked. This was something we had never discussed, and I was afraid of what he would say.

"Well, I just naturally thought you'd go with me—as long as they'll let you," he replied.

I breathed a sigh of relief. My heart stopped pounding. Then, thinking about his being in combat, I felt a lump of lead form in my chest.

"We have only a few days to pack up and close up the house," he said. "I'll take the L-2 to Marysville—store it in Dad's garage. Since that's where we'll eventually go to live, we might as well store the furniture there too."

I hated to leave Mr. Arganbright, but he agreed I should go.

I'd flown a few more hours with Bonnie in the past months but was still only half way through the private pilot course.

Carl, accustomed to moving from base to base, helped me decide what to pack for Barksdale and what we would store at his dad's.

To say that the next three days were hectic was putting it mildly. Carl rented a trailer to haul our furniture and household items. I would drive the car, pulling the trailer, and he would fly the plane to Marysville.

Thursday morning, the sun was just peeping over the horizon when we drove to the airport. After Carl took off, I watched the silver plane until it faded into a mere dot then disappeared into the wild blue yonder.

Feeling lonely, and apprehensive about the future, I got into the car, skirted the business district, and headed north on Highway 83. Towing a trailer, which jerked and swayed from side to side on the rough road, I kept the speedometer hovering at forty mph. Forty-five minutes later, I turned east on Highway 56, a better road, and increased my speed to fifty

As I drove, fearful of what lay ahead, my thoughts were chaotic.

The sun was just setting when I drove into Marysville. Carl was in the process of dismantling the wings of the L-2, which he had landed in a tiny pasture north of Dad's house. The next day he and a cousin completed the job, stacked the wings against the walls of his dad's garage, and jockeyed the fuselage to make it fit.

"Well, that's that," he sighed as he carefully closed the door. "That's where she'll stay until the war is over."

By bedtime, the trailer was unloaded, and our household goods and personal belongings were stored in an upstairs bedroom. Except for our overnight bags, everything we were taking with us was in the car.

We left at sunup the next morning.

Lillian had risen early and cooked breakfast, and Dad had pulled on a pair of overalls over his long underwear which, it seemed, he wore year 'round.

As we drove away, I turned and waved. The sight of Dad standing there, with tears in his eyes, chomping on the big, black cigar, reminded me of the first time we'd met.

Carl drove hard, and as fast as he could, over roads that weren't always conducive to speeding. We spent the night in a roadside motel in a small town in Arkansas and arrived at Barksdale Air Force Base shortly after noon on Sunday.

I waited in the car while Carl checked in. Although he had parked in the shade of a tree, the air was hot and steamy. When he returned, twenty minutes later, the back and the underarms of my shirt were wet with sweat.

"It's hot as hell here," he said, tossing a sheet of paper into my lap.

"That's a list of available lodging," he said. "Let's go to the officers' club and have a drink. We'll look over the list and make a few calls from there."

The coolness of the spacious club room was heavenly. Wide windows looked out on a patio and a huge swimming pool, crowded with swimmers.

"I'd like to join them," I sighed.

"We'd better try to find a place to stay first," Carl replied. "Hotel rooms are hard to come by, and I have to report in the morning; it'll save you a lot of trouble if we find something today."

He spent almost an hour on the phone. At last, he found an opening.

We might as well look at it," he said. "It's only a sleeping room but it has kitchen privileges. "We'll eat out most of the time anyway."

The room was small, but clean and neat; the kitchen was large and well-equipped, and included a washing machine. At the back of the house was a patio and a garden filled with flowers and shrubs. Mrs. Garner, the landlady, a large, good-natured woman, said that she spent most of her days at her job in Alexandra so we would pretty much have the house to ourselves. An added benefit was a shed we could use for storage.

Carl paid the first week's rent and we spent the rest of the afternoon unloading the car. By the time we'd taken a bath and dressed, it was dark.

"Let's go back to the base and eat at the officers' club," Carl said. "Maybe we'll meet a few people. Since this is where we're going to be living for the next few weeks, we'll drive around after dinner to check the place out."

He reported for duty the next morning. During the week, he was briefed and assigned a crew and an airplane. Thus began an intensive training period; mastering the B-29 Superfortress—a more complex plane than the B-24—and studying combat techniques, preparatory to overseas duty.

**World War II B-29 Superfortress Bomber**
(US Air Force archived photograph, Public Domain)

# B-29 Training

The B-29 crew consisted of eleven men—the pilot (Carl), copilot, bombardier, navigator, flight engineer, radio operator, radar operator, central fire control gunner, left side gunner, right side gunner, and tail gunner.

The men—all intent on crowding as much pleasure as possible into the short period of time they had left before heading into combat—were hard working, hard drinking, and hard playing.

The next few weeks, Carl spent long days in the air becoming acquainted with the plane and with his crew, as well as attending ground school and training sessions.

Bored, I whiled away the hours searching for something to do.

I spent most of my time at the officers' club, visiting with other wives. When Carl wasn't on duty, we got together with other crew members, and their wives and girlfriends. We ate out in the evening—at the officers' club and various restaurants in Shreveport. We also attended parties and dances at the officer's club. On days off we went sightseeing, and Carl and I, his crew, their girlfriends and wives, often went fishing at a nearby lake.

We learned, early-on, that the B-29 had some unexpected flaws. One of these turned out to be a tendency to catch fire.

Late one afternoon Carol, Carl's copilot's wife, and I were sunning at the pool at the officers' club. I was thinking we should probably be getting dressed. The men would be coming in from a flight soon.

I stood and was gathering up my towel, bag, and book when Carol shrieked.

"Oh, my gosh, Edna, look!" she was pointing toward a B-29 flying low over the club, the left outboard engine engulfed in flames!

As the plane disappeared beyond the trees, I jumped to my feet.

We raced to the dressing room and quickly donned our clothes, ears alert for a word or a phrase which might yield a bit of information about the burning plane. Who was flying it? Had it landed safely? No news had yet reached the club. Everyone was apprehensive. We all had someone on duty.

"Tim said it's nothing unusual—that they catch fire all the time," one of the girls remarked. "He said he's had two catch fire on him; but I don't think either were as bad as that one."

Once we were dressed, we went to the lounge and waited nervously for our husbands. The time passed slowly; they were past due. Other pilots and officers began joining their wives and there was still no news of the burning plane. Only speculation.

"We'd have heard by now if it crashed," Carol reasoned.

I was so nervous, I couldn't sit still so I stood and was about to circle the room for the second time when Carl and Carol's husband, Mike, appeared in the doorway to the lounge.

"Sorry. We had a little fire," Carl said as though it happened every day.

"I know. We saw."

He squeezed my hand and grinned in that special way of his, and we all went in to dinner.

Nothing more was said about the incident.

But to me, it was one more thing regarding this war to worry about.

Carl's Combat Crew

# Little Boy and Fat Man

C arl and his crew were scheduled to leave for overseas duty on Tuesday, August 14—less than a week away. My depression deepened with each day as the time approached.

I hadn't yet decided how I would spend my time in his absence. He presumed I would stay with his dad in Marysville; however, I was skeptical. I hardly knew them. Not only that, I would have nothing to do there but twiddle my thumbs, wait, and worry. On the other hand, if I returned to Liberal, Mr. Arganbright would welcome me with open arms. I would be in familiar surroundings and have a job to keep me busy while Carl was away.

Mrs. Garner, the landlady, was away, as usual. I was alone wandering about the house and yard, moping. To give myself something to do, I decided to start sorting our clothing and packing.

An hour later everything was neatly laid out on the bed; my clothing neatly stacked on one side. Carl's on the other. And the hollow place was there again in the pit of my stomach. More than the loneliness was the fear. The fire had been a reminder of the many dangers he would face in combat duty.

I turned on the radio. The news—discussing the uranium atomic bomb which had been dropped on Hiroshima the day before—only added to my depression, intensifying my fears.

For the next few days, "Little Boy" was the leading story in the news. It was mind-boggling to try to comprehend the extent of the destruction.

Then, on Thursday, August 9, came the report that a second bomb, a plutonium bomb dubbed "Fat Man" had been dropped on the city of Nagasaki.

The next day all flights were suspended!

Carl arrived home from the base early and turned on the radio; the airwaves were filled with speculation and news reports predicting the end of the war.

As flights continued to be suspended, we waited, nervously, to learn our destiny.

Then, on Wednesday, August 15, Emperor Hirohito announced the acceptance of the terms of the Potsdam Declaration and Japan's surrender to the Allies. On September 2, the instrument of surrender, ending World War II, was signed.

Carl and I were stretched out on the bed in our room, hands clasped, listening to the radio when we heard the loud honking of a car.

It was Carol and Mike.

"Come on!" Mike called. "We're going into town to celebrate!"

From blocks away we could hear the clanging and clamoring, the blaring of horns, the popping of firecrackers, and people shouting and singing. Crowds thronged the streets, stalling cars, so that occupants simply got out and left the vehicles where they sat. The noise was deafening.

Mike pulled into an alleyway where he had spotted an empty space, parked, and we walked to downtown Shreveport joining the thousands who were dancing in streets so crowded we could hardly work our way through. Everyone was hugging each other, kissing strangers, and shouting "The war is over! The war is over!"

The celebration lasted all night.

"What will happen now?" I asked, as Carl dressed to go to the base the next morning. "Will you still have to go overseas?"

"We'll have to wait and see," he replied.

As I waited for him to return, I marveled at the sudden calm. All the planes had been grounded, training classes cancelled, all activity ceased, awaiting orders. With no B-29s flying over the house, the silence was deafening.

"Nothing definite," Carl said when he returned. "The rumor is that we'll be sent to the West Coast and receive our orders there.

I sighed. "That's so far away."

"Not as far as Germany—or Japan," he said. "Look at it this way, Hon—at least, I won't have to be fighting a war."

Another week passed, then all pilots and crew members were told that they could stay in the Air Corps or, if preferred, muster out immediately.

I breathed a sigh of relief when Carl chose to leave.

# Mustering Out

Carl and those members of his crew who chose to leave the service were transferred to Savannah, Georgia for separation. Once there, we registered in a motel and spent our time waiting for government wheels to grind. The men reported to the base each morning for briefing, to fill out forms, and to be given physicals. During off time, we explored the city and the surrounding area and pursued Carl's favorite hobbies—hunting and fishing. I discovered that hunting ducks among the reeds along the shore of the Atlantic Ocean was radically different than hunting them on farm ponds on the prairie.

Then one morning, he reported in, as usual, and discharge papers were issued. The waiting was over. We were going home!

Two days later, we were driving north by northwest, heading home to Marysville.

The events of the past few weeks, the unexpected transition from war to peace so abruptly reversed the course of our lives, that we, like everyone else, were somewhat intoxicated by our new-found freedom.

With the threat of war no longer hanging over our heads, the future looked so bright that everyone was temporarily blinded by its brilliance and slightly mad with excitement. The transition had happened so rapidly we found it difficult to believe that we were really free—free of the dark clouds of war, the fears, the feeling that something out there was slowly propelling us toward a terrifying goal.

We drove at a leisurely pace and stopped often. We had plenty of time now. No more hurry. No more waiting expectantly for orders: "Report to base at 0600!"

I found myself looking at Carl appraisingly at times. What would it be like to live with him as a civilian? Out of uniform, he seemed different. I sometimes felt as though I didn't know this person at all. How would he change? Would I still love him? Of course I would! Still, a tiny question crept into my mind; had I fallen in love with the soldier? Or the man?

But at night, as I lay in his arms, I began to feel a contentment I hadn't known before. Long after Carl was asleep, I lay staring into the darkness thinking of us, of the past, and what the future might bring. I thought about the beginning of the war, and of the series of events that had brought us to this time and place. My life had changed so much since then—

As we drove over the bumpy road north from Savannah, up through Atlanta, Nashville, St. Louis, Kansas City, and on to Marysville, we excitedly discussed plans for the future, unable to believe that we actually had a future! The possibilities seemed unlimited.

"You know," Carl said thoughtfully, as he manipulated the heavily loaded car over the bumpy highway, swerving occasionally to miss a deep rut in the road. "Now would be a good time to go into business—especially the flying business."

As he talked, I grew more excited at what he proposed—at the possibilities.

"They say that we are on the cusp of the 'Air Age,'" he said. "The whole world is waiting to see what's going to happen next.

"Thousands of men learned to fly in the service. That means more airports to fly from will be needed, more airplanes to fly, and service and fuel for the planes.

"Take Marysville, for example. There's no airport there, and I've been thinking we might start one—make it a family business. I'm a trained pilot. We already have a plane. And my brother, Jim, with his mechanical training in the Air Force, could handle that end of it. There'll be a lot of men, exposed to flying in the service, who'll want to learn to fly—and we can teach them. All we'll have to do is lease a piece of pasture ground long enough for a runway, and we'll be in business!

"We'll start with the L-2, but there'll be a lot of mighty fine planes manufactured now that the war is over," he continued. "What with the tremendous technological developments made in the industry during the war, the new post-war planes with innovations we can't even imagine—a fantastic improvement over what small plane pilots are accustomed to flying—will be rolling off the production lines by the thousands."

Before we reached Kansas City, he had it all planned out.

Jim hit the home front about the same time we did. After discussing it at length over many a cup of coffee or bottle of beer, we figured we had the ideal set-up, our assets as follows:

- Carl had a multi-engine pilot rating (gratis Air Force), a war surplus L-2 Taylorcraft, 1,000 dollars, and lots of ambition.
- Jim had a mechanics rating (also gratis Air Force), 1,000 dollars, and lots of ambition.
- I had thirty-five hours toward a private pilot's license, 1,000 dollars, and lots of ambition.

It was decided since I, as yet, had no applicable talent, I could be the general flunky—keeping the books and that sort of thing—while continuing to work toward my private pilot license.

"That doesn't sound like much," I said.

"Don't worry; we'll find something for you to do," Carl said.

(If I'd only known!)

"Since Marysville has never had an airport, we'll have to build from the ground up," he said.

We all gave that some thought.

Carl Ungerer, Manager of Ungerer Flying Service

# Getting Started

Two days later, Carl and Jim had the L-2 re-assembled. They rolled it out to Dad's cow pasture, which would have easily fit into one of the ramps at the B-24 base back in Liberal. It would be impossible to fly out under ordinary conditions, so we waited—and we waited—for a wind strong enough, out of a northerly direction, to fly it out.

Then one morning we awoke to the sound of the wind whistling around the corners of the house. Carl leaped out of bed and looked out the window. The fruit trees in the orchard were bending rigorously to the south. A north wind. Just what we needed.

"Hey Jim! This is it!" he yelled out the door, then hustled into his clothes.

"Aren't you going to have breakfast first?" Lillian asked as they got into their coats.

"Later!" Carl called out over his shoulder as they rushed out the door.

By the time I dressed and got to the pasture, Carl was in the plane and Jim was spinning the prop.

Carl waved to me and yelled: "See you at George's pasture!"

Then he turned into the wind, pushed the throttle full forward, and released the brake. I held my breath as the plane sailed along for a short distance then leaped into the air, scaling the barbed wire fence by inches.

As Carl disappeared over the trees, Jim pulled up the stakes and threw them in the back of the car. I jumped in beside him. When we arrived at Uncle George's pasture the L-2 was circling, waiting until we arrived to land. In a wind this strong, Carl would need our help to keep the plane from flipping over while he tied it down.

Thirty minutes later, the plane was secured, the cockpit protected from the weather by the canvas cover Lillian and I had sewed from an old war-surplus tent.

"If the weather's decent tomorrow, we'll fly over the area and see if we can find a better landing strip, closer to town," Carl said that night as we sat around the table, well supplied with Dad's homemade wine and beer. "We can fly off George's pasture as long as we need to, but it's too far out and too rough for business."

"We got a letter from Frederick today," Lillian said during a lull in the conversation.

"What did he have to say?" Carl asked. "When is he coming home?"

Frederick, two years younger than Carl, had spent his tour of duty with the Army Ordinance Department. We'd all been wondering when he'd be getting out.

"Looks like any time now," Dad said. "Said he's anxious to get home."

The next morning, a slight breeze blew out of the northwest. I drove with Carl and Jim to George's pasture and watched as they readied the plane for take-off.

"We'll do an air surveillance of the land close to town, then fly up to Beatrice and fill up with gas." Carl said as he got into the plane. "We'll be out awhile so you might as well go home. We'll buzz the house when we're ready to come in."

Two hours later, they were back. When I arrived at the pasture, they were tying down the plane. Their beaming faces told me they'd found what they were looking for.

"It's an alfalfa field a half mile long and fifty yards wide just east of the poor farm[2]," Carl said. "My guess is that it's part of the farm itself. We made a trial landing; couldn't ask for a better landing strip."

Two days later, we signed a lease to the field. That afternoon Carl moved the L-2 in from Uncle George's pasture.

"We're in business!" he exclaimed when they came home for lunch. He threw two one-dollar bills on the table. "I took our first customer for a ride!"

The following Sunday, our "airport" was buzzing with curious onlookers. Not many small-town people had been up in an airplane back then, and we spent the entire day giving rides. At day's end, my pockets were bulging with bills.

"We've got a long way to go, but that's a start," Carl said. "Let's run an ad in this week's newspaper."

The next day, I placed an ad in *The Marshall County News*:

| | |
|---|---|
| *Flying instruction* | *$8 per hour.* |
| *Charter Trips* | *10 cents per mile.* |
| *Rides* | *$1.50.* |

The ad ran on Thursday, and on Sunday an even larger crowd showed up. The day was clear and warm for November. A slight breeze blew out of the northeast. We spent the entire day at the airport, answering questions and giving rides. Carl signed up two students: George, a young fellow from Kansas City, who worked for a local manufacturing company, and H. B. "Bus" Vincent, owner of Vincent Motor Company.

They both took to flying like a fish to water. A week later, we signed up two more students.

The next thing was to check me out in the L-2. Carl flew a couple hours of dual with me, after which I resumed practicing maneuvers in preparation for the private pilot check.

As GIs arrived home from the service, we began to get questions as to whether or not they would be allowed to take flying lessons on the new GI Bill Of Rights.[3] We contacted the Veteran's Administration and applied for a contract to train GIs.

Everything was looking up for Ungerer Flying Service!

We stayed with the folks until the house Dad had bought for us was available.

I like a lot of space but the rooms in the two-story, two-bedroom house were so large that the few items of furniture we'd brought from Liberal—a bed, a dresser, table and chairs, and a divan—left wide empty spaces throughout the house. With most of our money to be invested in the new business, we had little to spend on decorating. However, Carl's folks contributed kitchen appliances and an overstuffed chair and by gradually adding a few items picked up at auction sales, our first real home was soon quite comfortable.

Since we had only the one plane, and Ungerer Flying Service wouldn't yet support us all, Jim took a job with a local implement dealer while Carl and I spent our time at the "airport," waiting for business to pick up. Though slow, we were encouraged by the interest.

A wizard at saving costs in everything from building a house to preparing a vegetable stew, Dad discovered an unused barn which, he said, was "a steal." He proposed to buy it for us, help tear it down and rebuild as a hangar.

"Hell!" he said. "The lumber is good; it'll last for the next fifty years."

Since hangar space would be needed—for the L-2 as well as other planes soon to be added to our fleet—how could we turn down a bargain like that?

Weather permitting, Dad and Carl began dismantling the barn. That done, they began construction on the hangar. Jim pitched in when he wasn't at work.

From the first, I spent my days at the airport, living up to my job as "flunky," fetching tools, nails, drinks, and snacks for the men as they worked on the hangar, in addition to keeping the books.

We soon learned that a short flight over town usually brought visitors to our air strip and anytime a prospective passenger showed up, Carl left off his nailing and hammering to take them for a ride over the countryside.

[2] Poor Farms were county or town run residences where elderly and disabled people were supported at public expense. The farms declined in use after the Social Security Act took effect in 1935, with most disappearing around 1950.

[3] GI Bill Of Rights (The Serviceman's Readjustment Act of 1944, provided a range of benefits for returning World War II veterans. It was designed by the American Legion, who helped push it through Congress by mobilizing its chapters (along with the Veterans Of Foreign Wars); the goal was to provide immediate rewards for World War II veterans. The GI Bill included payment for flight training.

Edna in front of house.

# Hunting Season

Being another passion of Carl's, we went hunting as often as we could get away—even if for only an hour or two. My only previous hunting experiences had been riding along with Carl and Ted when they were stationed at Liberal, but Carl insisted I go along.

And so I learned to hunt.

First, I had to be correctly outfitted. Finding the right hunting boot was a problem. My size wasn't available locally, so we ordered them.

After I'd been equipped with the necessary licenses and proper guns—we hunted dove, rabbits, squirrels, quail, pheasants, and ducks. As time passed, I learned to shoot fairly accurately, except when it came to quail, which I was never very good at; by the time I got over the shock of one flying up from beneath my feet with a wh-r-r-r-r of wings, he was gone. Since pheasants and ducks were not so fast, I learned to bag these after some practice.

A hunter's biggest asset is a good hunting dog. Carl had taken care of this—we thought. He ordered Lady, a Springer Spaniel, and Dobber, an American Water Spaniel from a breeder back east.

I am a dog lover; I fell in love with them immediately. Lady was shaggy—liver and white—and Dobber was covered with liver colored curls.

As hunting dogs, however, they didn't turn out as expected. At the first sound of gunfire, Lady hid under the bed, or under the car, whichever was most convenient, while Dobber bounced around aimlessly, barking furiously at the sky. Carl soon learned that no amount of training would make either a hunting dog. So, although I had two good pets, we hunted without dogs.

Then, one morning, a shaggy coal-black spaniel trotted up our street, turned into the driveway, and made himself at home. Carl named him Blackie and when, a couple of weeks later, no one had claimed him, decided to try out his hunting skills.

Blackie, who from his appearance, should have had no aptitude whatsoever for the sport, proved to be a fantastic hunting dog. He and Carl became inseparable.

On his first trip to the airport, Blackie decided he liked it there. So, in addition to number one hunting companion, he also became the airport mascot.

I discovered on the first day of duck hunting season that flyers had a distinct advantage over other hunters when it came to bagging ducks.

After low clouds and a heavy mist set in, Carl returned from a dual flight early one morning, sent the student on his way, and rushed into the office.

"There's a big flock of Mallard ducks on Shoney's pond," he said. "While Jim and I wind up here, call Dad and tell him to get ready, then go home and get our guns."

Twenty minutes later, Dad, Jim, Carl, and I were speeding down a country road heading to Shoney's pond.

As we drove, Carl outlined his plan.

"They're lined up along the dam out of the wind," he said. "We'll circle around and come in from the north, then spread out atop the dam. The wind'll be with us so we'll have to make a quiet approach."

After parking, we spread out ten feet apart. As we crept slowly toward the dam on our bellies, frozen clods of plowed earth jabbed sharply at my knees and arms. When we reached the dam, Carl signaled and we all stood, guns at ready. A volley of shots rang out and what must have been a hundred ducks rose, in a body, from the pond. As the shots echoed through the cold air, I froze, awestruck, ducks falling all about me. In minutes, it was over. I hadn't fired a shot!

With Blackie's help, we retrieved our bounty and drove back to town. Leaving the ducks for Dad and Lillian to clean, Carl, Jim, and I returned to the airport.

I questioned Carl about the legality of what we had done.

"I don't know why it would be illegal," he said. "It isn't as if we were shooting them from the air."

A few days later, on a particularly muggy morning, Carl said:

"Why don't you take the L-2 and check a few ponds while I'm finishing up here?"

Skimming over the brown countryside in a deep autumn haze, the roar of the plane's engine drumming in my ears, the world seemed surreal.

Finally, I saw what I was searching for—a flock of Mallard ducks huddling at the sheltered end of a small pond. Not wanting to startle them into flight, I did a 180 and headed back to the airport.

We picked up Dad, and he, Jim, Carl, and I headed for the pond. We harvested five ducks. I bagged my first. We spent the remainder of the morning cleaning the ducks and preparing them for freezing, and the afternoon catching up on chores at the airport.

Throughout the duck season, the first plane out each morning checked the duck ponds within a ten-mile radius of the airport. We didn't always find ducks, and our schedule often prevented us going out, but we always knew where to find them if we could get away.

Carl and Edna

# Frederick

Dad hadn't arrived, and Carl was flying dual with Bus Vincent. I was alone when a car careened into the parking lot on two wheels.

Someone interested in flying, I naturally presumed as the driver got out of the car and took in the runway, and what would eventually be a hangar.

Grinning widely, he turned to me.

"You must be Edna," he said. "I've been hearing a lot about you!"

"Oh?" was my puzzled response.

He held out his hand.

"I'm Frederick," he said.

"Frederick! It's great to meet you! We've been expecting you."

A few inches shorter than Carl, at six-two, and Jim, at six foot, Frederick was, nevertheless, exceptionally well-built. He had a square jaw and clear blue eyes which crinkled at the corners. His wide grin revealed a row of very white, very even teeth. Though handsome, his features were a little more rugged than either of his brothers. His handshake was firm.

I liked his open frankness and suspected that he made friends easily

"Carl will certainly be surprised," I said. "We were expecting a letter or a phone call to tell us you were coming."

"I decided to surprise everyone," he said. "When the Army starts winding things up, they lose no time. In fact, I got here at almost the same time a letter would have arrived."

"Then you're home for good?"

"I still have to go back to Fort Leavenworth to muster out, but that won't take long."

"The whirring sound of a gliding plane reached our ears.

"Here's Carl now," I said.

We watched as the plane taxied toward the hangar then walked out to meet it just as Carl rolled to a stop and cut the motor.

He leaped out of the cockpit and gave his brother a bear hug.

"It's about time you got home—you old son-of-a-gun!" he said.

I recorded Bus's time on my clipboard and a few minutes later, Carl asked, "What time is Fred Burris's appointment?"

"Not until one," I replied.

"Do you mind watching things while Frederick and I run over to Dad's for a cup of coffee?"

"Not at all," I replied. "Stay as long as you like."

"You don't have to worry about dinner," Carl said when he returned an hour later. "We're having dinner with the folks. Judging by the way Lillian is bustling around that kitchen, looks like it's going to be a damned feast."

"What time?" I asked.

"Whenever we can get there. I told Lillian we had a student at five; she said no problem."

I called Lillian, offering to help for an hour or two, but she refused, so while Carl was flying with his four o'clock student, I drove home and dressed for dinner. It would be a gala evening. By the time I returned, Carl and his student had landed. Since George, our five o'clock student, was scheduled for a solo flight, I looked after things while Carl went home to dress. George was just landing when he returned.

"We'll gas it up in the morning," he said.

Together, we pushed the plane into what was only the skeleton of a hangar but which did provide a modicum of shelter.

When we arrived, the party was well underway. Dad was mixing drinks, and Lillian was dishing up food. The table, sparkling with a white cloth, her best china and silver, was loaded with colorful dishes of food. Wine glasses were filled with Dad's best homemade cherry wine.

Dad beamed. This was a festive occasion. All three of his boys were home from the war!

As we ate, I watched with amusement at the give and take between the men.

Dad—"Aw come on—don't be so stingy—fill up that plate!"

Jim—"Hell, you don't need to take the biggest piece!"

Carl—"All right! Who got the gizzard?"

Frederick looked at me and winked.

I remember that as one of the happiest nights of my life. This was my family. For the first time in my life, I felt I belonged.

"I see where your B-29 Superfortress is being redesigned to a peacetime aircraft called the Stratocruiser," Frederick said.

"Yeah; I read that," Carl said. "I guess they got that engine problem fixed. At 383 mph, it's broken all continental records.

"They say it'll carry up to a hundred passengers," he added. "With over-weather operation and the addition of sound proofing, air conditioning, and whatever it takes for passenger comfort, it should make a damned good intercontinental passenger plane."

"Maybe you should apply for a job piloting the plane"

"Nah! I'm happy right here where I am."

Lillian arrived with dessert.

After dinner, I helped Lillian clear the table and do the dishes while the men retired to the living room with their drinks. As we bustled around the kitchen storing leftovers in the freezer and washing up the dishes, we could hear a lot of guffawing and laughing among the men.

Lillian, who was only a year older than Carl, seemed more like one of us than Dad's wife. Although she seemed happy with Dad, I sometimes wondered if she didn't wish she could be around younger people more.

By the time we returned to the table, Carl was ready to go.

"Got an early student," he said. "Are you coming out tomorrow, Frederick?"

"Sure thing. I'll see you as soon as I can get the old bod up and going," he replied.

Three weeks later, Frederick was home to stay. He immediately set about making plans to open his own business—a welding shop.

"I've got a good location," Dad said. "If you and your brothers will do the work, I'll buy the materials and you can put up any kind of building you want."

In the weeks that followed Carl and I spent every day, from daylight till dark, at the airport. If he wasn't flying, Carl was either working on the hangar, keeping the runway in condition, or downtown working on Frederick's building,

As other pilots learned about our airport, we were getting more visitors.

Since my job was to mind shop, I greeted and talked flying with fly-in and drive-in guests, ran errands, chauffeured fly-in guests to their destination, scheduled flights, kept flying records, propped the plane, and serviced it when needed.

With all the men pitching in, the progress on both the hangar and Frederick's building was amazing.

"Isn't there anything you guys can't do?" I asked Carl.

"Sure," he replied. "Lots of things. But I guess you can't call us amateur builders; Dad's had us building things as long as I can remember."

Seeing how well the men worked together to get Frederick's business up and running helped me understand Carl better. He came from a family of "doers." I liked that. Perhaps that explained why he and I worked so well together.

Frederick Ungerer

# The CAA

Things were looking great for Ungerer Flying Service when, in mid-November, an official looking car drove into the parking area and an official looking man got out.

Carl, who had been servicing the L-2, introduced himself and me, and we all shook hands.

The man informed us that he was a CAA[4] inspector. Then he dropped the bad news; the set-up we had wouldn't work!

Both Carl and Jim must obtain civilian ratings, he said. We would have to cease flying until the proper ratings were obtained and specific modifications were made to the flying field. Once that was done, we would have to apply for CAA approval.

Carl's should be relatively easy, he said. He had only to pass a flight check with a CAA flight inspector. Also, considering the present condition and lay-out of the field, required alterations should be no problem.

Jim, however, would have to complete a nine-month course at an A and E mechanic[5] school before he would be allowed to so much as touch a wrench to a civilian airplane.

To say Jim was teed off is putting it mildly.

"What the hell is the 'CAA' and what right do they have to tell us what to do?" he exploded.

"The Civil Aeronautics Administration is the government agency that regulates United States civilian aviation activities. Actually, we should have known there were civilian regulations for operating an airport and checked with them before going into business. Anyway, whether we like it or not, we're under their control and what they say goes, and they say military ratings won't work—we have to obtain civilian ratings."

"But that'll set us back months!" Jim said.

As was the custom, the problem was being discussed around the folks' dining table on which sat a plentiful selection of drinks.

It was obvious Jim had no choice—not if he wanted to be a part of Ungerer Flying Service.

Their conversation spurred by a plentiful supply of alcohol, he and Carl had spent the evening cussing the damn fools who had put this obstacle in the way of our progress.

"Hell, I've been tearing airplanes apart and putting them back together for the past four years—from Piper Cubs to B-24s," Jim said. "And now some office jerk that doesn't know an aileron from a stabilizer says I've got to go to school and learn how to change the oil in a damned Taylorcraft! That would be like another nine months in the service!"

"I'm with you buddy." And Carl added his two bits. "They must think that after flying those big bombers in the Air Corps, maybe I don't know my own strength—that maybe I would tear the controls right out of that little L-2 in a power-off stall or something."

"Yeah. But all you have to do is take a damned test!"

Dad and I listened sympathetically.

Dad, as usual however, was practical.

He mixed our drinks and let them talk it out; then he rose from his chair, chomping on the ever-present cigar and said: "Okay. There isn't any use bellyaching about it all night—we still have to follow regulations so we might as well get to work and get it over with. Now, how about we all go to bed and get some sleep?"

The next morning, we had breakfast with the folks.

"I suppose you're right, Dad," Jim said as we ate. "We've got a good thing going here and, as much as I hate thinking about another nine months of training, we might as well do what we have to do."

Carl sighed with relief.

"I'm glad you decided to go ahead with it," he said.

Both he and Jim looked as though they hadn't had much sleep.

"Flying *is* going to be big business," Carl continued. "We've already had a taste of what we can accomplish."

"The time will pass before you know it," Dad said. "Then you'll all be set with a fine business. After all, what does a few more months matter?"

Jim found he could take the course and obtain his A and E license under the GI Bill at the Spartan School of Aeronautics, in Tulsa, Oklahoma. He could begin training immediately. The school was only a little over three hundred miles from Marysville, which would allow him to get home for an occasional weekend.

"Carl and Edna can keep the business going while you're gone," Dad said encouragingly. "They'll just have to hire a mechanic to do what needs done."

As it turned out, we needed a mechanic right off the bat. A week before Jim left, they cracked up the L-2.

Carl was scheduled to meet the CAA examiner at the Salina airport for his flight check. Jim, thinking to obtain more information about the A and E training, decided to go along.

On the appointed day, we awoke to find that a five-inch snow had fallen during the night—on top of a two-inch layer already on the ground. I drove them to the runway at eight o'clock. Carl's appointment was at ten. When we got out of the car, a strong north wind swirled the powdery white snow, stinging our faces.

"Do you think we'll be able to get it off the ground?" Jim asked through chattering teeth.

"The ground's pretty soft, and between the two of us we'll be carrying a lot of weight," Carl replied. "We do have a strong north wind in our favor though. Hell, since we're here, we might as well give it a try."

Though the open hangar provided shelter from the northern wind, the canvas covering was frozen stiff. After struggling to remove it, they wheeled the plane outside and Carl got into the front seat. Jim's teeth were chattering and his ears were beet red as he snapped the prop through several times.

"Contact!" he called out. The plane refused to start.

"Son of a bitch! Switch off! Throttle open!"

He pulled the prop through in reverse several times and they repeated the procedure several times. No results.

"I don't think she's going to start," Carl said, getting out of the plane.

"Hell, let's try it one more time," Jim said.

Carl got back into the plane. This time the motor sputtered then started.

"While it warms up let's walk up the hill and check out the runway," Carl said.

As they ducked their heads into the wind and walked fifty yards up the hill I stood by, shivering, using the plane as a windbreak.

After they returned, they spent a few minutes discussing the positives and negatives, evaluating the possibilities of getting the plane off the ground.

Factoring in their combined weight, and a 30-mile-an-hour north wind, it still looked iffy. Most of the snow had blown off the runway at the top of the hill, however, so they finally agreed that the odds were good enough to give it a try.

Carl climbed into the plane, handed me his overshoes, and motioned to Jim to pull the chocks. Jim climbed in and I stood shivering as they checked the instruments. I'd dressed warmly, but the sharp wind, blowing across the snow, penetrated my wool coat and pants.

Carl turned the plane into the wind and shoved the throttle open. The plane moved, slowly at first, then picked up speed as they reached the crest of the hill. I watched until they disappeared then waited to see her rise into the air.

Seconds passed. No plane. *Oh, God no!* I thought. My heart in my throat, I began running up the hill, stumbling through the snow as I went. I fell and began sobbing as I struggled to my feet, picturing mangled bodies in a tangled mass of steel and fabric. Then, through my tears, I saw the two of them trudging down the center of the runway.

They hadn't cleared the barbed wire fence.

"She got off the ground all right," Carl said, "but mushed back in—right into the fence."

"How bad is the plane damaged?" I asked.

"The cowling is tangled in the barbed wire," Jim said. "And the prop is broken."

When we arrived back at the folks' place, Lillian poured us mugs of strong, hot coffee and set fresh baked rolls on the table.

"I'd better call Salina and reschedule my appointment," Carl said, after we'd warmed up a bit.

"It won't be any trouble to replace the prop," Jim said. "All we have to do is drive up to Beatrice and get a new prop, loosen a few bolts, and replace the damaged prop with the new one. The damage to the cowling is minor and won't affect the plane's performance. We can straighten that out later."

"The only thing wrong with that solution is that *you* can't do it," Carl said after hanging up the phone.

"Do what?"

"Change the prop. Remember what that CAA examiner said."

"That I can't even touch a wrench to a civilian airplane," Jim mumbled.

Carl nodded.

"What if we don't tell them?"

"And what if they find out?" Carl shook his head. "We can't take that chance."

"Oh shit!" Jim said, getting up and storming out of the room.

"We still have to get the plane out of the fence!" Carl called out. "We'll have to push it back and that won't be easy in this snow."

"I'll go along and help," Dad said, getting up and pulling on his heavy coat.

We had to hire a mechanic to drive down from Beatrice, Nebraska—at five dollars an hour, in addition to the cost of the prop.

He arrived two days later.

"I didn't want to take a chance on flying," he said. "If your strip's anything like most of 'em, it would be too chancy."

"It is," Carl said.

Jim watched and fumed as the mechanic worked on the plane. He had obviously never worked on an L-2 before. At first, Jim offered instructions. That didn't work. Teed off, he took the wrench and changed the prop himself while the man looked on.

"Five dollars an hour it cost us for that dumb ass to drive down here to learn how to change a prop on an L-2!" he exclaimed.

It snowed again that night. The following week Jim left to begin the A and E course. Before he left, he straightened the cowling. The accident left a few scratches, easily covered by a coat of silver paint; otherwise, the L-2 was as good as new.

A few days later, the weather moderated. Carl made another appointment, flew to Salina, and took the flight check.

---

[4] To ensure a federal focus on aviation safety, President Franklin D. Roosevelt signed the Civil Aeronautics Act in 1938. The legislation established the independent Civil Aeronautics Authority (CAA). In 1940, President Roosevelt split the authority into two agencies—the Civil Aeronautics Administration (CAA) and the Civil Aeronautics Board (CAB). On August 23, 1958, President Dwight D. Eisenhower signed the Federal Aviation Act, which transferred the Civil Aeronautics Authority's functions to a new independent Agency (FAA), which later became the Federal Aviation Administration.

[5] CAA required aircraft and engine mechanical training.

# Ungerer Flying Service

Carl, of course, passed the flight check with flying colors and by mid-December the required improvements to the runway had been completed. Approved by the CAA, we continued student training.

We greeted the New Year with enthusiasm and optimism.

Thankfully, the weather turned out to be reasonably mild and, weather permitting, our four students eagerly resumed their practice maneuvers. Our list of GIs—who had missed out flying during the war and wanted to start flight training under the new GI Bill once we were qualified—was growing.

Things were looking up for Ungerer Flying Service! We ordered stationary bearing the new Ungerer Flying Service logo, applied for, and were granted, dealership for Taylorcraft airplanes. We ran advertisements in both *The Marysville Advocate* and *The Marshall County News* offering flight instruction and charter service, as well as rides providing "A bird's-eye view of Marysville."

Early in January, a free ride for the editor of *The Marysville Advocate* netted us a nice article on the front page of the newspaper. The headline read: *Carl Ungerer Opens Marysville's First Flying School.*

Not to be outdone, *The Marshall County News* ran a similar article the following week:

> "Flying is no longer a hobby," the article read. "Time was when many a county citizen remarked: 'I can't even afford to buy a car.' Today, you can hear the same remarks in Marshall County about planes."

The following week, Carl was asked to give a talk for a local boys' club, and we signed up two more students.

Business continued to be slow during the week but, if the weather was nice, our "airport" swarmed with people on Sundays, especially after church. Although we gave a lot of rides, most came out of curiosity.

A great deal of talk about the new "Air Age" circulated nationwide in both newspaper and on radio and, as the weather moderated a bit in January, an increasing number of people began dropping by weekdays to watch the plane take off and land. Some came so frequently Carl began calling them his "regular customers." Most were young people, but a few businessmen who were, we hoped, prospective clients, began to drop by.

Carl had his first charter passenger the first week in February. Having seen our ad in the newspaper, a local farmer who needed to make an urgent business trip to Shenandoah, Iowa, appeared at the airport to ask if Carl could fly him there and back the next day.

It was only eighty-five air miles. It should be no problem, Carl said depending, of course, on the length of time it would take him to conduct his business.

They took off at ten-thirty the next morning and, despite a strong headwind on the return trip, were back by four.

Both *The Marshall County News* and *The Marysville Advocate* gave us excellent coverage. *The Marshall County News* headline read:

Air travel is becoming an accepted part of the lives of Marysville residents. Resolving an urgent transportation need, demonstrating the extent to which air travel is rapidly becoming accepted as a part of the lives of Marysville citizens.

"Those articles are better publicity than any ad we could run," Carl said.

After the Iowa trip, we began receiving more requests for charter service. Soon Carl was flying passengers to Kansas City, Wichita, Omaha, and other surrounding towns.

When not flying or working on the hangar, Carl spent a considerable amount of time working the runway which needed constant attention to keep it smooth and free of ruts left by winter snows and wind.

Despite bouts of weather, which brought flying to a stand-still, we continued to run weekly ads in both newspapers and, in February, signed up two more students.

Meanwhile, with Dad's help, the hangar was slowly nearing completion.

One morning, when we arrived at the airport, the weather had closed in. Low hanging clouds limited the visibility to practically zero.

There would be no flying with students this morning.

"Why don't you and I go for a spin," Carl said.

"In this weather?"

"It's not that bad if we stay below the clouds; we'll stay close to the airport."

Though the runway was soft, the L-2 took off easily from the adjacent alfalfa strip. Once in the air, we "fence-hopped" for a while, then Carl climbed higher to check the ceiling. At three hundred feet, clouds skipped blithely about us and, at four hundred, the plane was completely enveloped in heavy, grey clouds. It was an eerie feeling; I breathed a sigh of relief when Carl glided down to a lower altitude where, even though our visibility was limited, I could see the earth.

"You'll never make an instrument pilot," he laughed, apparently enjoying his "busman's holiday."

Even though I was completely lost, Carl seemed to know our exact location at all times.

"How can you keep track of where we are?" I asked.

"It's easy as long as you know the country as well as I do," he replied. "I was raised here; I know every road, railroad, and water tank. I also know most of the farms.

"If you happen to be in unfamiliar territory in this kind of weather," he continued, "you check your map against the landscape. See that highway off to the left for instance; it's blacktopped, and it's running east and west, right? Then it must be Highway 36 leading into Marysville. But from what direction? Now, see the sign boards? You can see by the compass that we're headed west. Since you can read the front of the sign, that means we're east of town. If you look to the left, you'll see the railroad. And that farm just north of us? That's the Hoopers' isn't it? Well then, we know that the airport is about three miles west and a mile north so we turn until the compass reads west-north-west and before you know it we are over the airport."

And sure enough, just ahead I could see the dim form of the hangar through the mist.

"Thanks for the navigation lesson," I said as Carl cut the motor, opened the door, and swung one long leg to the ground in a single movement.

"Anytime," he grinned.

WAR VETERAN PILOT INSTRUCTOR NOW TRAINS CIVILIANS.

Carl Ungerer Opens Marysville's First Flying School.

# Headwinds

No sooner had the winter snows melted away, leaving the runways a bed of slush and mud, the March winds arrived. Although the strong gales dried out the runways, they whipped the plane about, often bringing Carl scurrying back to the field with a fledgling student.

It was one of those blustery March days that kept most people indoors. Carl and Dad were working on the hangar which, though going slowly, was gradually nearing completion. As usual, my job was to fetch tools, nails, drinks, and snacks. Midst the hammering and pounding, I could hear frequent expletives when blasts of wind snatched at the corrugated galvanized steel sheets they were struggling to nail to the roof.

I sat down in the car and picked up the *Kansas City Star*. Like everyone else, we were concerned about reports on the Cold War. The item in today's issue read:

> "Winston Churchill stepped up to the podium at a tiny college in rural Fulton, Missouri, yesterday, flanked by US President Harry Truman. The former British prime minister's subject was the cold war brewing between America and Soviet Russia."

The speech, titled "The Sinews of Peace," ended up sounding the alarm on the fracturing relationship between the post-war superpowers.

I looked up when a new Cadillac pulled in and a tall, heavy-set man, got out.

"Are you Carl Ungerer?" he called out.

Carl, hammer in hand, walked to the edge of the roof.

"Sure am!"

"Can we talk?"

Carl climbed down the ladder.

"What can I do for you?" he asked.

"Name's Peterson," the man said amiably, offering his hand. "I'm with Grosshan and Peterson Contracting Company, and I was wondering if you could take a letter to Limon, Colorado—and get it there before midnight tonight. It's a contract bid—and the bid closes at midnight."

Carl took an aerial map from the L-2 and studied it for a few minutes.

"That'll be around four hundred miles," he calculated. He looked at his watch. "Limon is five degrees south and I'll be heading into a stiff southwest wind. It'll take eight or nine hours, depending on the wind." He thought for a minute.

"Yes," he decided, "I can make it if I leave right away."

"I'll be right back," Peterson said, heading for his car.

While he was gone, Carl filled the L-2 with gas and gave it a preflight check. After talking it over, we decided I best go along. The flight would be long and rough, and I could relieve him at the controls.

Fifteen minutes later, Peterson was back with an eight-by-ten manila envelope.

"You two be careful!" called Dad who was still pounding nails on the aluminum roofing.

Five minutes later we were in the air.

The plane climbed swiftly, tossing to and fro in the wind.

Ignoring the flight pattern, Carl climbed to 500 feet. Crabbing to the south, he headed west. If Peterson was watching, he probably thought that transaction a lost cause when, after ten minutes in the air, we'd only reached the west side of Marysville.

"That wind's gotta be at least seventy miles an hour up here," Carl said, climbing steadily higher, hoping for less wind at a higher altitude.

At 5,000 feet we were still making no headway. Finally, dropping the nose, he headed earthward. When he leveled off, we were cruising just off the ground at a speed he calculated at about fifty miles per hour.

Our one advantage was that the further west you go, the flatter and more barren the Kansas prairie landscape. With Carl's experience and expertise, and nothing in our way, the trip was grueling but the danger minimal.

Growing up, I'd often heard western Kansas referred to as "the Kansas desert" which was exactly how it appeared that breezy March day as we flew westward.

Flying just off the ground, Carl's shoulders were tense, as he skillfully skimmed over barbed wire fences and leaped telephone lines. The air glowed red from the dust. Four-foot tumbleweeds rolled and tossed before the wind. Pheasants, startled from shelter by the low-flying plane, sailed across the prairie. Jack rabbits darted wildly this way and that and, occasionally, a coyote leaped from a fence-row and loped away across the plain.

At times, it seemed that the wheels almost skimmed the ground. My face felt sandy and my eyes and muscles ached from the strain.

We could estimate our speed by checking the time at the fence lines— evenly spaced at one mile apart.

"If this wind doesn't go down, we're going to play it awfully close!" Carl shouted over the roar of the engine.

When the prairie stretched ahead flat and barren as far as we could see, Carl yielded the controls to me, stretched and flexed his back. Since I was flying from the back seat, my view was limited, so I had to maintain a slightly higher altitude. Even though no obstacles lay in my path at fifty feet, I was tense and nervous.

At two o'clock, we landed for gas, a soda, and a candy bar. Carl's eyes were red and bleary but being out of the plane for only a few minutes gave us a chance to stretch our muscles and the cold drink soothed our parched throats.

An hour before sundown, the wind velocity diminished, and we climbed to a higher altitude. After the heat and the dust and the rough air of the past eight hours, it felt good to climb to a cooler, calmer, altitude. Carl pried his fingers from the controls, stretched his legs, and rotated his shoulders. From this vantage point the world seemed surreal and unrealistic.

"We're playing it awfully close," Carl said, checking the map. Pointing at the gauge, he added. "And, we're almost out of gas."

We were crossing Kansas's western border and the map showed no airport east of our destination.

The sun was settling rapidly toward the horizon when we spotted a small town. The map listed no airport, but we saw a field that looked as though it might be used for a landing strip. Taking a chance, we landed on a smooth, makeshift, runway not very different from our own "airport." At the far end, stood a T-hangar. No one was around but, again, lady luck was on our side. Beside the hangar stood a barrel of gas and a five gallon can.

Carl siphoned off five gallons, wrote a quick note, and left it and some bills under a rock on top of the barrel.

Soon after taking off, our destination hove into sight. However, the sun was nearing the horizon, the earth was darkening and lights were flickering on in the town and over the sparsely settled prairie. Once the sun disappeared completely from sight, the sparkling lights of our destination, beckoning in the deepening dusk, seemed so near and yet so far.

Hoping to have enough light to see to land, Carl inched the throttle forward to gain speed.

I breathed a sigh of relief when the outline of the small airport on the far side of town became faintly discernible.

"See if you can locate a windsock or a windmill so we can get an idea of the wind direction and velocity," Carl said.

I pointed to the right. "There's a windmill," I said. "The wind is in the north. I can't tell exactly, but it doesn't appear to be too strong."

"Okay. We'll land to the north and hope for the best. It's going to be pretty dark by the time we touch down, but we should be able to make out those metal hangars. If I land to the left of them, we should be okay."

As we headed in, we could barely make out a grass field with narrow mowed strips marking the runways. As we glided closer to the runway, the hangars were faintly visible. By the time we reached the southern boundary, we could hardly make out the buildings much less the runway.

"We're too high!" Carl yelled, fumbling for the spoilers. The plane stalled and dropped heavily to the ground. He hit the brake and the L-2 rolled to a stop about ten feet short of the gas pump.

Cutting the switch, he took a deep breath. "Whew! That was a little *too* close!"

We climbed out of the plane and stretched our muscles.

"Looks like we're about a mile from town so I guess we're in for a walk," Carl said. "Think you're up to it?"

"Doesn't look as if I have a choice," I retorted. "Unless you want to carry me!"

Feeling our way in the dark, we drove in the stakes and tied the plane down where it sat.

When Carl helped me over the fence I was shivering—from nerves rather than cold. He took my hand, and we headed down a dark, rutty road toward the lights of the town.

Our feet and our rear ends were numb from the strain of sitting in one position for so long. It felt good to stretch our legs.

We had no trouble finding the hotel where we were to meet a C.A. Andrews. It was the only one in town.

The only lighting, a dim electric bulb hanging over the check-in counter, cast dark shadows over the lobby so dismal and depressing I shivered.

When we entered, a tall, thin, swarthy man rose from a creaking divan. His suit hung limply from his body and his western style hat completely shaded his eyes.

"I'm C.A. Andrews," he said. "You Carl Ungerer?"

Carl nodded.

"I was beginning to think you weren't going to make it," Andrews said. "Do you have a letter for me from Peterson?"

Carl handed him the envelope.

"Thanks," he said and, without another word, turned and left the hotel.

"Damn, that was weird!" Carl said.

"I wonder why he didn't meet us at the airport?" I thought aloud. "He must have heard the plane when we flew in."

"Good question," Carl said, shrugging his shoulders.

The meeting with Andrews only added to the unreality of the day's events. Feeling as if we were involved in espionage rather than a business transaction, I had a sudden compulsion to look over my shoulder.

"Well, our part of the bargain is over," Carl sighed with relief. "I guess this is where we spend the night." He rang the bell on the counter.

A small, dwarf-like man appeared from down the dark corridor. Carl signed the ledger and paid for a room. We followed him down the hall. He entered a room and pulled a string hanging from the ceiling. Another dim bulb cast a yellow light over the small, sparsely furnished room. At least, it looked clean.

"I'm starved," Carl said after we'd washed the layer of dust from our faces. "How about you?"

"I could eat a bear," I said. "As tired as I am, I don't remember when I've felt so hungry."

"Just hope we can find something still open," he said.

We didn't have to look far. The main street was only two blocks long. Catty-cornered across the street a red and green neon sign blinked "Charlie's Café." A combined beer joint and café it was, apparently, the only establishment that remained open after dark.

Three men sat at the bar drinking beer, and a man in a dirty white apron, chewing on a toothpick, leaned on the back-bar.

When we entered, the juke box was blaring county western music, and the long, narrow room smelled strongly of beer, burned grease, and creosote. The floor was littered with scraps of paper, bottle caps, and cigarette butts.

Having had only a Coke and a candy bar since breakfast, we had only two choices—to go hungry or risk a case of salmonella. Carl headed for a corner table as far as possible from the juke box.

The big man, who apparently served a triple role as bartender, waiter, and cook, came to the table and swiped it with a dirty towel.

"What'll you have?" he asked.

"How about a couple of beers to start with, and a couple of steaks—make mine rare and the lady's well-done—with French fries."

The beer perked us up, and the steaks turned out better than we'd expected.

"Well," Carl said as we crossed the street, back to the hotel, "this has been quite a day. I'm ready for some shut-eye, how about you?"

Despite the spare furnishings, the bed was fairly comfortable, and we spent the next ten hours in blissful oblivion.

We ate breakfast in the one other café in town, a much cleaner establishment than the one we'd patronized the night before.

When Carl paid the tab, he asked about transportation and was told there was no taxi service.

We stood for a minute looking up and down the street, deserted except for some children playing hop-scotch at the far end of the block.

"Looks like we're in for another walk," Carl said, and we set off for the air strip.

The air was fresh, and the sun was warm. I didn't mind walking, but the only time Carl ever walked by choice was when we were hunting.

A stocky, red-faced man greeted us when we arrived.

"You stretched your luck pretty close last night, didn't you?" he asked.

"Just a little," Carl replied.

After commenting briefly on the luck of some fool pilots, he filled our tank with gas, propped the plane, and waved us off.

"Not the friendliest town I ever landed in," Carl said as we taxied out for take-off.

"You can't expect to always get the breaks—even when you pay the preacher regularly." Carl said, once we were airborne. The wind had switched 180 degrees and was blowing strongly from the north northeast.

"Oh no!" I moaned as he pointed the nose toward the ground.

The sun was well overhead when the wind diminished in velocity.

"Thank God!" Carl said and began climbing.

We continued the flight at a normal altitude and reached home well before dark, tired but happy that Ungerer's Charter Service had successfully completed a difficult, but profitable, mission.

The following Thursday, *The Marysville Advocate* reported the letting of a contracting bid to Grosshan and Peterson Contracting Company of Marysville. The story ended with, "Ungerer charged $70.00 for the special flight but the successful bid was for $450,000."

"That does the business more good than any advertising we could run," Carl said, repeating himself.

The next day, I revised the ad we ran in both *The Marysville Advocate* and *The Marshall County News:*

> Charter service: 8 cents per mile. Round trip from Marysville to Kansas City - $24.00, Lincoln, Nebraska - $14.00, Topeka, Kansas - $15.00, Wichita, Kansas - $32.00.

# A Wedding, A New Office, and The Doctor Learns to Fly

Dr. J.W. Randall, the family doctor, was one of the most outstanding physicians in northeast Kansas. A man of action, he kept up with new developments in the world of medicine, and the world in general. His fifty years didn't prevent him from taking on new challenges.

He showed up at the airport for a ride one Sunday afternoon. A few days later, he called and asked if Carl could fly him to Kansas City the following day.

"Doc Randall wants to start taking flying lessons!" Carl said when they returned.

"Isn't he kind of old to take up flying?" I asked.

"Not if he passes his physical. Actually, fifty isn't all that old, and Doc *is* sharp. I let him handle the controls on the way back from Kansas City; he catches on quick. He wants to start immediately, so I told him to come out at seven o'clock tomorrow morning."

"Doesn't look as though Doc is one to waste time," I said.

The next morning, he was the first one out. I spun the prop and watched them taxi off, Dr. Randall focusing on the instrument panel, listening intently to what Carl was saying.

They returned an hour later.

"How did he do?" I asked after he drove away. "Do you think he'll continue?"

"He did good," Carl said. "Of course, it's possible that he'll go for a couple of lessons, then decide it's not for him; we'll just have to wait and see."

In spite of being twice as old as most of our students, Dr. Randall proved to be our most enthusiastic, surprising everyone with his dedication and perseverance. He flew every morning that first week, practicing his maneuvers methodically and religiously.

After that, if the weather wasn't suitable for flying when he arrived at the airport, he stayed anyway, studying the maps and the books on meteorology, navigation, etc.

The townspeople marveled that Dr. Randall would take up flying at his age, but as far as he was concerned, his fifty years had nothing to do with his ability to fly. He had the money, he was physically fit, and he wanted to fly. So fly he did.

April proved to be an eventful month for the Ungerer family.

First, the building to house Frederick's new welding service nearing completion, he and his fiancée, Viola Schidler, were married on the ninth. They set up housekeeping in the house Dad had prepared for them across the street from Carl and me.

Everything was looking up for Ungerer Flying Service as well. Carl and Dad laid a concrete ramp and put the finishing touches on the hangar; capacity, five planes—if you tipped one up on its nose.

"One of these days we're going to need at least that much space," Carl said. "Before you know it, we'll have a whole fleet of airplanes."

We now had nine students flying regularly, and the lengthening days meant more time students could spend in the air. Mid-month, we signed up two more students, our charter service was growing, and the Sunday afternoon rides helped to balance the books.

Also on the bright side, more veterans were signing up for training on the GI program.

We had complied immediately with all the requirements and were puzzled as to why it was taking so long for the Veteran's Administration to approve our application.

April also brought diminishing winds.

Not that we weren't still at the mercy of the weather. Whereas it had been only a phenomenon to be tolerated before we went into the flying business, it had now become a virtual dictator. The state of the weather controlled our business, our time, and therefore, our lives. We were, it seemed, at the complete mercy of the Gods.

At times we could fly through an entire day, but then there were days when the April rains brought flying to a standstill.

We watched the sky and the windsock, one ear turned to the radio and the weather news, and waited for the wind to lay, the rain to stop, the runway to dry.

To me, once a photographer, this was a strange new world. While I was often at a loss, Carl seemed to take everything in stride—always confident in what he was about to do.

I had obtained a cardboard box to keep my files in, borrowed a card table and a folding chair from Lillian, and set up office in the hangar. However, due to the wind blowing papers about, it was often impossible to work there.

Again, Dad came to the rescue. He found a discarded chicken shed and moved it in next to the hangar. Though somewhat shabby, the frame was sturdy, and Dad worked diligently, hammering nails into the hard, oak lumber, cursing around a mouth full of nails as only Dad could curse. Occasionally, when the hammer struck too close to his thumb, he released a string of expletives. Before I knew what was happening, he had converted the chicken shed into an office.

Dad never ceased to amaze me. It wasn't only his ingenuity; the manner in which he got things done was astounding. Everything he undertook was approached in a great hurry and in what appeared to be a haphazard manner—as though it was vitally important to get the job over and done with so he could get on with something else.

Somehow his projects always came out right—and so it was with the office. By mid-April, he pronounced it ready for occupancy. As Dad said, it "wasn't fancy," but by the time we'd furnished it with a used desk and chair, a file cabinet, a new typewriter and adding machine, record books, and stationary, it was as efficient as I could have wished for.

It was spacious enough to serve a dual purpose. The office area occupied one end of the room, while the end near the door we equipped with a large table, folding chairs, and a divan. This was assigned as a waiting area as well as space to conduct ground school.

Once completed, Dad had a sign—UNGERER FLYING SER-VICE—made and installed over the entrance.

"You'd never guess that this once served as home for a flock of laying hens!" I exclaimed.

Viola Shidler Ungerer, the New Bride

# Growing a Flying Service

Having only one plane made it difficult to find time but, weather permitting, and the L-2 available, I flew as often as I could.

One morning as I flew the flight pattern after a dual flight, I admired our base—the new office; the hangar, now boasting a concrete ramp and a new coat of silver paint, glittered brightly in the sun; the windsock, hanging from the leading edge of the eave, fluttered in a gentle breeze.

"It's beginning to look like a real airport, isn't it?" Carl bragged.

The plane touched down gently on the grassy turf. I taxied to the corner of the hangar where the gasoline barrel rested on a make-shift rack.

As we got out of the plane, Carl eyed the gasoline barrel.

"While you fill the tank, I think I'll call the oil company and see about getting an underground tank and a gasoline pump installed," he said.

As the weather grew warmer, it brought more people to the airport. They came, not only from Marysville, but from surrounding towns and area farms as well. Our upstart of an airport seemed to have become a recreational center, especially on Sunday.

The biggest crowd came directly after church. Some brought picnic lunches and spent the afternoon visiting with friends while watching the plane take off and land. We often heard them kidding among themselves, daring each other to go for a ride.

Some Sundays, Carl hardly got out of the plane from noon until dark.

"The novelty won't last forever," he said. "It's good though that so many people are becoming acquainted with flying. A lot of them will be our future customers."

Dad and Lillian were always there, ready to help. Dad was a great bull-shitter; he seemed to know everyone, and he'd often kid some on-looker about being afraid to fly.

"How come I haven't seen you up there, Harry?" he'd ask.

"Hell, you ain't gonna catch me up in that damned contraption," the man would reply.

"Aw—you're just scared."

"Not as long as I've got one foot on the ground, I ain't."

But Dad never gave up. He often succeeded in talking a man into going for a ride—sometimes even paying for it himself.

Other ex-Air Corps pilots who, like us, had built their own aviation business, often flew in from surrounding towns, adding to the excitement. As Dad remarked, after one particularly busy Sunday "A hell of a good time was had by all."

"And we didn't do too bad financially," I said.

Carl rubbed his butt and said: "Well, this is what we signed up for! If today is any indication, Ungerer Flying Service is going to do pretty good!"

"I can't believe there are so many people who have never flown before," I said.

"Hell, it hasn't been all that long since you started flying yourself," Carl said.

Although the Sunday rides were our bread and butter in the beginning, an added advantage was, that in only a short time, there were few people in Marshall County who had not become, as Carl said, "on speaking terms with an airplane." As he predicted, with the passing of time, many of them took advantage of our charter service. Others learned to fly, and some of these ultimately purchased a plane.

Meanwhile, Dr. Randall was making rapid progress. Carl flew with him to Belleville and Salina and pronounced him ready for his solo cross-country.

"How's the schedule for Thursday afternoon and Friday morning?" Carl asked a couple of days later.

"Let's see—Fred is scheduled to fly Thursday evening, and George has a dual appointment Friday morning—" Due to working hours and the fact that the air was smoother in early morning and late evening, these continued to be our busiest times.

"See if you can reschedule Fred and George. Dr. Randall wants to take his solo cross-country Thursday—leave early afternoon and stay overnight. There's a medical convention in Omaha Thursday night; he thinks it would be great if he could fly to Hastings after lunch on Thursday, then up to Omaha, attend the convention, then fly home Friday morning."

"That's a rather ambitious solo cross-country; do you think he can handle it?"

"I wouldn't let him do it if I had any doubt. I've let him take over the controls flying into Kansas City several times. He's cautious; I can't see that it would be a problem for him."

"That means we won't be able to fly at all from Thursday noon until Friday noon."

"That's all right."

To be honest, I was glad for a little slack. I was behind on the books, and the house could use a little attention as well.

Carl used the time advantageously smoothing out ruts in the runways.

We expected Dr. Randall around ten o'clock, so we slept in Friday morning, took our time, and arrived at the airport at nine.

I was deeply engrossed in bookwork when Carl came into the office.

"Doc is overdue," he said, a worried expression on his face. "I told him to let me know if he couldn't make it by ten."

A glance at my watch told me it was slightly past ten-thirty.

"He shouldn't run thirty minutes over—unless he didn't get away from Omaha on time. There's hardly any wind—not enough to delay him this much."

"He probably got away late" I was saying when the telephone shrilled loudly in my ear.

Carl picked up the receiver, listened, then hung up, shaking his head.

"Who was it?"

"Doc. He forgot to buy gasoline before he left Omaha."

"Oh, no!"

"He's all right—luckily. He almost made it. He landed in Carter's wheat field and was calling from there."

"What about the plane?"

"It's all right, he says. The old codger was as calm as if he'd just landed here at the airport. Asked if I would drive out with a can of gasoline and fly the plane in. Carter's going to bring him into town so he can get to the office."

I left a note on the door while Carl filled a five-gallon can with gasoline.

"Lord, I'm telling you, we didn't know what to think when we saw that plane headed into our field!" Mrs. Carter exclaimed. "We didn't think it was actually going to land—but then it did, and Dr. Randall came climbing out, as cool as you please. He mumbled something about running out of gas and wanted to use the phone. Ron's taken him into town."

"We'll just put some gas in and get it out of your way," Carl said. "We appreciate your letting us use the field."

"Will you have any trouble taking off?" she asked.

"I'm sure not," Carl said. "The ground seems pretty solid and there's a good breeze."

After he put the gasoline in the tank, I propped the plane then waited as he taxied to the far end of the field. The L-2 took off after only a short run.

"Thanks!" I said, waving to Mrs. Carter, who was leaning on the fence watching. Getting into the car, I drove back to the airport.

By twelve, the plane was serviced and ready for the one o'clock student.

Dr. Randall, none the worse for his experience, came out Monday morning as scheduled. He offered to pay for our having to go after the plane, but Carl waved him off.

"Just glad you made it all right," he said. "Maybe you learned something from the experience—always be sure your gasoline tank is full."

Ungerer Hangar

# The Blue Bird

Carl and I arrived at the airport shortly after five on Monday morning. Our first student of the day would be arriving soon. We shoved open the heavy steel doors, and Carl stood for a moment looking into the hangar.

"The L-2 looks lonesome in there all by itself, doesn't it?" he said thoughtfully. "I think it's about time we bought another plane. We've got eleven students now, and we're not going to be able to handle student training and charter flying with one plane for much longer."

Aircraft manufacturers had retooled early-on for post war production, and the sound of rivet guns, drop hammers and compressors were being heard nationwide as new, revolutionary designs were making their appearance. When nothing else demanded our time, Carl and I poured over magazines and brochures, studying the specs of the new models rolling off the production lines.

We already had the Taylorcraft dealership, and our distributor in Salina had told Carl last week that he had planes available.

After Bus Vincent, our first student for the day, took off, flying solo, we went into the office. Carl picked up a brochure and, again, we weighed the values and advantages of different planes—specifications, performance statistics, and pricing—on the post war Piper Cub, Taylorcraft, Stinson, and the Aeronca Chief, as well as the Cessna. Produced in Wichita, Cessna was well known as "the first light plane manufacturer in America." We had discussed doing so but hadn't applied for a Cessna dealership. However, that would be no problem should we decide on a Cessna.

"I kind of like the looks of the new side-by-side Taylorcraft," Carl said. "If it's half the plane the L-2 is, it would serve us well."

"This article says that Taylorcraft is the world's largest builder of side-by-side airplanes; and that they are, quote, the 'best buy in the sky,'" I said.

"The new one has more power than the L-2. Cruising speed, ninety-five miles per hour—plus a twenty-four gallon gasoline capacity, which gives it a cruising range of 500 miles. That would be a definite advantage in charter work."

"What about the Cessna?" I asked. "The fuselage is all metal, and it has a new safety landing gear."

"It's more costly," Carl said. "And it's more plane than we need right now. I think we'd better wait on that until we have more and better pilots. The Taylorcraft is less expensive; it looks great, has wheel control, is economical and easy to operate. I think it should suit our needs perfectly for now. "And," he added, "the distributor is in Salina—which is convenient."

He checked the flight schedule.

"I have a dual with Bill right after lunch," he said. "After I fly with him, I think I'll go into town and talk to the banker."

The banker proved to be more than agreeable.

"I wondered when you were going to get around to it," he said.

The next morning, Carl called Red Taylor, who operated the Taylorcraft distributorship in Salina, and asked if he had a new BC12D we could pick up by Sunday.

"A plane is available," Red said. "The problem is, it's still at the factory in Alliance, Ohio, and I don't have anyone to go after it. If you want to pick it up at the factory yourself, I'll knock two hundred dollars off the price."

"How soon will it be available?" Carl asked.

"I'll call the factory and get back to you," Red said.

A short time later he called back to tell us the plane would be ready by Thursday morning.

"I'll go along," I said after he hung up. "You'll need someone to fly the L-2 back."

"That would be a good idea, but I don't think you've had

enough experience in big city airport traffic. You can go, but we'll take the train."

I rescheduled student appointments for Wednesday and Thursday, and we left Wednesday morning. We had reserved berths and, after a good night's sleep, pulled into a deserted railway station in Alliance at seven Thursday morning feeling fresh and ready for the flight back to Marysville.

When we got off the train, there wasn't a taxicab in sight. We walked two blocks up a street that must have seemed drab, even on busy days. Finally, we rounded a corner and found a taxi. The driver was asleep at the wheel, so Carl rapped sharply on the hood. The man came to with a start. When Carl asked if he was for hire, he nodded his head, grabbed his cap from the seat beside him, screwed it on his crew cut, put a cigarette in his mouth and took his post at the wheel, ready to go.

We'd had breakfast on the train, so we drove straight to the factory. When we arrived, we could hear a buzz of activity. Production was already underway. The cab driver let us off at the office. Once inside, we waited while the red-headed receptionist dusted her desk, took the cover off her typewriter, and combed her hair.

Then she turned to Carl. He handed her the purchase order. She looked it over, spoke into the intercom, and said our plane was being checked over and would be ready shortly. She asked if we would like a tour of the factory while we waited. I nodded enthusiastically. Flipping another button, the receptionist spoke into the mike. A moment later, a short, thin man in a yellow t-shirt and khaki trousers appeared.

He led us through a series of doors and down a long hall. The further we went, the louder the noise. At last, we emerged into a long room. Airplanes parts were stacked everywhere, and workers were sitting, lying, and standing among them busy at work.

We followed the long moving ramp running the length of the room. As it moved forward workers at each side added nuts, bolts, and various parts until, at the end of the line, an airplane complete with wheel pants, several coats of blue and silver paint, and a serial number rolled out of the building and took its place with identical planes lined up on the hill back of the factory.

Our plane was out for a flight check, our guide informed us. As soon as it came in, we would be set to go.

We returned to the office, signed release papers, received copies, and followed the guide to the flight line where our plane was waiting.

It was beautiful!

The fuselage was blue, the wings silver and, as described in the brochure, it boasted side by side seating, wheel control and, in addition to the gas tank in front of the cockpit, a six gallon tank in each wing fed by gravity to the main tank at the flick of a switch. This gave her a range almost twice that of the L-2 which could remain in the air only three hours without refueling. It also boasted a one-way radio which allowed the pilot to obtain weather reports, flying conditions, and landing instructions. Its fabric cover, waxed and polished to the nth degree, glistened in the morning sun.

We climbed in, adjusted our seat belts, and the line man spun the prop. The engine purred as smooth as a kitten as Carl taxied to the runway for takeoff. It felt strange to be sitting side by side, rather than in tandem.

After checking the maps, Carl turned the plane into the wind. The take-off was smooth in the calm morning air and the plane was much less noisy than the L-2. We could actually talk in our normal voices! We were elated; our first new plane! A few minutes on course, Carl turned the controls over to me. I was surprised at how easy it was to fly. After I'd checked out all the new gadgets, Carl took over, and we laughed just because things were going so well, and because we were acting so silly. Releasing the controls, he let the plane fly itself while he put both arms around me and gave me a bear hug and a shake that rocked the plane.

I took the maps out of my bag. We'd charted our course from Alliance to Marysville, before we left home so, after making sure we were on course, we relaxed and sat back to enjoy the scenery.

By now I was exhausted from the morning's exertion so I rested my head on Carl's shoulder and went to sleep. I slept until we landed for gas and a bite to eat.

Since I'd never flown a side-by-side or a wheel-controlled airplane, Carl took off. Once we were on course, I took over and he leaned back for a nap.

It was around three o'clock when a few clouds drifted in. The further west we flew, the more dense they became. Soon, rain showers were skipping blithely about us. I woke Carl to ask if we should look for a place to land. He checked the map, found no landing strip near our position and told me to steer clear of the thunderstorms and keep on course. Then he went back to sleep.

The air was rough and, as the plane pitched and lurched through the turbulent air, I became increasingly nervous. The rain showers came more frequently and the visibility, at times, was only a few hundred feet. I wished Carl would stay awake—for moral support if nothing else. However, I wasn't one to question my husband's judgment, so I flew on while he dozed, his head on my shoulder.

Suddenly, I sat up straight and blinked twice. Looming ever larger through the mist, was a blue and silver ghost of a plane, identical to the one I was flying!

I acted strictly on reflex, jerking the wheel to the right and down. Fortunately, the pilot of the other plane went in the opposite direction and we missed colliding by what seemed inches.

The sudden maneuver woke Carl.

"What happened?" he asked.

"We almost collided head-on with another plane."

I was shaking like a leaf.

"Are you OK?" he asked, taking over the controls.

"Yeah," I replied. "I just need a little time—"

It stopped raining soon after; the clouds began to lift, and the sun came out. After checking weather conditions, Carl climbed to six-thousand feet to take advantage of a thirty-mile-an-hour tailwind. We reached Marysville well before dark.

The Blue Bird
(Photo by "Armchair Aviator" D. Miller, Flickr - Used per Creative Commons Lic. 2.0)

# Doctor Randall Buys a Plane

The new Taylorcraft was an outstanding success.

*The Marysville Advocate* ran a picture with the caption: *Marysville's First Post War Plane.*

"You'd think we were the property of the city," I laughed when I saw the article. "First, *I* was Marysville's First Airborne Bride, *You* are Marysville's First Flying Instructor, *I* am Marysville's First Woman Pilot, *This* is Marysville's Airport, *We* are Marysville's Flying Ungerers, and now *This* is Marysville's First Post War Plane!"

We'd placed an ad in both newspapers before leaving for Alliance, inviting the public to come out and take a ride in the new plane. Both the ads and the article ran on Thursday, May 2. On Sunday, "Blue Bird" made her debut. A sizable crowd turned out, and both Blue Bird and the L-2 were in the air for most of the day, Carl taking rides in the new plane while students practiced their maneuvers in the L-2.

As usual, Lillian brought sandwiches, and Dad helped keep traffic under control.

"Isn't it great to have two airplanes flying at the same time!" I exclaimed when Carl took a break for a bite to eat.

"Ungerer Flying Service is on its way!" he replied.

Dr. Randall arrived at the airport shortly after noon, flew an hour solo in the L-2 and took two rides in the new plane. The next morning, he came out, bringing his wife and two daughters with him.

"I want another ride in the new plane," he announced.

"I have a couple ahead of you, if you don't mind waiting," Carl said.

"We'll wait."

I visited with Mrs. Randall while Carl and Dr. Randall were out.

They were out much longer than usual and, when they returned, Dr. Randall insisted that his wife and two daughters go for a ride. That done, they sat in their car for another hour, watching the planes take off and land.

It was well after sundown when the last car drove away. We serviced the planes, rolled them into the hangar, and drove home, weary but happy. Tomorrow, Carl would start checking out the more advanced students in the new plane.

The next morning, Carl was flying with a student in the L-2 when Dr. Randall arrived at the airport, unannounced.

He climbed out of the car, looked toward the flight line where Blue Bird was tethered, then came to the office.

"I don't have an appointment," he said, seeing me check the schedule. "I just want to talk to Carl."

"He'll be out another twenty-five minutes," I said. He turned and walked toward Blue Bird.

I watched from the door as he walked around the plane, occasionally caressing the smooth fabric.

"It's too bad you aren't checked out in it," I said, joining him. "You could take it out."

"Oh, I didn't come out to fly," he said, wiping an imaginary speck from the gleaming prop. "I want to buy the plane."

We hated to part with her so soon, but we *were* operating a business, and the commission on the sale would make a down payment on another plane.

That afternoon, Carl called Red Taylor.

"Congratulations!" Red said. "Yeah. I should have one ready for pick up sometime Wednesday."

Wednesday afternoon, Carl and I flew to Salina to pick up our new plane. Other than the serial number, it was identical to the one we'd sold Dr. Randall.

"Three planes!" I exclaimed as we rolled them into the hangar that night. "Ungerer Airport is growing by leaps and bounds!"

Even though we had more rain in May than in April, the proverbial rainy month, we managed to get in a good amount of flying. Our charter service increased steadily as the public became accustomed to the idea of chartering an airplane for, as the newspapers stated, *a more rapid and convenient means of travel.* Carl made trips to Kansas City, Omaha, St. Louis, and Chicago, as well as several flights closer to home. As time passed, we flew a great many interesting people—and things—including machinery parts, movie film, dogs, letters, people who needed medical attention, and corpses.

As we became acquainted with other veteran pilots who, like Carl, had started airports of their own, we found that enthusiasm ran high throughout the area as the post-war "Air Age" progressed. Predictions, both real and unrealistic, ran rampant about the future of aviation.

"Do you think the time will really come when the airplane will replace the automobile in long distance travel?" I asked Carl as we drove to the airport one morning.

"I don't know about *that*," he replied. "But if this *is* the 'Air Age,' we're certainly in the right place—and our job right now is to make the time and place for airplanes right handy."

All eleven students were making progress toward achieving private pilot licenses, and men returning from the war continued to inquire as to when training would be available on the GI Bill. Some who had joined the Air Corps hoping to fly had "washed out" of the Air Cadet course; others had been assigned to other duties and never been given the opportunity to fly. To learn at the government's expense would be the answer to many dreams.

We awoke to the persistent patter of rain on the roof.

I sighed happily and snuggled closer to Carl. A day off! A rare opportunity to relax—to catch up on housework.

After breakfast, Carl hiked over to his folks, leaving me the car to shop for groceries. An hour later, he called and said that he and his dad were going downtown on business. Wonderful! I had the day to myself. I cleaned until the house shone, did my shopping, then took a long, hot bath and donned a house dress. Carl returned as I was heading downstairs to prepare dinner.

"Hey! The house looks great!" he said, looking me up and down. "And so do you!"

"Thank you, Sir."

"I'm glad you haven't started dinner," he said then. "Lillian insisted we come over there and from the way her kitchen smells, she's been having one of her cooking marathons. Seems like when she gets started she doesn't know when to stop."

"I'll go change then," I said. "While I'm doing that, why don't you take a bath and put on fresh clothes?"

"Dad and I made arrangements to build a new runway today," he said as we dressed.

"A new runway?"

"We stopped by the post office and there was a letter from the Veterans Administration. Seems like one of the requirements for our obtaining a government contract for training students is that we'd have to add another runway."

"Now they tell us."

"Yes. Dad and I leased the land to the east. I measured it out for a northwest/southeast runway. It'll be shorter than the north-south runway—only 1280 feet—but long enough to meet CAA requirements. I made arrangements to rent the equipment and do the work myself. It shouldn't take long, given a break in the weather."

The delicious odor of home cooked food greeted us when we walked in the folk's door. Dinner was on the table; wine poured.

"What kind is it?" I asked picking up my glass and sipping the light, sweet wine.

"Cherry," Dad said. Picking up his glass, he sipped the wine and smacked his lips.

"Two years old. Best I've made in a long time. We had a good crop that year—after I started sittin' out in the orchard with my shotgun to keep the starlings off."

After we ate, I helped Lillian gather up the plates and carry them to the kitchen. When we returned to the table with plates of apple pie, Carl and Dad were talking about Dr. Randall.

"He's doing great," Carl was saying. "The boys have a tendency to piddle around sometimes. But not Doc. You'll always see him out there in the practice area, practicing his maneuvers."

When we arrived at the airport the next morning the sun was just breaking over the horizon. The sky was clear, and the windsock hung limply from its vantage point on the hangar. Carl walked to the top of the hill to check the condition of the runway.

"It's a little soft," he said when he returned, "but not too much."

"After all the wind we had last week when everyone wanted to fly, it's too bad you don't have a student this morning," I said as we pushed the planes out of the hangar.

"I have," Carl replied.

"Who?"

"You," he said. "We need to get you working harder toward that private license."

He was right. I'd been flying when a plane was available and, though I was stacking up hours, I hadn't been practicing the maneuvers. I had a lot of catching up to do to meet the qualifications for a private pilot license.

Once Frederick had his business up and going, he began taking flying lessons and had recently challenged me.

"Hell, I started from scratch," he said. "At the rate you're going, I'll bet I get my license before you get yours!"

I settled myself in the front seat of the L-2. Carl propped the plane and once he was settled in the back seat, I took off. We flew for about an hour while Carl put me through the basic maneuvers. Although somewhat rusty; I did fairly well.

"You just need to practice a little more on your maneuvers and take your cross-country," Carl said when we landed. "Also, be more careful to log your flights. You've been a little negligent there."

"Yessuh, boss," I replied, my arm circling his waist as we walked to the office where the first student of the day was waiting.

We had decided that, since I was most familiar with the L-2, I would take my flight check in it. The students came first so it was several days before I had another chance to fly. I went out a couple of times during the mid-day hours and, despite the turbulence, diligently practiced the maneuvers.

"It may not be as pleasant, but there's one advantage," Carl said when I came in after a particularly bumpy ride. "You are not only mastering the maneuvers, you're learning to cope with adverse wind and weather conditions."

We used a business trip to Salina with a side trip to Belleville to log in my dual cross-country. All I needed now was a time when the plane was available, and the weather suitable, to fly the solo cross-country. Although I had flown solo to several surrounding towns, including Lincoln and Salina, I hadn't flown the required triangular route, getting signed verification at three separate airports.

Finding the time when the plane was available was the problem. Then, one morning, one of the students was called in to work and postponed his appointment until the following day.

I decided to fly one of our easiest and most popular routes—to Belleville, Hastings, Nebraska, and home.

"You couldn't have asked for a more perfect day for a cross-country flight." Carl said as I climbed into the cockpit.

He was right. The sky was cloudless, the air calm, with a gentle breeze blowing out of the northeast.

I took off to the north, flew the flight pattern, headed west, climbed to 500 feet and leveled out. Although Carl preferred traveling at higher altitudes, I liked flying lower to enjoy the view of the countryside. Once airborne, I leaned back and looked about savoring the beauty of the rolling green hills, the river with its border of green trees and shrubs, winding through the valley; the lush fertile land planted with various crops.

The flight to Belleville was a no-brainer—I had only to follow Highway 36. Forty minutes after takeoff, I landed, got the required signature and took off for Hastings.

I was back home two and a half hours after I left.

When I arrived, Carl was working on the new runway. It was almost completed.

Three days later, Carl pronounced me ready for the flight check. As he'd suggested, I'd logged all my flights of late—including those flown for reasons other than practice. The fact that I'd accumulated almost twice the required number of hours, should be in my favor, he said.

All I need do now was to wait for decent weather, and for the plane to be available.

So far, we had applications from eleven GIs who wanted to start taking lessons as soon as the contract was approved.

On the day the northwest/southeast runway was ready, Carl and I completed the forms and posted them, so they'd go off to the Veteran's Administration the following day.

"Hopefully, that will take care of everything they need," Carl said wearily.

May continued to be uneventful until, the last of the month, a tornado struck northeast of town, leaving a large amount of damage in its wake. Carl flew the photographer from the *Marysville Advocate* over the area to take shots for the newspaper. Thank God, no one had been injured.

Mrs. Carl Ungerer flies, writes columns, and performs other duties at Airport.

# Irish McCalla and Noodling

With the coming of June, the rain began—again. The Marysville newspapers reported 8.60 inches for the month with a total of 20 inches for the year. Much of the time, the runways were too soft for students to fly.

Carl used the alfalfa strip paralleling the runway to fly a few charter trips, as well as tours for curiosity seekers wanting an air view of the Blue River which was threatening to overflow its banks.

July brought dry weather, strong winds, and stifling temperatures. Since heavy turbulence prevented students flying during the middle of the day, there was always a scramble for available time in early morning and late evening.

While Carl flew, I tended to my usual chores. Onlookers and visitors, asking innumerable questions, added substantially to my duties.

When Carl wasn't training students, giving rides, or on a charter trip, he always had planes to service and runways to keep in condition.

When there was no possibility of flying, we often participated in one of Carl's favorite pastimes—hunting or fishing. Depending on the season, we'd head for a local lake or river bank with fishing poles, or to the open fields to hunt pheasants, quail, ducks, rabbits, or squirrels.

As Carl predicted, the Sunday pleasure rides had fallen off. However, pleasant weather usually brought out a crowd of onlookers and even though, with the passing of time, rides were fewer in number, they added much needed dollars to our bank account.

Our charter service was often more lucrative than training students.

During the summer Nellie McCalla, who had graduated from high school in the spring and was spending the summer with an aunt in Marysville, began showing up at the airport almost daily on her morning walk. (She had to watch her weight she said.) She was always accompanied by several girlfriends.

Nellie was tall girl, pretty, and well-built. She and her friends usually arrived mid-morning, purchased Cokes from the machine, and hung around, watching the planes take off and land, listening enthusiastically if some of the students happened to be doing a little "hangar flying," often exaggerated for the girls' benefit.

A couple of times Nellie asked Carl to fly her to Pawnee City, Nebraska to visit her parents. It was only forty-five miles by road, less than an hour's drive, but Nellie liked flying.

It was along about this time that she started insisting her friends stop calling her Nellie—to call her "Irish."

The last time Carl flew her to Pawnee City, her friends were waiting when they returned.

"I flew the plane back," I heard her say as they walked off. There were numerous "oh's" and "ah's" and questions.

"No sweat," Nellie said. "It's actually easier than driving a car. I could have my private pilot license in no time."

She didn't sign up for flying lessons, however, and when, a couple of months later, Nellie stopped showing up at the airport, we figured she'd gone back home. Then we heard that she'd gone to California.

Several months passed and we began to hear rumors: "Irish" McCalla had wound up in Hollywood, been discovered by a producer, and was now the star of a moving picture called "Sheena, Queen of the Jungle."

Liberal with his time, his money, and his advice, Dad, our staunch supporter, was there for us anytime we needed a helping hand. He knew more "short cuts" to get things done than I knew existed and was always available for a "touch" when the first of the month came around and we hadn't taken in enough to meet our bills.

He was also a morale booster. Thinking we were working too hard, he encouraged us to "take it easy." He and Lillian would sometimes appear at the airport on a windy afternoon, the car loaded with fishing equipment and a picnic lunch.

"Let's take the afternoon off!" he'd say. We seldom turned him down.

It was on a hot July afternoon that I was introduced to "noodling" (taking fish in its natural habitat). Though illegal, that never seemed to worry Dad. Whereas success in fishing with a pole depends mostly on luck, getting into the water where the fish have the advantage makes it physical.

Carl and I were, as usual, playing catch up with some of the ground work. It was in the high 90s in the shade; the windsock stood straight out, and dust devils swirled gleefully up and down the runways.

The planes had been rolled into the hangar, out of the wind, and Carl was trying to secure the hangar doors to prevent their banging. I was at my desk, dripping with perspiration, sipping on a Coke, when Dad and Lillian and friends, Joe and Hazel Cooper, drove into the parking area.

"Lock up!" Dad yelled. "Let's go noodle a couple a catfish!"

I'd never noodled, but I knew that it meant a hand to hand combat with catfish in its natural environment. The idea of tussling with a slick, slimy, horny catfish in four feet of muddy water sent chills up my spine. However, it was so hot and uncomfortable in the office that getting into water, for any reason, overcame the distaste, so I agreed, and we did as Dad suggested—locked up and went fishing.

I avoided contact with the fish at first, but everyone seemed to be having such a good time, I decided to give it a try. *Perhaps, once I catch one, I'll learn to enjoy it,* I thought, so when a small bullhead got caught in the net next to my elbow, I reached down, put my thumb into his mouth, as I'd been instructed, and held him up for the others to see. Suddenly, the fish clamped down with his saw teeth. I screamed and shook him loose.

Dad painstakingly explained what I'd done wrong but after that, I left the "noodling" up to the others.

We ended up with a gunny-sack full of catfish and carp and by the time we changed into dry clothes and returned to the airport, the wind had died down and the first evening student was just driving up.

# GI Training, KAW and
# Marysville Municipal Airport

"I sent Dan out to shoot takeoffs and landings in the Blue Bird," Carl said, entering the office. "Keep your eye on him while I run to the post office. And keep your fingers crossed!" he called back as he went out the door.

He was impatient. August already, and still no word from the VA even though, in the past eight months, we had complied with all the government requirements and completed a seemingly endless supply of forms.

He had been gone only twenty minutes when I saw the car speeding up the road, leaving a heavy trail of dust. He turned into the parking lot on two wheels. His face beamed as he strode toward the office.

"It came!" he exclaimed, picking me up and whirling me around. "The VA approval came!"

At last! We had fifteen GIs, the number allotted, waiting to begin training.

Usually calm and cool, no matter the circumstances, I'd seldom seen Carl this exuberant. He had obviously been more concerned than I'd thought.

"Start making appointments!" he said and went out to check on Dan who was still shooting spot landings.

The following week, *The Marysville Advocate* asked if I would like to write a "Flying" column, reporting on airport news and activities. It proved to be an immediate success. *The Marshall County News* asked to publish it as well.

The wheels of progress turned rapidly. Carl spent every available minute in the air and all fifteen GI students had logged an hour or two when we learned that everything was going to change—and not exactly as we had planned.

I had just seen Bud Shortle off for an hour solo time and was working on the books when Carl returned from the Chamber of Commerce meeting.

He was exceptionally quiet—thoughtful.

"What's wrong, Honey?" I asked, looking up from my desk.

He cleared his throat.

"The city has applied for a grant to build a municipal airport," he said.[6]

"They what?"

"It isn't as bad as it sounds," he said. He sat down, leaned back, and put his feet up on the desk. "Actually, I suppose it could even turn out to be a good thing. All the Chamber members are thrilled at the prospect. It will be great for the city—and for all concerned—even us, they say. Although I can't help wondering about that."

"But why? We're doing a good job; why do they want to interfere?"

"Because they can. The government is making grants available to municipalities for the construction, expansion, and improvement of airports.[7] Actually, it's a good idea. It means more and better runways, new and improved buildings. The report is that the runways will be blacktopped and equipped with landing lights."

He paused. "I'm to be appointed airport manager."

"You mean we'll be working for the city."

"As airport manager only," he replied. "We'll continue running our own business, own our own planes, train students, provide charter service, and all that," he said.

He got up and stretched.

I still felt depressed. We had devoted our lives for over nine months to building the business. It was our dream. We had worked damned hard to make it a success and were proud of what we had accomplished.

"That's life, I guess." Carl said. "Progress is progress; things change. It may be for the better, who knows? Maybe we did too good a job—suppose?"

He gave me a peck on the cheek and went out to greet his next student for an hour of dual. I glanced at the windsock. The wind was going down. They would have a good flight.

I sat down at my desk and thought over what Carl had told me. I wondered that he wasn't as upset as I was; didn't he resent being reduced to the role of caretaker?

*Oh, come on!* I told myself. *As Carl said, he would just be exchanging his services as airport manager for the privilege of using the facilities for his own business. We'll just be leasing from the city instead of someone else. With Carl as airport manager, we'll no longer have to pay rent. Not only that, we'll have more updated space to work from.*

It didn't seem to help; I still felt frustrated—and resentful. Had there not been an airport here—an airport we had built, the city wouldn't have had an airport to improve!

*It'll be all right,* I assured myself, turning back to the forms spread out on my desk. We had to believe that everything would work out for the best.

"Where will the new buildings be?" I asked Carl the next morning.

I followed him outside and across the ramp. He pointed to the northwest.

"Up there," he said. "On top of the hill."

We walked slowly to the area he'd indicated.

"What all does the city plan to do?"

"Well, in addition to new runways, they will build a new administration building with waiting room, rest rooms, office space, and six T-hangars. The present runways will be leveled, broadened, and lengthened, and they'll build another—northeast by southwest. They are all to be blacktopped, and landing lights will be installed for night-flying."

"It all sounds very posh."

"You'll like the administration building," he said. "Plans show that it will have broad windows with a view of, not only the runways, but also most of the flight pattern."

"Sounds wonderful. I'll just have to get used to the idea. I've gotten sort of attached to things as they are."

He put his arm around me and we walked slowly back to the office.

"I feel better about it than I did yesterday," he said, trying to sound cheerful. "Yeah, like you said, we'll just have to get used to the idea. 'Onward! Upward!' as they say."

"When is all this to take place?"

"They've already submitted the application. As soon as it's approved, the city will ask for bids for various construction jobs. Who knows how long that will take? By this time next year we may be operating from a brand new, improved airport."

"What will happen to our buildings?"

He shrugged. "We'll continue to hangar our planes here; probably lose our renters though. No doubt, they'll move to a hangar at the new location."

"Wonder what Jim will think about this?"

"Like us, he'll probably have mixed emotions. However, the only thing we can do is to go along with the city and wait to see how it plays out."

Carl returned from the next Chamber of Commerce meeting to report that the city had purchased the land. Pending approval of the grant, bids would be taken for construction of the administration building and reconstruction of the runways.

The city had agreed with his request that one runway be accessible at all times while construction was in progress.

"We might as well look at it optimistically," Carl said. "Once it's completed, we'll have a better field to operate off of. We won't have to worry about mowing or grading, and we won't be hampered by runways we can't use because of mud or snow. And think about the beautiful new office you'll have—much better than this old chicken coop."

"I just happen to be attached to this old chicken coop," I retorted. "There was a lot of hope and hard work built into it."

I still couldn't help feeling sad. Our dream was no longer ours alone. Now that the airport belonged to the city, there would, of necessity, be adjustments. Some good. Some not so good. I wondered how much difference it would make.

Our next surprise was that a new airline, Kansas Airways (KAW), had been established, and the city had started a financial drive to raise $12,000 to support Marysville's inclusion on their route.

Originating in St. Francis, flights would include stops in Goodland, Colby, Atwood, Oberlin, Norton, Phillipsburg, Mankato, Belleville, Clay Center, Marysville, Topeka, Lawrence, and Kansas City.

Representatives of Kansas Airways, flying a five-place Cessna, made their first official landing at the Marysville airport on August 15. Two weeks later, a nine-passenger, twin engine Beechcraft was put into service.

The newspapers headlined the event as *A New Era in Transportation for Marysville*.

Our runways were not as good as some on the route but were better than others, and even though the plane had to bypass Marysville occasionally because of muddy runways, the fact that a government grant for airport improvement was forthcoming made Marysville an excellent inclusion.

---

[6] AIRPORT IMPROVEMENT PLAN  On May 24, 1946, President Harry S. Truman signed the Federal Airport Act which provided funding for airport construction and improvements. The act provided for $500 million in grants for airport projects. The maximum federal grant for an eligible project would provide half the project's cost. Local sponsors would issue bonds to finance the balance of the cost.

[7] All projects had to meet CAA standards for location, layout, grading, drainage, paving and lighting. January 9, 1947, regulations governing the administration of the Federal Airport Act received final approval. Two days later CAA announced

the 1947 construction program, listing 800 airports for either construction or improvement. The National Airport Plan contained requirements involving 4,431 locations.

Kansas Airways

# Jim Returns

S trong winds over the Labor Day holidays followed by rain and muddy runways kept the planes grounded much of the time early in the month. By mid-September, however, all fifteen of our GI students were well into the program.

Twenty-six students, training in only two planes, was impossible, so we added a used plane—a BC12D to our fleet. Still, with three planes and one instructor, I was kept busy juggling the schedule to work them all in. Turbulence during the day continued to add to the challenge. The more advanced civilian students sometimes braved the turbulence, but most were morning or evening flyers.

Carl knew from the first hour of training which students would make good pilots, and which would not. He discouraged two of the new GI students early in training.

"It isn't worth the risk," he'd say, as the student climbed glumly into his car.

I learned that training students under the GI Bill increased my work exponentially when, a few days after receiving our approval, my desk was buried in government forms—to be completed and submitted to the government the first of each month. In addition to those required by the VA, I also kept each student's logbook, the airplane and engine logs, Carl's logbook and mine, as well as financial records for the business.

Our days, beginning before dawn when we rolled the planes out of the hangar and tied them down on the flight line, were long and strenuous.

By the time the sun peeped over the horizon, the first student arrived, sleepy-eyed, for his morning lesson. Soon, another two or three appeared and, God willing and weather permitting, others came out for lessons during the day. When the last student landed at night, Carl and I together serviced the planes and rolled them into the hangar.

We held ground school classes in meteorology and navigation three nights a week, and it was often ten or eleven o'clock when we arrived home, tired and hungry.

When he wasn't flying with a student, Carl gave rides and took charter trips and serviced the planes. In addition to struggling with the never-ending stack of forms, I greeted visitors, helped service the planes, and propped planes for solo students when Carl was out.

Although I refused to admit it, I seemed always to be tired. Working from dawn until well into the night seven days a week was taking its toll. I sometimes wondered how Carl kept going with twenty-four students demanding his time.

We were counting the days until Jim would complete A and E training. His return would take a great deal of the pressure off both of us. During his absence we had been flying the planes to Beatrice or Salina for checkups and service.

*Perhaps after he comes home, Carl and I can take a day or two off*, I thought; although that seemed too much to hope for.

He arrived home the latter part of the September. His first day at work was on a Sunday which turned out to be a beautiful day. All three planes were in the air from dawn until dark. We had more Sunday visitors than we'd had for some time, and if a student wasn't scheduled to fly, a newly licensed pilot was waiting for a plane, or someone was waiting to take a ride. It was good to have Jim there, not only to service and prop the planes, but also to help greet people and answer questions.

Judging by the crowd, the public hadn't lost interest in flying as Carl had predicted. In fact, public interest seemed to be increasing. I attributed this, in part, to the KAW airline, and also to the numerous new post war planes—Taylorcrafts, Cessnas, Stinsons, Ercoupes, Bonanzas and others—which landed frequently at the airport; and, of course, to the families and friends of our numerous students.

Days like this helped make up for those when inclement weather kept us grounded.

Despite the numerous changes in our circumstances, Carl was optimistic about our future.

Kansas Airways, flying a twin motor, nine passenger Beechcraft, carrying both passengers and express, now stopped in twice a day; once on the east flight, once on the west. By late-September, $8,000 of the $12,000 sought to support the airline, had been raised, and the quota needed was dropped from $12,000 to $10,000.

Ungerer Flying Service was responsible for the selling of tickets for the flights and aiding passengers in any way necessary. To our advantage, rather than having to do the work ourselves, the city would now provide men and equipment to clear the runways during inclement weather and keep them in condition.

In spite of the city's dedication, however, the airline had by-passed Marysville twice because of muddy runways. When the airline added a north-south line, flying a five-place Cessna, which was thought to be better capable of handling soft runways, we were placed on that route.

With the three of us, our days were still hectic but, even so, Carl and I *were* able to relax a little; take an hour off now and then, sometimes scheduling an appointment a little later or leaving early if no dual was scheduled.

"I think what we've got ourselves is a combination business, a school, a circus, and a headache," Carl laughed one morning as the three of us rolled the planes out of the hangar.

"Well," I said, "isn't it what we asked for?"

And it did have its rewarding moments.

Since it was necessary that I spend so many hours at the airport, housework was of secondary importance. I'd never been good at housekeeping, but I did like my house clean and neat. When I could get away from the airport, I'd slave away cleaning, polishing, shining. I expected it to stay that way. Of course, it didn't.

Both Carl and I were guilty of coming in at night, dead tired, and dropping everything in the nearest corner. In no time, the house would be a mess again.

Carl, good-naturedly, didn't seem to mind.

"As long as there's a strip wide enough for me to get to the table and the bed, I'll be okay," he'd say.

I couldn't neglect the work at the airport, but it bothered me to see everything get so far behind at home. I found myself actually looking forward to a day when the weather prevented our flying.

It wasn't only that I'd have time to give the house an occasional cleaning; it was a pleasant feeling to look out the window to see rain or snow and get back into bed. It meant a few extra hours of rest and relaxation. On days such as this, we'd sleep until eight or nine o'clock and then enjoy a leisurely breakfast—with enough time for hotcakes. After breakfast, lingering over coffee, we discussed things we seldom had time to talk about.

"At least, this will give us a chance to catch up a little on the ground work," Carl said one such morning, as we drove to the airport. While I worked on the books, Carl helped Jim go over the planes. After lunch, I stayed at home and gave the house a good cleaning, washed and ironed clothes, and cooked a decent dinner. That night, we topped off the day by going to a movie; a rare treat.

Although that might not sound like a "day off" to most women, to me it was luxury. Is it any wonder that I still look forward to a bad weather day?

As enjoyable as a day away from the airport was, keeping the planes in the air was a priority if the business were to succeed. We felt extremely lucky that, housework or no, bad weather didn't come often that first year.

But to get back to my housekeeping:

Since my mother had never taught me the fine art of keeping house, I was at a disadvantage from the start. In the beginning, I tried to establish a schedule. That didn't work. The airport came first and, as the days passed, I was usually so exhausted when we arrived home at night that I prepared what was easiest and fastest for our supper. Quick meals became our way of life.

I thanked God for Spam, a canned meat product I'd become familiar with during the war. I kept several cans on hand and our evening meal often consisted of Spam and eggs, served at the kitchen table, with a head of lettuce and a couple of tomatoes for a salad. More often than not, I left the dishes on the table and less than an hour after arriving home, we were in bed, the alarm set for four o'clock when, as Carl said: we'd "hit it again."

Grocery shopping was a problem. I learned, early on, that it was unwise to buy many perishables, as I never knew when I'd have time to prepare them. So, I relied chiefly on canned foods. When there was time, I turned to the freezer which contained a plentiful supply of meats from our hunting and fishing expeditions.

Coming downstairs to a sink full of dirty dishes and an empty refrigerator one morning, we headed for the nearest restaurant.

"I think we should hire a housekeeper," Carl said as we ate.

"Can we afford it?" I asked.

"What do you think? You keep the books."

Once at the office, I did some figuring.

And so Mrs. Zabronski entered our lives.

Jim Working on Plane

Edna Bell-Pearson

# Mrs. Zabronski

A lthough our workload was heavy, things were going as smoothly as could be expected at the airport.

They weren't, however, going so well at home.

Relieved that I no longer had the house and meals to worry about, I had placed a lot of faith in our new housekeeper. A big woman, Mrs. Zabronski should have had no problem handling our housework. We soon learned better. Her "housekeeping" left much to be desired. Even so, had our meals been properly prepared and ready on time, her laziness might have been acceptable. As it was, we often came down for breakfast in the morning, or arrived home for lunch at noon, to find nothing on the table. "It won't be but a minute!" she'd say leaving us to cool our heels until the meal was on the table.

"Call Mrs. Zabronski and tell her to have lunch ready by eleven-thirty," Carl said one morning, hurrying into the office. "Tell her it *has* to be on time; that I have a charter trip to Wichita at twelve-thirty.

"Where are the Cessna brochures?" he asked then. "While I'm waiting for Ron to take care of his business, I'll check in at the Cessna factory and look over their new planes."

I took the brochures from the file and spread them out on the desk.

"I might as well talk to the distributor about a dealership while I'm there," he added.

The Cessna 120 had rolled off the production line earlier in the year as had the 140, an upgraded version to which flaps had been added.

Mrs. Zabronski answered on the tenth ring.

"Mrs. Zabronski, we have to have lunch by eleven thirty today," I said.

**114**

"Oh, no! I haven't even taken the chicken out of the freezer. It won't be ready until at least twelve-thirty!"

I sighed.

"Mrs. Zabronski, Carl has a charter trip this afternoon; we have to eat by eleven-thirty at the latest."

The line went silent.

"Why don't you open a can of soup and serve it with a sandwich made from the ham left over from yesterday. Open a can of peaches for dessert. Just make sure everything is on the table by eleven thirty." I hung up.

"It's a quarter after eleven," I said. "Best we head for home."

When we arrived, Mrs. Zabronski was leisurely slicing the ham, the table was bare and the unopened can of soup sat on the drainboard.

Carl was furious. He stomped up the stairs to wash up.

Not only was lunch not ready, the breakfast dishes were still in the sink, unwashed. Sensing our anger, Mrs. Zabronski remained silent while I opened the can of soup, emptied it into a pan and set it on the stove to warm. While she fried the ham, I set the table.

By the time Carl came downstairs, lunch was ready. The three of us sat down at the table (She had insisted on taking her meals with us).

Silence hung heavy in the air; then Mrs. Zabronski began to talk. (Mrs. Zabronski dearly loved to talk).

"God damn it, woman!" Carl said angrily. "Will you please shut your damned mouth?"

She paused, an astonished expression on her face.

"Well—" she started to say huffily then, seeing the look on Carl's face, she resumed eating.

As we drove back to the airport, I talked about Cessna airplanes, carefully avoiding any mention of Mrs. Zabronski.

The afternoon passed slowly. Only three students were scheduled to fly. Jim had taken the afternoon off, so I propped the planes for them and spent the afternoon on bookwork.

I thought about calling Mrs. Zabronski. I was hesitant to let her go. It would be impossible for me to keep up the house without help.

Perhaps I should start looking for someone to replace her.

George McAnany, the last student for the day, came in shortly after five.

"Are you planning to hang around for a while, George?" I asked.

"Got nothin' else to do," he replied.

"Would you mind keeping your eyes on things for a while? I need to run home for a minute."

"Sure thing," he replied. "Don't worry about coming back for Carl. I'll help close up and bring him home."

"I appreciate that. If you need me, just call."

When I arrived home, dinner was almost ready. The kitchen was clean and neat. Mrs. Zabronski had prepared the chicken and, in an obvious effort to make amends, had baked a chocolate pie—Carl's favorite.

I decided, however, not to pull any punches.

"I thought I'd better come home and see how things were going before Carl arrived," I said.

"I'm sorry about what happened at noon," she apologized. "Time just seems to get away from me and—"

"Mrs. Zabronski," I broke in, "What happened today cannot happen again. We hired you to make things easier for us—not more difficult. When you don't do your part, it causes us a great inconvenience. Your constant chatter and gossip is also annoying; it irritates Carl."

"I'm sorry, Mrs. Ungerer. I really am. And I promise, from now on it's going to be different. I swear it!"

"I don't know—" I started to say when she broke in.

"Just let me try," she begged. "I like working for you real well and I can do it right."

"All right," I relented. She seemed sincere, and domestic help was hard to find. "We'll try a little longer. However, after this, Carl and I will eat alone. We like to discuss business matters privately, and this will give us time to talk. You can eat either before we do or after, whichever you prefer."

She turned as if to argue but, instead, closed her mouth tightly and continued stirring the gravy.

"We'll eat in the dining room tonight," I said and headed up the stairs to freshen up. Halfway up, I stopped and leaned over the railing.

"Put on an extra plate," I called. "George is bringing Carl home. We'll ask him to stay for dinner."

When I came down later, Mrs. Zabronski had set the dining room table for four. I quietly removed one of the plates and returned it to the kitchen.

Lady and Dobber's barking announced the arrival of George and Carl.

When Blackie joined the family, he always followed at Carl's heels, ignoring Lady and Dobber, no doubt feeling they weren't worth his time. As a result, I made sure to give them extra attention, so they wouldn't feel left out.

I went to the door.

"You might as well stay for dinner, George," I called out. "We already have your place set at the table!"

His grin told me that was exactly what he'd been hoping for.

"I'll mix drinks while you two wash up," I said.

While we ate, Mrs. Zabronski, obviously furious, banged pots and pans so loudly we could hardly hear each other talk. I got up from the table and quietly closed the door.

Carl looked at me and raised his eyebrows.

"Later," I said.

"Anything happen while I was gone?" he asked as we were dressing for bed.

"The Standard Oil boys stopped in. Said they'd catch you next time."

"Those boys are on their toes. We need more aviation boosters like them,"

"They're certainly doing all they can to be sure we small airport operators get off to a good start."

He nodded in agreement.

"I came home early to have a talk with Mrs. Zabronski. I told her we'd try it a little longer, and that you and I would eat alone from now on."

"Good," he said. "I just hope she'll start having our meals on time."

It had to happen; Mrs. Zabronski pulled her final stunt.

After her plea to stay on, I hoped she would at least make an effort to keep things up, and she did tolerably well—for the next ten days.

My head was deep in the books when Carl stormed into the office after a trip to the post office.

"Whatever is wrong?" I asked when he entered the office, banging the door furiously.

"I stopped by home," he said. "And that woman is having a God-damned party—in our house! She is serving dinner to four of her relatives—complete with *our* wine and *our* food!"

"Oh, no," I said.

"I'd decided to stop by Dad's, and when I drove by the house, I saw two cars in the driveway. Naturally, I stopped to see what was going on. You should have seen the look on their faces when I walked in."

"What did you say?"

"Nothing. I was so damned mad, I was afraid to say anything."

"As soon as you get back from flying with Pete, I'll go home and tell her to go," I said. "We may have to eat out for a while, but we'll just have to manage until we find someone else."

It was a couple of hours before I could get away. When I entered the house, Mrs. Zabronski was nowhere to be seen. The kitchen was clean; there was no sign that a party had been going on. Hearing a noise upstairs, I went up to find her hurrying about, packing her suitcase. She looked up.

"My son is coming to pick me up in a few minutes," she said. "I was going to leave you a note. I guess it didn't work out very well, did it?"

I didn't reply; shaking my head, I went downstairs to write her last check.

# Mrs. Jones

J im eased Carl's workload a great deal but, for me, housework
continued to be a major problem.

"Perhaps we could hire someone to work at the airport part
time," I suggested.

After considering the idea, we discarded it as impractical. Finding someone capable of handling my odd mixture of duties would
be a challenge.

"No way!" Jim said. "There's no one that could keep this place
running as smoothly as you do!"

Then Nadine Watson told me about an elderly lady who was
interested in keeping house for us.

Her daughter brought her to the airport for an interview.

My hopes had been high, but when Mrs. Jones entered the office, my heart fell. She was a sweet-faced, little old lady with blue
eyes and white hair. I liked her immediately but doubted she could
handle our two-story house. Although she suffered from arthritis
occasionally, she said, she was confident she could do what we
needed done. The wage she asked for was much less than we'd
paid Mrs. Zabronski. All she wanted, she said, was a pleasant home
and something to keep her occupied.

"What about climbing stairs, Mrs. Jones?" I asked. "We live in a
two-story house and your bedroom and the bathroom is on the
second floor."

"I can manage as long as I take it slow," she replied.

"Also," I said. "Carl and I keep very strange hours. We usually
have breakfast at four-thirty in the morning and our evening meal
is sometimes as late as ten o'clock at night. As for lunch, it may be
at any hour during the day and often must be ready at a moment's
notice."

"My husband and I lived on a farm, so I'm used to long hours," she replied. "He died recently, and I get lonely living alone. All my children, except Rose here, live back east. They've all invited me to move in with them, but I want to stay here."

"I've tried to get her to move in with me," Rose interrupted.

"I love you, dear, but you and Bill have your own lives. I would feel useless living with you. I want something to do—to be with someone who needs me."

"You would be by yourself most of the time if you worked for us," I reasoned. "Carl and I spend all our days at the airport—unless the weather prevents us from flying."

"That doesn't matter; I'd know you'd be coming home sometime," she said, smiling. "And meanwhile, I'd have something to do to occupy my time."

I thought for a moment.

"All right," I decided. "We'll give it a try."

Her face lit up.

Despite her arthritis, Mrs. Jones proved to be a gem. The house was always tidy; our meals were deliciously prepared and always on the table when we were ready to eat. She moved so quietly and unobtrusively that we hardly knew she was there. She preferred eating her meals at a regular time so having our meals alone was no problem. I suspected that, unlike Mrs. Zabronski, Mrs. Jones sensed our need for privacy. In addition to that, we'd never eaten so well. She was an expert at cooking up delicious pots of stew or a baked dinner. She often spent an entire morning picking out nut meats to add to a cake she was baking.

# The Ace

We awoke to dark skies and a steady drizzle.

"Do you think it'll let up?" I asked, studying the low, overcast sky as we drove to the airport.

"I don't think so," said Carl who was often more accurate at predicting weather than the meteorologist we tuned in on the radio each morning.

"I'd say it's settin' in for a spell," he said. "Oh well, maybe we can catch up a little on the paperwork; maybe give the boys some extra ground school training."

He drove past the office and up the hill on the edge of the runway. The car left deep ruts in the soft ground. He turned and headed back.

"The ceiling is over four hundred feet," he said. "We could take off on the sod in an emergency."

Jim hadn't shown up, and by the time we'd lugged open the hangar doors, the rain had diminished to a fine mist. Carl stood in the hangar door studying the sky.

"Now what?" I asked.

"Make some calls and see if you can schedule a ground school class for tonight—or tomorrow night," he said.

"On what?"

"I think meteorology would be a good subject," he laughed.

Most of the students would be at work, so there was no hurry to make the calls. I sat down at my desk, pulled the stack of logbooks forward, took one from the stack, and painstakingly began entering figures. With twenty-nine students to keep track of, the task sometimes seemed insurmountable. I didn't complain; Carl's responsibilities were much greater than mine.

I heard Jim arrive. As I worked, I could hear him whistling cheerfully, the two of them laughing, the occasional sound of metal on metal and the opening and closing of an engine cowling.

About an hour had passed when Carl entered and stood at the door for a minute, then he walked around the desk and bent over, his cheek next to mine.

"How would you like to have a date with an old washed-up pilot tonight?" he said.

"Washed out, maybe," I laughed. "But certainly not washed up! What did you have in mind, Sir?"

"I was thinking that, since it's going to be raining again tomorrow, you can catch up on that stuff for a while, then take off, get all dressed up, and I'll take you out to dinner and to a movie?"

"That would be marvelous!"

"That's what *I* thought. It's been much too long since I've had a real date with my favorite girl."

We had a great evening out; I even felt lighthearted as I attacked my books the next morning.

It had rained all night and was still raining when we arrived at the airport the next morning.

Entering figures on the stack of government forms before me, I was so deeply engrossed in my work that I startled when the telephone rang.

"Hi, Edna. Red Taylor here. Is Carl available?"

I went to the door. Carl was just coming from the workshop.

"Red Taylor is on the phone," I said.

"What does he want?"

"He didn't say."

He picked up the phone.

"Hi, Carl," Taylor said. "I've got a proposition I thought you might be interested in."

"I'm always interested in a good deal," Carl replied. "What have you got?"

We'd signed up two new students to replace the two Carl had washed out. With a total of twenty-nine students, we could still use another plane.

"Taylorcraft has put out an economy plane designed to be used as trainers," Red said. "It's a lighter, less expensive model of the BC12D. What the company did was leave off some of the equipment not necessary for training—like extra gas tanks—and cut back on the dope.[8] Sells for considerably less than the custom models. I got a break on the price by taking five of them. Now I find I can't handle the financing on all of them right now, so I'll let you have one of them at my cost. As many students as you've got, I figured you could probably use it.

"You figured right," Carl said. "How much?"

Red quoted a figure.

"Sounds great," Carl said. "I'll take it."

He replaced the receiver.

"We just bought another airplane," he said, repeating their conversation. "How's that for an answer to a prayer? Out of the blue a plane falls in our lap—at cost!"

"Can we get the financing?" I asked.

"For a deal that good, we'll manage—even if I have to put the touch on The Old Man." He sat down opposite me at the desk. "Let's do some figuring!"

Although our monthly income had increased, our expenses had increased right along with the business. After a checking our budget, Carl decided we could handle the additional payment.

"It doesn't leave anything for a down payment," he said. "I'll try to talk the banker into waiving that."

"We've been making our payments on time and he knows we're doing okay," I said.

"If he won't approve the loan, we've still got Dad."

"I'd rather not go to Dad unless we have to. We're still behind on what we owe him."

"He understands. He knows the money's coming. In fact, I think he gets a kick out of being a part of the business.

"Just wish I could get the old codger to fly," he added.

I laughed. The argument between Carl and his dad about his learning to fly had been long ongoing.

He stood, shoving back his chair. "I'm heading for the bank," he said.

I walked with him to the door then watched as he ducked his

head and ran for the car. The rain, which had slowed earlier to a mist, had developed into a steady downpour.

I returned to my desk.

An hour later Carl was back.

No problem," he said, shaking the water from his leather jacket. "The bank agreed to the terms I asked for."

"When will we get the plane?"

"As soon as the weather clears up,"

At ten o'clock Monday morning, he and I flew to Salina in the Blue Bird to pick up the new plane.

"The runways should be dry enough by mid-week for the students to fly," he said as we taxied out for take-off. "When we get back from Salina, we'll start lining up appointments. I'll fly dual with the advanced students in the new plane. Shouldn't take long to catch up on some of the time we've lost."

I fell in love with "The Ace" the minute I saw it. It was a brilliant red—my favorite color.

"Let me fly it back!" I exclaimed.

"You might fly around the field with her a time or two first," Red said. "It's a little hotter than the others."

I had no problem handling it. A couple of take-offs and landings was all it took.

"Land on the alfalfa strip," Carl reminded, waving me off.

As I took off, he was getting into the Blue Bird.

I landed in Marysville well ahead of Carl proving that the Ace was, indeed, a faster plane.

Although we'd purchased the Ace for training students, I claimed it as my own and never flew anything else if it was available.

The weather, which had turned crisp and cool, was perfect for flying.

Even though we now had four planes at their disposal, twenty-nine students were a lot for one instructor to handle, Carl was finding it difficult juggling his time when a flight instructor by the name of Marion Hoover stopped in one morning and asked for a job. His credentials were good, his licenses in order. Carl hired him.

Marion proved to be a very good instructor. With him on the job, the students began catching up on time lost. Several were nearing the end of the course and would soon be ready for their flight checks. Two of the more earnest GI students had signed up for the commercial course. Luckily, each time one of them completed the course, another was waiting to take his place.

The last of the month, we had two days of rain. The weather cleared Wednesday afternoon. Thursday morning dawned bright and sunny, and we were able to fly for the next several days.

---

[8] Aircraft dope is a plasticized lacquer that is applied to fabric covered planes. It tightens and stiffens the fabric which renders them air-tight and weather proof. The number of coats applied can add or detract from the weight of the aircraft.

Edna as Office Manager

# I Learned About Flying From That

"We've put it off long enough," Carl said one evening as we hangared the planes. "It's time you went for your flight check. Make the appointment, and we'll make the time."

Although I'd logged twice the number of hours necessary to qualify for a private pilot license, we'd been so busy I hadn't made time to go for my private pilot flight check.

Carl had another year as a civilian instructor to qualify as an examiner so most of the students flew to Salina to take the test.

The next morning, I called Salina and made an appointment for Thursday afternoon.

When Thursday arrived, the sky was clear, the sun warm and bright; a perfect day for flying. Since I'd done most of my flying in the L-2, we'd kept it free for the afternoon.

Shortly after lunch, I took off for Salina.

From the beginning, nothing went as planned.

Because of an unforeseen headwind, the flight took longer than anticipated and when I arrived, twenty minutes late, Red Taylor had gone out to fly with a student.

I'd felt confident about my ability to pass the test but, as I waited for him to return, I began thinking of the many times I'd spent flying about the countryside instead of practicing maneuvers. I became increasingly nervous.

An hour and ten fingernails after I arrived, Taylor returned. Rather than the pleasant smile I was used to, he had a dark scowl on his face. Not a good sign. I fidgeted nervously as he gave his student pointers about wing-overs and pylon eights. He was still scowling when he approached the L-2.

During an unexpectedly long, and intensive flight check—a grueling session of stalls, spins, 720s, pylon eights, and spot landings, he hardly spoke a word except to bark out orders.

When we landed, he was still scowling. Exhausted and apprehensive, I followed him to his office. I didn't realize I'd been holding my breath until he began filling out a temporary private pilot certificate.

When he handed me the slip of paper, he smiled for the first time.

"I'm sorry I was so rough on you," he said. "But I had a twofold purpose: first, the number of aviation accidents and fatalities have risen rapidly since the war's end, and we're trying to cut down on that. We're going to have to be more exacting if the industry is going to grow. This means better pilots and better planes.

"Second, although you're not going to be flying commercially, you *are* involved in the business. I wanted to know you were up to the job. Carl has done a good job. I was proud of your performance."

"If I'd known you were going to be that rough on me, I'd have been scared to death," I said.

He laughed.

"If Carl does half the job with the other students, he'll be turning out some mighty fine pilots—the kind we want!"

He held out his hand.

Women who earned a private pilot's license were still a minority back then. When I came out of the office, there was a lot of back-slapping and congratulations. Someone bought me a Coke and after a lively session of "hangar flying," I looked from the sun to the windsock and calculated I had just about enough time to get home before dark.

For the benefit of my audience, I made a "hot-shot" take-off to the southwest, flew the flight pattern and pointed the nose of the plane northeast. According to my calculations, I should wind up directly over the Marysville airport in about an hour, with fifteen minutes of daylight to spare. The air was as smooth as flying on a magic carpet, and I was exuberant. Figuring I'd flown the route so often I knew it by heart, I carelessly tossed the map in the back seat. Then I settled back to wait for the time to pass.

I was singing a snappy tune, and dreaming of a brilliant flying career when, at about the half way point, I looked out to check my position.

It didn't check!

A quick look at the sun told me this was no time to get lost. Rolling the seat back, I unfastened the seat belt and stretched until I reached the map. Locating a check point, I discovered I was seven miles off-course and thirty miles from home.

I could make it; just barely.

Then I saw something I really didn't want to see—a black, broiling cloud formation on the northwest horizon. Having lived in Kansas through the Dirty Thirties, I knew what that meant! It loomed larger, more menacing even as I watched.

At the rate it was traveling, there was no chance in hell I could outrun it, or make it home, before it struck. Unless I got on the ground pretty damned quick, I would be engulfed in a black cloud of violent winds, dust, rain—and probably hailstones. This little old fabric-covered airplane wouldn't stand a chance!

I looked frantically about for a place to land. All I could see was ridge after ridge of rough, hilly terrain.

Then, just off the right wing-tip, I spied a small field nestled between two hills. No more than a quarter of a mile long, a tree-lined stream ran down the middle of it and a house and barn lay at one end. I might—just might—be able to make it.

A quick look over my shoulder told me I had no choice.

Jerking the carburetor heater on, I closed the throttle and headed in.

I strained my eyes, trying to see if any ruts, bushes, or rocks lay in my landing path, but the light was fading fast; I could only hope for the best.

I was skimming along only a few feet off the ground when I realized I wasn't going to make it. The plane stalls out at forty-two miles per hour, the airspeed was indicating fifty, and the end of the field was coming up fast! I was trying to force the plane down when the barn loomed in my path.

Slamming the throttle forward, I jerked back on the stick and made a sharp, climbing turn. As I flew by, the weather cock perched on the corner of the eaves struck a chord in the back of my mind. The wind had changed—I had been trying to land downwind!

My hands clammy, my forehead dripping with perspiration, I made a sharp 180 degree turn.

This time, I'd better do it right!

Fingers of the storm were clutching at the plane which was tossing and vibrating violently in the turbulent winds. Large drops of rain splattered the windshield and it was now so dark, I could barely make out the field. Mid flashes of lightening, I could see mere shadows of trees and bushes, so I lined up parallel to them, using them to judge my altitude. When I figured I was near the ground, I jerked on the spoilers and pulled back sharply on the stick. The storm struck just as the wheels touched the ground. As soon as I felt the plane settle in, I applied the brakes and held onto the stick with both hands.

Luck was with me. Due to the strong headwind and soft earth, the plane rolled to a stop inches from a dense thicket.

"Thank God!" I muttered as I snapped the seat belt, jumped out of the cockpit and grabbed hold of a wing spar to keep the plane, rocking violently in the wind, from flipping over.

My legs were so weak I could hardly stand. I was wondering how I was going to keep it upright while I retrieved the stakes and got it tied down when I saw a lantern approaching.

While his son held onto the struts, the farmer helped me drive in stakes and tie the L-2 down; then we dashed for the house in a driving rain.

"Some storm!" the man said once we'd reached the shelter of the porch. "You made it just in time, young lady!"

"Name's Woden," he said extending his hand. "And this here's Ma and Junior."

"Lord a mercy!" Mrs. Woden said. "It's a girl! Well, let's don't just stand here talkin'; she's darned near drowned."

Gasping for breath, I could only nod.

My clothes were plastered to my body and rivulets of water streamed from my hair down my face. Mrs. Woden handed me a towel, and I followed her into the bedroom. She helped me out of my clothes and into a warm robe then folded me in a blanket.

"I need to call my husband," I said then. "He'll be frantic."

Carl's first words were: "What does the plane look like?"

I refused food, but Mrs. Woden insisted I sip on a warm glass of milk. While we waited for Carl to arrive, they plied me with questions.

"I swear when I saw that silver plane come practically flying out of that storm then saw you standing there, dripping wet, I thought for sure the good lord had sent us an angel! A drowned one, maybe, but an angel all the same."

I burst out laughing.

"Well, I'm no angel," I said. "Although I wondered there for a few minutes if I might wind up being one!"

They all laughed.

"I *did* play it a little too close," I admitted in answer to their questions. "Actually, flying is as safe as driving an automobile if one doesn't allow oneself to get into a compromising position, such as I did tonight."

On the drive home, Carl didn't have much to say. Nor did I. I didn't know whether he was angry with *me* or just worried about the plane. Not a word was said about whether or not I'd passed the test.

It rained all night. Though it ceased the next morning, the clouds hung low and the sky looked threatening, as if it could start again at any time.

"It looks as though it might set in for quite a spell," Carl said.

We spent the day catching up on chores we were behind on—both at home and at the airport.

"By the way," I teased. "You haven't even asked if I passed the flight check."

He looked up and grinned.

"I had no doubt about that. I figured if you could handle the plane in a storm like the one last night and not crack up, you'd certainly have had no problem passing a flight check."

"It wasn't all that easy!" I retorted. "In fact, there for a while, I was afraid I wouldn't."

I told him what Red Taylor had said.

It was still cloudy the next morning, but the sky looked as though it might clear. We decided to drive out to the Woden's, check on the L-2 and the possibility of flying it out of that pint-sized field.

Jim went along, as did George McAnany, who drove up just as we were leaving.

When I surveyed my "landing strip," I told myself that there was no way that I could have made a safe landing there.

Lying between two steep hills and bordered by trees and dense brush, the field was short, narrow, and rough. A tree-lined creek running through the center made it even more hazardous.

Was it my quick thinking—my expert flying skills—that brought me safely out of the storm?

*Not likely*, I thought.

I wasn't about to take the credit; someone whose skills were far superior to mine had guided my hand that day.

I *had* learned a valuable lesson; on subsequent flights, I watched the time closely, kept my map handy, my eyes on the horizon, and thanked God for watching over fools and little children.

As we walked across to where the L-2 was tied down, our boots sank into the soft mud.

Mr. Woden and Junior came out to join us. I waved to Mrs. Woden who was standing at the door.

"Think you can fly it out?" Mr. Woden asked.

"I'm not sure," Carl said, shaking his head thoughtfully. Not a leaf stirred and the windmill was at a stand-still.

Jim looked the plane over.

"Looks OK," he said. "Don't see a scratch on her."

Carl walked down the center of the field, testing its firmness.

"Soft," he said, returning to the plane. "Hardly any wind. I don't know—

"Hell, as long as we're here, we might as well give it a try," he said then. "If I don't get up enough speed by the time I reach the fence, I can always shut her down."

They removed the tie downs and it took the four of us to turn the plane around in the mud and point it down the field. The wind was now stirring a little out of the east so that, at least, was in our favor.

"I'm not as heavy as you are," Jim said as Carl started to get into the plane. "Why don't I do it?"

"Talking about weight," I spoke up. "I weigh sixty pounds less than either of you. If any of us can get it out of here, I can. Besides—I'm the one that got it in here."

Carl shook his head.

"Come on!" I coaxed. "I can do it! If it won't fly, I'll do as you said—cut the throttle."

I wanted to do this; after all, I was the one that got it in here, and I wanted to prove to myself that I could get it out.

"OK," Carl relented. "But I don't want you taking any chances, hear? If you don't have enough airspeed by the time you get to the fence, cut the throttle. Don't play it too close. Do you understand?"

I nodded, giving him a light kiss. "I'll be all right."

To cut weight, I removed my boots and my coat, then climbed into the cockpit.

Carl spun the prop; the engine started on the first try. I let it warm up a bit then released the brake and eased forward on the throttle. Nothing happened. It was mired too deep in the mud.

I pulled the throttle back and stuck my head out the door.

"Try it again!" Carl yelled. "We'll give you a shove."

I shut the door and pushed the throttle wide open. With Carl on one strut and Jim and George on the other, the plane started moving. They dropped off as it picked up speed.

I was rapidly approaching a four-wire barbed wire fence when I looked down at the airspeed indicator—just under forty-two miles per hour—flying speed. I had to make a quick decision. Should I take a chance on clearing the fence? Or cut the throttle and settle back into the mud?

Beyond the fence, the ground fell away sharply. Although I had promised Carl not to take a chance, I felt confident that I could make it. I pulled back on the stick.

I cleared the fence by inches and when I felt the plane settle, dropped the nose and held the plane steady until it picked up speed. I was flying just off the ground through a deep gully between two low-lying hills. As the airspeed increased, I slowly began to climb, leveling out below the clouds. Once I reached the airport, I avoided the mud-soft runway, landed on the alfalfa strip running along its edge and taxied to the hangar.

"I almost had a heart attack when I saw the plane settle into that gully," Carl reprimanded me when they arrived.

"Would you have stopped if you'd been flying it?" I asked.

"That's different," he replied.

"Yeah. If it had been you, *I* would have been the one doing the worrying."

"One thing for sure, Carl," Jim broke in. "Neither you nor I could have got her outta there."

"You've really scared the hell out of me with your flying lately,"

Carl said. "A few more incidents like the last two, and I'll be a basket case!"

As for me, I had felt more in control during that take-off than when I'd landed in the field two days before with the storm lashing at my tail.

I grinned to myself the next day when I heard Carl bragging to Dr. Randall that I had not only landed in that tiny field in the dust storm, but had also flown the plane out.

"I wouldn't a given two cents for that airplane when I saw what she was going to do," he said.

The newspaper ran my picture, standing by the L-2, accompanied by the caption: "Edna Ungerer, Marysville's first licensed woman pilot!"

Edna Ungerer, Marysville's First Licensed Woman Pilot

# A Bohemian Dance

Although owning a private pilot license wasn't *that* unusual—a lot of female pilots had accomplished amazing deeds during the war—I became a local celebrity. It was embarrassing when people pointed at me on the street or turned and stared.

It seemed odd that even with jet propulsion and space rockets now making headlines, a woman pilot was a novelty. I guessed it was because jet propulsion and space rockets were something to read about, while I was the real thing. Flying was still glamorous—at least to country folk. Until we opened the airport, a lot of people in the community had never seen an airplane up close, much less a woman pilot.

One advantage of my new status was that it brought new spectators to the airport.

"I'm not allowed to take passengers for hire on a private license," I'd reply when asked how much I would charge to fly around the airport once or twice. "If you'd like to go for a ride, Carl can take you—"

*What am I—a circus performer?* I wondered when the reply was: "Oh, we don't want to fly! We just heard about you and was wondering how much it would cost to see you fly."

Carl thought it would be good publicity so, if we weren't too busy, I sometimes took a passenger along and circled town a time or two.

I also thought it strange that so many preferred riding with me, a newly licensed pilot, rather than with Carl. Somehow, flying with a woman seemed to give them confidence.

Frederick had been flying as often as time and weather allowed, and an airplane was available. The last of November, he and Fred

Burris took the flight check and received their private pilot licenses.

Once Jim obtained his, there would be four licensed "Flying Ungerers."

"You and Carl never go anywhere," Jim said one morning when he and I were alone in the office. "Why don't you go to the dance with me and my date tonight?"

"Better ask Carl," I said. "I'd love to go but it's up to him."

"I won't just ask him, I'll tell him! It's about time you guys started getting out more."

"My gosh, Jim!" I said. "Even if we wanted to go, I don't have anything decent to wear! I haven't bought anything new for over a year."

"Just dig down in your closet, girl. I'm sure you'll find something," he said.

Carl said okay and, although it hadn't been worn for a while, I found a dress I had hoped would be suitable.

The dance was in full swing when we arrived. Not only was the hall crowded, groups were gathered around cars in the parking area. Sponsored by the Bohemian community, just over the Nebraska line, the dances were held almost every Saturday night in a building that had once been a schoolhouse.

Carl and Jim had attended since they were teenagers and, although I'd heard of them, I had no idea what to expect.

"It's something like a square dance," Carl explained.

My heart began to pound with excitement as we stood just inside the door watching the dancers whirl to the "Flying Dutchman." Suddenly, I was lifted off the floor by Carl and the friend he'd been talking with. Harvey was as tall as Carl and my feet hardly touched the floor as we whirled around the room.

This was, without doubt, the wildest, most exciting dance I had ever attended. Nor had I ever met people so friendly or seen so much drinking. Since drinking was not allowed in the hall, we were frequently asked to join someone at their car where bottles of bourbon were passed around, followed by a chaser of Coca Cola or Seven-Up, kept cold in tubs of ice.

Though I always took a sip, I never felt tipsy. "You dance it off," Carl said.

It was raining when we arrived home just before dawn. We awoke at noon.

"I don't think I was ever so glad to see it rain," I said as we dressed. "After last night, I don't think I could have faced a busy Sunday at the airport."

Carl and I began going out more frequently after that—to dances, picnics, ball games, and other social affairs. When we received an invitation to join the country club, Carl agreed.

"It'll be good for business," he said.

In spite of unpredictable weather much of the time as winter approached, we succeeded in keeping the planes in the air more than we'd hoped.

Three more GI students completed their training, took their flight checks, and received their private pilot licenses, and three new students enrolled bringing the number back up to the maximum allowed.

With twenty-nine students both Carl and Marion were kept busy with student training, plus charter flights to points not served by Kansas Airways. From the time he returned home, there was a constant flow of requests for Jim's mechanical services, and I seemed never out of bookwork and other odds and ends to occupy my time.

Our bank account gradually began to show a profit.

Edna

# Marysville and the National Airport Plan

H aving gotten off to a rough start, Kansas Airways was threatening to close down. In an attempt to salvage the airline, the company substituted a smaller plane—a five-place Cessna—for the nine-place Beechcraft, cut service to five days a week, and added more towns to the route.

The company—assuring the council that Marysville would continue to be served—made several stops early in the month. Then, on October 25, the announcement came that service would cease, but only until new plans could be put into effect. The airline had been operating under "too extravagant management," they said; service would resume after reorganization.

Although the City Council had been led to believe that other towns on the line had invested more, we learned that only one other city had invested as much in Kansas Airways as had Marysville.

Although unfortunate for the city, KAW's cessation was a positive for Ungerer Flying Service. It meant an increase in charter service, plus less work for me.

With favorable weather to our advantage, student training was progressing rapidly. Two new boys had soloed, others were taking cross-countries and preparing for their flight checks.

Carl was thinking of adding another plane to our fleet.

We were considering another Taylorcraft when the announcement came that the Taylorcraft factory in Alliance, Ohio had been destroyed by a fire. We then learned that the company had gone into bankruptcy.

"Damned good airplane," Carl said when he heard the news. "But it looks as though we aren't going to be buying Taylorcrafts for a while. Looks like it's time for us to invest in the Cessna."

We first ordered a 120 which we sold soon after to Bus Vincent.

"We might as well go for the 140," Carl said.

The 140 was definitely an upgrade. It, too, had a metal fuselage and fabric covered wings—but was installed with flaps—which would be an added asset for training commercial students. It also had a radio and a starter and was equipped with a Continental 85 horsepower engine. The cruise speed was 105 mph, fuel capacity twenty-five gallons with a range of 450 miles.

"The 170 will be coming out after the first of the year," he said optimistically. "The 140 should cover the requirements for training commercial students until then."

Beautiful fall weather was bringing Sunday crowds to the airport again, but with twenty-nine students vying for time in five planes, sight-seeing rides were rare.

"Since we're adding more planes, we're going to need more hangar space," Carl said one evening after he and Jim and I had jockeyed the planes into the hangar, tipping the L-2 on its nose to get all five planes in.

He ordered material, and he, Jim, and Dad began building two T-hangars.

Once the hangars were completed, Elmer Anderson, a Marysville implement dealer who had been keeping his Ercoupe in Seneca since before Ungerer Flying Service went into business, rented one of them. Dr. Randall rented the other. With the acquisition of the Cessna, this left the L-2 parked overnight on its nose so the men enclosed the space between the two T hangars to increase our storage capacity.

I had been secretly hoping that the city wouldn't follow through on their plans to take over the airport. Then Carl returned from the November Rotary meeting with the news that Marysville was one of

152 Kansas airports on the National Airport plan. The city had received the grant application forms for airport improvement. (The Federal Airport fund totaled $524,000,000. The State of Kansas was allotted $7,265,422). Estimating the total cost of improvements at $50,000, Marysville had requested $35,000.

On November 15, George McAnany, our very first student, took the flight check and received his private pilot license.

Cessna 170
(Photo by Mark Harkin, Flickr - Used per Creative Commons Lic. 2.0)

# Christmas

December weather also proved to be relatively moderate. We had an occasional flurry of snow, but not enough to prevent students flying—at least not those willing to brave the cold. Because of work schedules, mornings and evenings continued to be our busiest times, we managed to fly enough hours during the day to keep everyone on schedule. The shorter days made this more difficult, but we made use of every minute.

I was looking forward to our first dance at the Country Club. I had bought a new dress for the occasion. Carl and I and Jim and his date planned to go together.

On the day of the dance, I took off early and went home to dress. Reveling in the fact that I had all the time needed to get ready for the party, I took my time.

As I dressed, my mind flickered over all that had happened in the past year. It seemed unbelievable that Carl had taken our first customer for a ride—in the L-2, flying off a leased alfalfa field—just a little over a year ago. We now had twenty-nine students, five airplanes, two runways, four hangars, and an office. Frederick and I had our private pilot licenses, Jim his civilian mechanic's license, and was working toward his private. And we had "graduated," three students!

And tonight, miracle of miracles, I was caught up on the bookwork and forms!

After I'd bathed and dressed in my new blue dress, my Christmas present to myself, I stood looking at my reflection in the mirror. With all that had happened, I felt like a different person; it seemed odd that I didn't look any different than I had the year before.

I heard Mrs. Jones slowly climbing the stairs. Since cold weather had set in, her arthritis was making the climb more difficult. I wished we had a room for her on the first floor. How much longer, I wondered, would she be able to carry on?

"My, you do look pretty in blue," she said, pausing at the door.

"Thank you, Mrs. Jones," I said. "It's been so long since I've really dressed up, I don't quite know how to act."

I looked at the clock. "Carl should be home any minute—"

"I hope you won't mind if I don't come down," she said. "Dinner is ready. All you have to do is dish it up."

"I've run his bath and laid out his clothes," I said. "Will the food be all right until he gets dressed?"

"Indeed, it will. The roast is in the warming oven; it'll be just fine."

As she returned to her room across the hall, I heard the sound of the car turning into the driveway. A moment later, Carl came bounding up the stairs.

He stopped in the doorway and gave a long, low whistle.

"Wow!" he said. "I'd forgotten I was married to a real, live girl!"

"Silly," I said, going to him and raising my lips for his kiss.

He stepped back, his arms behind his back and, bending over, barely touched his lips to mine.

"Mustn't touch," he teased.

"You're in a rare mood," I laughed. "Hurry up and get yourself in that bathtub and get dressed. Mrs. Jones has dinner holding in the warmer. While you're dressing, I'll go down and mix us a nice tall glass of bourbon and Coke."

"Hmmmm—that do sound good. A nice hot bath, a sip of whiskey, and a nice long taste of you is just what the doctor ordered."

I laughed as he danced his way into the bathroom. As I headed for the kitchen, I could hear him singing over the splash of water in the bathtub.

Opening the door to the liquor cabinet, I reached for a bottle of the bourbon we bought by the case at the Nebraska state line liquor store. During the war, rum had been the drink of choice, whether we liked it or not. Most of the time, we were lucky to find that. After the war, we had switched to bourbon. I mixed the drinks, including a weak one for Mrs. Jones. Perhaps it would relieve her backache and help her to relax.

I delivered Carl's drink then rapped on Mrs. Jones's door.

"Thought a little nip might relieve your back a little," I said.

"Bless you child," she said, giving me a wide smile.

Jim and his date arrived just as we finished eating.

"Would you like a drink?" Carl asked,

Jim shook his head.

"No. Let's go on over. We can have a drink when we get there."

When we arrived, the ballroom was crowded. Everyone appeared to have turned out for this, the first major dance of the season. I made a quick appraisal of what the other women were wearing and gave a sigh of relief. The dress I'd chosen seemed "right" for the occasion.

After the waiter took our drink orders, we sat, watching the crowd. Occasionally, someone stopped by the table to say hello and chat a bit. I knew several of the men—at least by sight—but not many women.

*I guess that goes with the kind of business we're in*, I mused.

Working from dawn until dark in what was, literally, a man's world, gave me little opportunity to make women friends.

Our drinks arrived just as the music began. Carl raised his glass.

"To a very successful first year for Ungerer Flying Service," he toasted.

Then he stood up and bowed.

"Mrs. Ungerer, may I have the honor of this dance?" he asked in mock formality.

"I'd be delighted, Mr. Ungerer," I replied.

"Have I told you lately that I am very proud of you?" he whispered in my ear as we danced.

When the music stopped, a man I recognized as owner of one

of the car dealerships, and a one-time charter customer, approached and introduced his wife. As we made our way back to our table, others smiled and spoke. When we danced again, another couple approached and suggested we change partners and soon we were mingling and dancing with others and being introduced to other members of the club.

The evening had almost reached an end, and I was dancing with one of our student pilots—a businessman—when Carl cut in.

"I haven't had much of a chance to dance with my wife all evening," he complained.

The band swung into the strains of "Auld Lang Syne."

"It's been a beautiful evening," I said. "I hate for it to end."

We awoke the next morning to find the ground white. Huge snowflakes, falling heavily and steadily, glowed under the street lights.

"Well, it had to come some time," Carl said as we snuggled back into bed. "We should be happy that we've had good flying weather for as long as we have. We got a good enough head start on old man winter; we should manage to survive a few days of adverse flying conditions."

"Know what I'm going to do?" I said. "I'm going to do our Christmas shopping, wrap the gifts, put up the tree, and then I think I'll plan a Christmas party."

"A party?" Carl said. "All that sounds expensive."

"We'll start with you and me going shopping today," I added.

We'd heard several cars pass by; the streets were clear.

"I hate shopping," Carl groaned.

After breakfast, he shoveled the driveway while I picked up our bedroom and dressed. Although he hated shopping, he remained cheerful throughout the "ordeal," carrying packages, sometimes offering his opinion about a gift selection.

"What shall we buy for Mrs. Jones," I asked.

"On that one, I don't have a clue," he replied.

I finally decided on a lovely blue flannel nightgown and matching robe.

"She'll like that," he agreed.

By the time we returned home, we had purchased gifts for almost everyone on the list. The two or three remaining would require a little more thought.

Mrs. Jones had dinner on the table when we arrived. After we ate, we walked over to the folks' for an evening of canasta. Delighted with the falling flakes, sparkling in the light from the streetlamps, I hummed *"Oh what fun it is to ride in a one-horse open sleigh—"* as we trudged through the snow.

"How much money can we spend on a Christmas party?" I asked the next morning,

"About a dollar two ninety," he teased. "What do you have in mind?"

"We don't have room for a formal affair, so I was thinking of an open house party. It'll go a long way toward promoting the airport. Everyone can come and go as they please, and it will entail a minimum of effort. All we'll have to do is keep the bar, table, and buffet stocked with food and drink—no table settings to worry about—we'll use paper plates and paper napkins. And we won't send out invitations. We'll just post notices inviting all our students and clients."

"That's a lot of people. It could get pretty expensive."

"That's why I asked you how much I could spend. We can keep it simple—or not—depending on how much we want to put into it."

"Let's start with simple."

"I'm thinking that we're probably talking about a hundred people or so. Liquor will be the most expensive item, but we'll get the case discount on that. As for food—we can serve anything from hors d'oeuvres to a complete meal—any thoughts on that?"

"None at all."

"You're not being much help. Okay, I'll stock up on cheeses and lunch meats, crackers, potato chips, nuts, and candy—I think we can have a pretty good party for around three hundred dollars—and we can charge it off to advertising."

We planned the party for Christmas Eve. As it turned out, my calculations were slightly off. Over two hundred people came—many of whom stayed long past the first drink. The cost was twice what I'd estimated. The important thing was that a good time was had by all, and the party was the talk of the town for weeks after.

"I think we should make it an annual affair," I said. "Not only was it good for business, it was a lot of fun."

"That's what I like about you," Carl said. "Underneath that 'anything for a good time' front of yours, you have a hell of a shrewd head for business—for a woman."

I socked him on the shoulder.

Christmas day was cold, but clear. Carl flew the new Cessna, and Jim and I flew the Blue Bird to Frankfort, where members of Lillian's family were gathering for Christmas dinner. Since Lillian had prepared a number of pots of food and Dad was taking a keg of wine, they chose to drive over.

Mrs. Jones was having dinner with Rose and her family.

The weather moderated after Christmas. Several couples we'd met at the country club stopped by the airport, the students made the most of the break in the weather, and the hours flown covered our expenses for the month.

I had ordered flying suits from an Army Surplus store—khaki colored, with nine zippered pockets. Made of wool, they were warm and ideal for the cold winter weather. In an article complimenting us on a successful first year, *The Marysville Advocate* ran a photo of the four of us, dressed in our new flying suits, captioned *"The Flying Ungerers."*

The Flying Ungerers

# 1947: A New Year

New Year's Day started late for Carl and me. To celebrate the success of Ungerer Flying Service in 1946, and the arrival of 1947, a brand-new year with wonderful things to come, we attended the New Year's party at the American Legion, then went out for breakfast with our friends, Nadine and Bill. Since both Carl and Bill Watson had flown bombers during the war, they had a lot in common, and it hadn't taken long for Nadine and me to become friends.

We didn't arrive home until 4:00 AM.

It started snowing around midnight, and the accumulation was sufficient indication that there would be no flying on New Year's Day.

At ten o'clock, I opened my eyes, got up, and looked out the window. It had stopped snowing, but a foot of snow covered the ground.

We had a lazy breakfast and, rather than dig the car out of a snow drift, walked over to Carl's folks.

"Doesn't look like we're going anywhere today," Carl said as we mushed our way through the snow. "The roads, as well as the runways, will be drifted closed."

When we arrived, Lillian was making coffee, and Dad was sitting on the stool in the bathroom in what he called his "long handles." When he heard us come in, he opened the door a crack, and stuck his head out.

"Let's go hunting!" he called out.

"Hell," Carl said. "You can't even get downtown right now. Snowed all night."

Dad came out of the bathroom pulling one overall suspender

over his shoulder, letting the other hang down his back.

"That's a helluva note," he grumbled, yawning, wiping the sleep from his eyes.

He opened the door and Carl followed him onto the back porch where they stood appraising the situation.

Lillian winked at me.

"He's been grumbling ever since he got up about what the hell they were going to do all day," she said.

"Son of a bitch!" Dad hissed through his false teeth. "A hell of a way to spend New Year's Day."

"Sure is a humdinger," Carl responded. "I just hope it's not a sign of what's to come throughout the year. Last year was bad enough—sometimes good, mostly erratic—a hell of a year to try to build a flying business."

"Let's get a cup of coffee," Dad said, leading the way back to the kitchen. "Whaterya gonna do today?"

"Thought I might try to get the city to come out and clear the runways," Carl replied.

"They'll have everything they've got out on the roads," Dad snorted, pouring coffee into two of the four brown mugs Lillian had set out on the counter. "Might as well sit down and take a load off."

Carl sat.

I poured myself a cup of coffee, and Lillian began breaking eggs into a frying pan.

"None for me," I said.

"This is a hell of a way to start the New Year," Carl said, then, turning to Lillian, said, "I'll take two."

Eating was Carl's second favorite hobby.

"You already ate two at home," I reminded him.

"That was before all that strenuous exercise, walking over here," he said, buttering a slice of toast and spreading it liberally with homemade strawberry jam.

"One thing about Carl," Dad said, "Never was a time that boy couldn't eat."

After eating, the men moved to the dining table and began a game of pitch. I helped Lillian wash up the dishes and we joined them. When Jim got up, he played in her place while she cooked his breakfast.

In spite of the men's grumbling about the weather I was thoroughly enjoying myself. A pleasant, leisurely day—a day with no demands on my time—was rare.

Frederick showed up during the afternoon and when the light began to fade. Dad brought a pitcher of cherry wine up from the basement, and Lillian, who had spent most of the day in the kitchen, turned on the lights and went to put dinner on the table.

"If we're going to stay, I'd better call Mrs. Jones and tell her not to cook for us," I said.

I felt guilty leaving her alone all day on a holiday.

"Oh, I don't mind, dear," she said cheerfully. "Both Rose and my daughter back east called for a chat. It was rather pleasant to spend the day lying around, being lazy."

As usual, Lillian had done herself proud.

After dinner, Carl stood up.

"I just want to make a toast to how well things have turned out for the Ungerer's," he said. "Jim completed his A and E training, Frederick got his business up and going, Edna and Frederick got their private pilot licenses, and Ungerer Flying Service now has seven planes hangared on the field, counting the one we sold Dr. Randall and Elmer Anderson's Ercoupe. This time last year, the only plane we had was the L-2. All in all, I think we're doing pretty damn good!"

"Yeah! Yeah!" Everyone shouted, and we downed our drinks.

Frederick stood up.

"And I want to make a toast to the old man without whom none of us would be where we are today," he said. His toast was followed by much clapping and hooting.

The conversation turned to Dad's latest project. Weather be damned, he had recently purchased another house—to be moved to a property he owned just down the street from us.

"What the hell," Dad said. "I've still got one son who's gonna be needin' it one of these days. Gotta plan ahead."

Everybody laughed and patted a red-faced Jim on the back.

After dinner, we switched to canasta. As we played, most of the discussion consisted of activities at the airport and all we had accomplished in our first year in business.

"It took me long enough to get my private license," I said. "Now I can start working on my commercial."

"Getting my A&E license took most of the year." Jim said. "Now that I'm home though, I'll start working on the private. I've got in almost twenty hours; it won't take me long."

The conversation switched to the newspaper article and photo of the four flying Ungerers.

At eight o'clock, Carl stretched and yawned.

"I'm getting sleepy," he said. "How about we head for home?"

"A hell of a way to spend the New Year!" Dad complained.

"I enjoyed it," I said. "We haven't had many opportunities to goof around all day this past year."

The weather turned severely cold, and it was several days before snowplows got around to clearing the runways.

"I don't think anyone is going to want to fly in weather like this anyway," Jim said.

Once the road was cleared, Carl and I drove to the airport to see if we could start one of the planes in case of an emergency. While Carl shoveled the snow piled up against the hangar door, I huddled in front of the oil-burning heater in the office.

It was all the two of us could do to inch the heavy, ice-laden hangar door open. We rolled the L-2 out. The wind had blown the ramp clear except for an ice-crusted, layer of snow. Carl chocked the wheels, and I climbed into the cockpit.

Starting an airplane on a bitterly cold morning was, as Carl said, a matter of persistence and "outguessing the temperamental sons-a-bitches."

I primed the engine and held the brakes while Carl called out the signals:

"Switch off, throttle closed!"

"Switch off, throttle closed!" I echoed.

He pulled the prop through several times.

"Contact! Throttle cracked!"

"Contact! Throttle cracked!"

He spun the prop.

The engine sputtered but refused to start.

"Prime it!" he called. I primed it again.

"Switch off, throttle closed!"

"Switch off, throttle closed!"

He pulled the prop through again.

"Switch on, throttle cracked!"

Again the plane refused to start.

"Son of a bitch! Must be loaded up," he said. "Switch off, throttle open!"

"Switch off, throttle open!" I said, and he pulled the prop through in reverse several times.

"Okay! Contact, throttle closed!"

Twenty minutes later, the plane sputtered and started. My fingers, drenched with gasoline from the primer, were numb with cold. They ached so that the pain crept up into my arms. I removed my gloves and held my hands between my legs to warm them up. My heart went out to Carl who had struggled so hard to start the plane in the bitterly cold wind.

I wondered if it had been worth it.

We left the L-2 running and took refuge in the office which, by now, was tolerably warm.

That afternoon, Carl ordered what was called a "hotstick," an electric heating rod which, inserted in the oil tank overnight, would make the plane easier to start. Thankfully, it arrived only two days later.

The next day, the city cleared the runway and Carl and I took off in the L-2 for a short flight to check flying conditions. We stayed out only a short time.

"None of the students will want to go out in this weather," I said once we'd hangared the plane and were back in the office which had warmed up considerably while we were out.

"You're right about that," Carl said, shaking off his gloves and rubbing his hands together as we huddled over the stove, letting the warmth penetrate our heavy clothing.

"What shall we do now?" I asked.

"Let's take a drive and see if any game is out and about," he replied. "I'll call the Old Man and see if he wants to go along."

Thirty minutes later, equipped with guns and ammunition, Carl, Dad, Lillian, and I drove south over a newly cleared road.

"You girls watch for tracks in the snow," Dad said. "When you see something, Carl and I'll get out and hunt it down."

Apparently, the wildlife had sought refuge from the weather. An hour later, we had bagged only one cottontail.

"They're a hell of a lot smarter than we are!" Dad exclaimed. "I'm cold as a son of a bitch. Let's go home!"

As the cold spell lingered, there was no flying and no flying meant no income.

"Do you think we should let Mrs. Jones go?" I asked one morning. "Now that I don't have a lot to do, I'll be able to handle the housework."

"We should probably keep her on," he replied. "This is only temporary and if we let her go, we might have trouble replacing her when we need the help.

"Don't worry about it," he added, "you've earned some free

time."

Secretly, I'd have hated to let her go. I was fond of her, and she took pleasure in making her home with us. She considered us "her kids."

"Thank God, we had good flying weather through most of the fall so we're not in bad shape financially," Carl said. "We should have enough in the bank to meet the bills for a while—even with George's retainer, Jim's salary, and payments to make on two planes."

"We still have two or three months of winter to go."

"Hopefully we'll have a break in the weather now and then which will help us squeeze through. We have plenty of students."

Three new ones had signed on, and two of the old ones were considering commercial training.

"With Jim here to keep the planes up, we've cut maintenance costs, and if things get rough, the three of us can take a cut in salary for a spell. You and I could handle it, and I'm sure Jim wouldn't mind."

"As long as we don't have to put the touch on Dad. I'll be glad when we can start paying him back; we owe him over three thousand dollars."

"We should be able to start paying him back come spring as the weather warms up and the days get longer. Dad would rather the business stabilizes before we start worrying about paying him back. He's been around long enough to know that it takes money to make money."

Not only had Dad helped us out financially this past year, but he was our ardent promoter. No matter who he was talking to he always brought up the subject of flying. On top of that, he and Lillian never failed to be there to help out in any way they could, from building a hangar to cooking meals and helping out on busy days.

"Let's schedule a ground school class in meteorology for tomorrow night," Carl said.

Only six students attended. The following day the temperatures moderated a little. Except for the cold, it was a perfect day for flying. However, only two students showed up.

Then, suddenly, the sun was shining, the temperature climbed above freezing and students scrambled to get back on schedule and make up for time lost.

During January, they all took advantage of the breaks when they came; several soloed and two took their solo cross-country. Two of our GI students, Vance Meinecke and Robert Craven, the first to "graduate" on the Veterans training program, took the flight check and received their private pilot license.

Airport activity picked up as outsiders flew in on business trips, or to visit friends and relatives, and local pilots came and went.

Standard Oil Company continued to be an avid airport supporter. We always looked forward to visits by company representatives who flew in periodically "just to make sure that everything was up to par."

We also had a visit from the VA representative. He pronounced everything in order and seemed pleased that we were doing so well.

The last of the month, officials from Kansas Airways met in Marysville to discuss re-organization of the feeder airline which had ceased operating in late October after only fifty days of service to Marysville.

 Carl attended the meeting.

"How did it go?" I asked when he returned.

He shook his head.

"The company is still having financial difficulties," he said. "The Beechcraft has been repossessed. It seems unlikely to me that they'll resume service anytime soon, if ever."

As it turned out, he was right.

Ungerer Repair Shop

# Coyote Hunting

"If I can catch a plane available, I think I'll go out for a while today," I said as we drove to the airport a few days later. I was eager to start working toward a commercial license and with all the students trying to catch up from the cold spell, I hadn't been getting in much time.

"The Cessna is free for the next hour; why don't you go out first thing," Carl said. "In the meantime, I'll make some calls and see if I can get more students out during the day.

Jim arrived about the same time we did. The Cessna was stored up front, so as soon as we rolled it out, I got in.

The sun was just creeping over the horizon and the air was bright, fresh, and calm. I took off on the runway to the north and, as the plane gathered speed, I suddenly jerked the wheel back to avoid what appeared to be four large dogs loping across the runway. As I flew over, I saw that they were not dogs, but coyotes; apparently a mother and three pups.

As I flew the flight pattern, I watched them disappear into the brush.

Carl was sending a solo student on his way in the Ace when I landed an hour later.

"Jack Barrett said he's seen them skirting his pasture, heading this way, two or three times a week," he said when I told him about the coyotes. "Said they've been around three or four years. It's only recently that they've gotten so brave as to venture onto the runway. We'll have to keep an eye out. It would wreck a plane to strike one, and we sure as hell don't want anyone getting hurt. Post a bulletin for students to be on the look-out for them."

Later, Carl took a rifle and walked to the north end of the runway. He saw tracks but found no coyotes.

"We're going to have to do something about those coyotes before they cause an accident," he said a few days later after a dual flight with a student. "There were two on the north end of the runway when we came in to land; I had to take over and give the plane the throttle to keep from hitting them."

They began to appear on the runway ever more frequently, and a large, grey male coyote was often seen sitting at the top of the hill.

It became a game between Carl and the coyotes. Anytime one was seen, he would grab the rifle and take off in that direction. But they always succeeded in avoiding him, disappearing into the cornfield or along the brush-lined fence.

At night, during ground school classes, the howl of the coyotes could be heard and on a moonlight night, we could see them on the rise of the hill outlined by the light of the moon.

"One of these days—!" he threatened.

I had learned a lot about hunting since I met Carl Ungerer and was getting pretty good at shooting a handgun, a rifle, and a shotgun. By now, I had bagged quite a few ducks, pheasants, rabbits, and squirrels—but I hadn't been introduced to hunting coyotes. Until—

We arrived at the airport one morning following a light snowfall during the night. It hadn't snowed enough to prevent flying, but the two students scheduled to fly called and cancelled.

We started the planes, warmed them up, and tied them down on the flight line, ready for anyone who happened to show. Then we waited.

Thirty minutes later, no one had shown. Or called.

We were standing around the stove in the office, warming our hands in front of the fire, when Jim said, "I think I'll head home for a while. Call me if you need me."

"Let's take a ride," Carl said after he left. "Might as well show these fledglings that a little snow can't keep *us* on the ground."

As we headed for the flight line, he said: "Let's take the L-2.

You fly."

I got into the front seat, and he spun the prop.

"This is the first time we've been up together, just for fun, for a long time," I said as we taxied out for take-off.

I leveled off at five hundred feet, circled over town, then cruised over the countryside, wiggling the wings at some of our farmer friends out doing morning chores.

Carl tapped my shoulder, and I turned to see him pointing at something just off the left wing.

At first glance, they appeared to be dogs, but after a closer look I saw they were coyotes. They stood out clearly against the snow.

I felt Carl shake the stick—the signal to turn the controls over to him. He made a sharp turn to the left and dived straight at the coyotes who took off at a mad dash, looking back over their shoulders at the huge flying contraption diving at their tails.

As we drew closer, I counted five coyotes fanned out against the white, snow-covered field. Carl pulled up and headed back toward the airport, two or three miles away. When we landed, he spun the plane around and taxied rapidly to the ramp, "Wait here!" he shouted. Leaving the plane running, he jumped out and ran into the office.

Seconds later, he returned carrying the 12-gauge shotgun.

"Take off!" he shouted, buckling his seatbelt.

By the time we were in the air, he had the gun loaded. He took back the controls and headed the plane toward where we had last seen the coyotes.

When we arrived, they were nowhere in sight.

"Damn it!" he exclaimed. "I was afraid of that!"

He circled the area a couple of times, then we spotted them, trotting in a single file down a narrow, grassy ravine. Carl pointed the nose of the plane toward the ground, heading straight toward their retreating tails, zigzagging the plane to keep them running straight away rather than scattering in different directions. He was skimming just over the ground when they broke from the ravine.

"Take the controls!" he shouted once they were out in the open field.

I did as he said and somewhat nervously tried to maneuver the plane as he had done. I had never before been asked to chase coyotes in a plane but, since I was a dutiful wife, I flew the plane.

Trying to keep five coyotes together, running in a straight line, was challenging.

"Lower!" Carl shouted. "Lower!"

We were already skimming the ground.

Three of the coyotes broke away. We still had two. Carl opened his window and pointed the gun.

"Keep them just to the left of the nose," he shouted. "As soon as I fire, pull up!"

I nodded, one hand firmly on the stick, the other on the throttle.

There was a loud explosion in my ear; I pushed the throttle forward and pulled up. Out of the corner of my eye, I saw one of the coyotes somersaulting end over end. It came to rest in a twisted heap between a pile of cactus and a prairie dog town.

Carl took the controls and began circling the area again. I was shaking but had no idea whether from fright, cold, or excitement.

He turned back to where we'd first spotted them and circled until we spotted a lone coyote skulking alongside a brush-lined creek bed. As we headed toward him, he looked warily up and over his shoulder, made two or three laps in a circle, then stretched out into a dead run, heading for a clump of hedge.

I took the controls again, and Carl shot just in time for me to pull up and over the trees.

Beginning to get the hang of it, I climbed to a couple hundred feet, as Carl had done, and circled the area. However, the other coyotes had evidently headed for hiding places in bushes, ravines, holes—wherever coyotes hide. Although we spent several minutes circling a wide area, we didn't see another coyote.

Carl took the controls, landed, and taxied back to where the first coyote lay. Why leave them for the buzzards, he said, when the bounty would cover the cost of our gas.

Cutting the motor, we crossed the ravine to where the coyote lay, and dragged it back to the plane. After we'd retrieved the other, Carl tied one to each wing strut with a length of baling wire he found wound around a fence post. We flew back to the airport, our trophies swinging beneath the wings.

Jim met us at the door of the hangar.

"That's quite a haul you made there," he said.

Although I had never participated, I'd listened to tales about the great sport of hunting coyotes in cars in western Kansas. I knew it took a lot of skill to keep the coyote in gun range while speeding over the open prairie, or a rough field of wheat. To hit the target from a vehicle whipping and jolting over rough terrain was said to be quite an accomplishment.

This was the first time I'd heard of hunting them by plane.

A student who worked for *The Marshall County News* arrived for his lesson shortly after we landed and took our picture which appeared in that week's newspaper, along with an article about our "hunting trip."

The following week, *The Marysville Advocate*, not to be scooped by *The News*, published a photo of me with the Cessna, along with a report on my duties at the airport and a speech I'd been asked to give to the Kayettes, the local chapter of a national youth group.

In spite of our struggles with the weather to keep our students flying and the planes in the air, we were getting superb publicity!

The following week Carl introduced me to coyote "round-ups."

It doesn't sound very sporting, but you'll find little sympathy in the Midwest for the coyote, a perpetual nuisance to the farmer—raiding chicken houses and poultry flocks. If he gets hungry enough and bold enough, he'll attack young calves and sheep as well. Constantly on the lookout, farmers keep shotguns or rifles handy.

Coyote "round-ups" were considered not only a means of eliminating the coyote, but a sport as well.

In Marshall County, coyote roundups were held, usually on a Saturday or a Sunday, during the fall and winter months.

"Hunters line up on roads surrounding the area and, at the appointed time—usually around nine o'clock—begin walking toward the center," Carl said, explaining the sport to me the first time we went out. "The coyote keeps moving to avoid the hunters and as the circle closes in, finds himself trapped in the center of a human circle, within shooting range of dozens of guns. Occasionally one may escape through the line but that's almost impossible after the hunt has progressed for any length of time."

"It sounds dangerous," I said. "Do the hunters ever shoot one another?"

"Never heard of that happening," he replied. "They're all seasoned hunters and very cautious."

"It doesn't sound very sporting."

"It isn't meant to be. The hunts are held for the sole purpose of eliminating coyotes. If someone doesn't eliminate *him*, he will eliminate the farmers' chickens, turkeys, ducks, pigs, lambs, calves—anything available.

"Occasionally a coyote breaks through the line—but he still has to reckon with a shot in the rear or being chased by an airplane aiding in the hunt.

"Hunting coyotes by air isn't recommended by safety experts," he added, "but *is* indulged in, especially by pilots in the prairie states."

Carl and I attended the hunts as often as we could get away from the airport. If weather and runway conditions permitted, we sometimes flew the lines of the hunt, giving chase to any enterprising coyote that succeeded in breaking through the barrage of fire.

Carl had sawed off the gun barrel and the butt of the 12-gauge shotgun for better maneuverability in the close confines of the cockpit.

The L-2 made a perfect coyote-hunting plane. In the many times we hunted coyotes, I had only one close call.

One Saturday, Carl having no dual scheduled for a couple of hours, we left Jim in charge, cranked up the L-2, and headed for the site of a hunt in progress. When we arrived, it was well under-way. A large crowd of hunters, clad in layers of warm clothing and carrying shot guns, were advancing rapidly toward the center of the circle.

The morning was cold and damp, and several inches of snow covered the ground.

"This section is infested with coyotes," Carl said. "As many as thirty-five have been killed here in past hunts."

As usual, I was flying the plane, and Carl was doing the shooting.

His skill with the cropped 12-gauge, had enabled us to bag a number of coyotes since that first excursion.

The hunters were about fifty feet apart when suddenly we saw a bustle of activity on the west line. Although we couldn't see the coyote, bursts of flame and smoke in the foggy air indicated that a coyote had broken through, drawing fire from a number of guns.

We were cruising at about 300 feet, so I cut the throttle and glided in that direction.

That coyote must have had a dozen lives for when we closed in behind him, he was clear of the line a hundred feet and heading for a grove of trees.

I maneuvered the plane low to the ground, the nose pointed at the retreating tail.

"Shoot!" I yelled, my eyes on the grove of trees ahead. I'd about given up when Carl shot. Mr. Coyote went into a somersault and I pushed forward on the throttle.

Nothing happened!

Then the L-2 coughed and sputtered. It had iced up! This was a frequent occurrence in cold, damp weather—if you were not watching what you're doing. In the excitement of the coyote chase,

I'd forgotten to pull on the carburetor heater!

I jerked it on and the motor sputtered again and took hold just in time to make a climbing turn, grazing the groping top branches of the trees.

"You barely made that one!" Carl yelled.

No need for me to reply.

When we'd reached a safe altitude, I turned back to where a group of men were dragging the coyote from the edge of the woods. *A couple of seconds more,* I thought, *and it would have been me they were dragging out of there.*

I resolved never again to become so excited over a hunt that I didn't have the presence of mind to watch my airplane.

Ungerers Hunt Coyotes by Plane

# Flying in Winter and Jim's Romance

February brought alternating blizzards and spring-like weather. Despite cold temperatures, most of the students doggedly stuck to their flight schedules.

After servicing the planes and storing them in the hangar for the night—a slow process, since they had to be angled just so, to make room—we placed "hotsticks" in those scheduled to fly early the next morning.

Ground school, held three evenings a week, was well attended.

New concerns about the Cold War, which had been in the headlines since shortly after the end of World War II, arose in February when the British government announced it could no longer afford to finance the Greek monarchical military regime in its civil war against the communist-led insurgents.

In response to this, President Truman delivered a speech that called for the allocation of four hundred million to intervene in the war, thus unveiling the Truman Doctrine.

"I told you that SOB was going to get us back into a war," Dad fumed.

Although Carl never said much, I knew the European situation weighed heavily on his mind.

In addition to the European situation, we also wondered whether it was for better or for worse for Ungerer Flying Service that plans for a grant for airport improvement had been submitted and were pending approval.

"The class two airport, to be constructed in Marysville, should be well on the way toward completion by the end of the year," Mayor J.A. Beverage had announced optimistically. "The city engineer is preparing to begin the survey, which will be submitted to the CAA for approval, after which construction will begin."

**167**

It was a welcome boost to our income when Dr. Randall, who had been flying as frequently as possible on both business and pleasure trips, decided to trade in his Taylorcraft for a Cessna 140.

"As much as I fly, it's time I upgraded," he said. "The Cessna's heating system is better and since it has a starter, I won't have that to worry about."

"That sale came at a great time!" Carl said. "It will insure that our bills are paid this month."

He made only one charter trip in February—to Kansas City—despite strong winds and flurries of snow. Mid-month, he and Jim flew to Wichita to see the 170, Cessna's first four-place plane.

In the past six months, Jim had dated several girls but had never been serious about any of them—then he met Nelda.

He brought her to the airport after lunch one day late in February.

"This one must be special," I said, as I watched them walk, hand in hand, toward the flight line.

As they moved from plane to plane she, like me, evidently favored red because they spent considerable time examining the Ace. Jim seemed to be explaining the plane's various attributes.

A few minutes later, he brought her to the office and introduced her. Her name was Nelda Bargmann. She was very pretty. She was dressed in blue jeans and a bright plaid shirt and wore a matching ribbon in her hair. She was slightly taller than I—and slender. Her wide, blue eyes were friendly, and she wore her curly hair in a short bob. Both being blonds, she and Jim made a handsome couple.

Nelda soon began hanging out at the airport occasionally. She always asked me if there was anything she could do to help.

Although he was going out almost every night, after spending from daylight to dark at the airport, Jim still managed to hold up his end.

Jim and Marion Hoover had taken over most of my outside duties and, with the housework in Mrs. Jones capable hands, I felt that, even though the bookwork had increased along with the number of students, I could still find time to work on my commercial license.

Carl didn't think it was necessary.

"I might as well," I said. "If I get a commercial, I'll be able to help take some of the load off your shoulders."

# A Blue Bird in an Oak Tree

As suddenly as it had appeared, the snow was gone, and it was spring. Then, the March winds began to blow—incessantly—keeping the planes grounded most of the time for the first two weeks of March. It blew, not only during the day, but early morning and late evening hours as well, cutting back significantly on the number of hours students could fly.

Some of the students were falling so far behind in their schedules that Carl worried they would lose interest.

"Looks as though the powers that be are determined to make it as difficult for us as possible," Carl said, staring out the office window. The windsock was standing straight out. "We haven't met expenses for two weeks now; we have the maximum number of students we're allowed, but we're completely at the mercy of the elements."

"It *has* to let up soon," I said.

But it didn't.

Then slowly, the wind moderated. We took advantage of every minute we could to fly. As a result, three more GI students completed the course and received their private pilot's licenses.

Then we had our first accident; the first of two.

The first occurred when Ray Minger, who had soloed during a break in the high winds early in the month, cracked up the L-2. While shooting landings, he came in too low and hit the telephone lines at the north end of the field. The plane nosed in, washing out the landing gear and prop. Ray suffered only a minor scalp wound and required no medical attention.

As if that wasn't bad enough, a bizarre incident, causing a great deal more damage, occurred the following week.

Dan Brungardt, a quiet, easy-going student, took his flying seriously. Precise when practicing maneuvers, he had soloed in less time than the average student.

I was confident he'd turn out to be one of our better pilots.

Carl agreed.

"If he continues the way he's going, it won't take him long to get his private license," Carl predicted early in his training.

We discovered, too late, that although calm and cool in routine practice, Dan wasn't worth a darn in an emergency.

It was a beautiful Saturday morning. All the planes were out. Dan had taken off in the Blue Bird; his assignment—to practice rectangles, lazy eights, and pylon eights in the designated practice area northeast of the airport. Before taking off he did the pre-flight check as usual. Everything was in order—he thought. However, he overlooked one small but crucial item; the left-wing tank was in the "on" position.

All went well until he reached the practice area and began flying pylon eights. Suddenly gasoline began spraying over the windshield.

Dan panicked—and turned off the switch to the engine instead of the offender—the left-wing gasoline tank. Now that he had no power, he looked around for a suitable place to land. He was flying at an altitude of only five hundred feet but, luckily, he happened to be flying over a smooth, flat field. It shouldn't have been a problem to make a safe landing had he not, nervously, misjudged the distance. He undershot the field and landed in the top of the tallest oak tree in Marshall County.

Uninjured, he climbed down the tree, walked to the nearest house, a quarter of a mile away, and called the airport.

Listening as he related what had happened, I was incredulous.

"Are you all right?" I asked.

"I'm fine," he replied, unperturbed. "Except I scraped my leg on the tree as I climbed down."

*Thank God!* I thought, breathing a sigh of relief. "What does the plane look like?"

"W-e-l-l—" he replied. "It's still in the tree."

Carl had just come in from a dual flight when I hung up the phone.

"What?" he asked when he saw my face.

"You won't believe it—" I said.

"Good God!" he exclaimed as I described what had happened. "What the hell is going to happen next?"

"Thank God, he wasn't hurt," I said.

"You stay here and watch the office," he said. "Jim and I'll drive out and pick up Dan and see what we can do about the plane."

Dan was waiting at the farmhouse when they arrived. The plane—still perched perilously in the top branches of the tree, the wings drooping limply at its sides—looked dejected, like an enormous, broken bird.

"Do you have time to go out again?" Carl asked as they drove back to the airport.

Dan consulted his watch.

"Not now," he replied. "I'm late to work already."

"Okay," Carl said. "But you'd better get yourself out here at six o'clock sharp in the morning."

"Do you think he'll come back?" I asked when Carl told me to reschedule another student, so Dan could fly in his place.

"We'll see," he replied. "His chances of becoming a pilot depends on whether or not he makes that flight."

"How bad was it? The plane, I mean."

"Pretty bad. I don't know what the hell is going on, but do you realize we just wrecked our second plane in two weeks? I suppose we should expect an accident now and then, considering the number of hours we fly and the stunts some of the students have pulled, but this is ridiculous."

He leaned back in his chair and sighed.

"Thank God, he didn't get hurt! It's ironic; as few trees as there are in that area, that's where he would land!"

Dan appeared promptly at six the next morning. He seemed nervous but determined. Carl flew with him through several routine practice maneuvers, made three take-offs and landings, and got out of the plane.

"He'll be all right," he said confidently as Dan took off.

"Well, old buddy," Carl drawled sarcastically that afternoon as he, Jim, and I stood looking up at the Blue Bird, still hanging in the tree top, "Looks as though we're about to find out exactly how much you learned at that mechanic training school."

I'd gone along. There was no way I was going to miss seeing the Blue Bird perched in a tree top.

"I reckon you're right," Jim said, scratching his head. "But first, how're we going to get the damned thing down from there? They didn't teach me that!"

"Any ideas?"

"We might shoot it out."

We all laughed.

"It looks sad," I said. "Like a bird with broken wings."

"Well, let's get back to town and get some men and equipment together," Carl said. "It's had all day and it doesn't look like it's going to come down by itself."

Late that evening, they drove into the airport, the wings of the Blue Bird on the back of a flat-bed, towing the fuselage behind.

"It's going to be a major job to repair it," Jim said. "Meanwhile, we're going to be short a couple of planes until I can get them going again."

"You've got your work cut out for you, that's for sure," Carl said.

"Just thank God no one was hurt—and they *are* both repairable," I said.

"The L-2 won't take much time," Jim said. "I'll get it out first."

"Considering the number of students we have, we'll have to make use of every minute of flying weather we can," Carl said.

"I thought we were doing that now," I retorted.

"We'll just have to do it better."

Having two planes out of commission was a problem. The next morning, we discussed problem number two. Although Dan should have caught the error in his pre-flight check, Marion had serviced the Blue Bird, and Carl felt he was responsible for the left-wing gas tank switch being left open. Nothing was said, but I was sure Marion could sense a touch of hostility.

"I'd fire him if we didn't need him so badly," Carl said.

At our next two ground school sessions, Carl emphasized the importance of thorough preflight checks.

A week later, Jim had the L-2 back in the air. He looked at the Blue Bird, a sour expression on his face.

"This one isn't going to be as easy," he said.

The first of the month, Marion gave notice. He'd been offered a job back in Wisconsin, at an airport near his hometown, he said. Fortunately, George Wirth, of Byron, Wyoming, a pilot Carl knew in the Air Corps, contacted us soon after Marion's departure. Wirth had just received his civilian instructor's rating, and Carl hired him immediately.

Mid-month, Carl and I flew to Wichita to pick up a new Cessna 140 to replace the one Dr. Randall bought. While there we took a tour of the Cessna factory and saw the new all-metal Cessna 190 and 195, a five-place business plane with a rotary engine which, we were told, would be in production soon.

A few days later, Fred Burris, who had recently received his private pilot license, decided the 140 was just what he needed for his business. When Carl called the factory about a replacement, the company suggested we try out the new version of the 140. This model sported a "jump seat"—a seat which replaced the baggage compartment allowing the plane to carry two passengers.

By the time Jim had the Blue Bird back in the air, Dan Brungardt had completed the course. He passed his private pilot test with flying colors.

Blue Bird in an Oak Tree

# Flight Breakfasts

I was sitting in the office, my feet propped up on my desk, when Carl came in from flying a dual.

"Well—this is the first time I've seen you sitting around with nothing to do for a long time," he chided.

"Oh, I have plenty to do," I said, nodding at my desk. "I've just been thinking."

"And what are you thinking about that's so important?"

"About something that would fit into our schedule, would be fun, not cause you more work, and bring in more income."

"Wow! I'd like that! Come up with anything?"

"Yes, a flight breakfast."

"You mean get a group of people together and fly somewhere and have breakfast."

"Exactly! Others are doing it. It'll stimulate public interest, give the new private pilots an incentive to fly, add a few dollars to our income—and everyone has a good time!"

"I see you've got it all figured out," he laughed. "When do you propose to do this?"

"Why not schedule it for this coming Sunday? Looks like the weather will hold; we still have time to get an ad in Thursday's paper."

"I was thinking we'd go to Lincoln," I added. "The airport has a good restaurant, and we can be there and back in time to get in some serious flying."

"Sounds good. See what you can do."

By the end of the day, I had pilots and passengers lined up for all five planes.

Dr. Randall said he and his wife would go.

I would fly the Ace and take Bob Griffith as a passenger.

Bob Griffith had been hanging around the airport for two or three weeks. He always came directly to the office where he sat around for an hour or so, asking questions which I answered patiently, encouraging him to take flying lessons. He hindered my work but, considering him a prospective customer—possibly even a buyer—I tolerated him. As owner of a local business, he had the money, he had the time, and his interest in flying seemed genuine.

Carl, less enthusiastic, called him my "boyfriend."

"What do you want to bet that his only reason for hanging around out here is to talk to you?" he said.

"Nonsense!" I protested. "He always acts like a perfect gentleman, and we only talk about flying."

"All the same," Carl laughed, "I'll bet you a quarter that you never get him to take up flying."

"It's a bet!" I replied, even more determined to sell Bob Griffith on taking flying lessons and maybe even buying a plane.

We met at the airport shortly after dawn Sunday. It was a beautiful sunshiny morning; the air was calm, and perfect for flying.

Bob and I were the last to take off. It was a beautiful sight to watch the planes lift into the air, one by one, just as the sun peeped over the horizon. Once on course, the other planes fanned out before us. Bob was delighted as I pointed out familiar farms and towns below.

"You'll see people coming out of their houses to watch the planes fly over," I said.

When we were about half way to Lincoln, I asked if he would like to take the controls and see what it was like to fly the plane himself. He smiled but shook his head.

Undaunted, I pointed out another community appearing up ahead off to the left of the nose.

As he leaned forward to look, he casually placed his arm across the back of the seat, his hand resting on my shoulder. At the same time, his other hand dropped to my knee.

*Oh, Oh!* I thought.

As his hand moved slowly up my thigh, pulling my skirt above my knee, I pushed the left rudder forward and pulled sharply back on the wheel, negotiating a wing-over to the left. Then I reversed the controls and made another to the right.

After I brought the plane back to straight and level flight, I turned to Bob.

"Wasn't that fun?" I said cheerfully. "That's only one of the maneuvers you'll learn when you start taking lessons."

Not only was the plane back on course; so was Bob. His hand, no longer on my thigh, was covering his mouth as he reached for the ice cream container in the baggage compartment.

I babbled on about flying maneuvers, but Bob was strangely silent for the remainder of the flight. When we landed at the Lincoln airport, he sought out Carl and told him he wouldn't be joining us for breakfast or the return trip; he'd decided to spend the day with a friend in Lincoln.

Mrs. Randall and I were studying the menu, discussing what we should order for breakfast, when I looked up to see Carl looking at me with a sly grin on his face.

The flight breakfast was a huge success. As word got around, pilots began vying for a plane to fly on the next one.

Bob Griffith didn't show up at the airport the next day—or the next. When a week passed and he hadn't made an appearance, Carl said, "What happened to Bob? I won't say 'I told you so' but it looks like you lost a bet."

"Looks like it," I grinned and tossed him a quarter.

In spite of murky weather on Sunday, eight planes carrying sixteen people took off for our second flight breakfast—this time to Seneca. The flight yielded us a bit of publicity when *The Marysville Advocate* ran a photo with a caption in Thursday's newspaper.

Though the March weather had made flying iffy much of the time, the wind died down toward the end of the month, and we had beautiful flying weather. Students vied for time to get back on schedule and, for over a week we kept the planes in the air all day, almost every day. Carl and George, our new instructor, flew extra hours of dual to help those who'd gotten behind catch up. The flurry of activity gave both our income and our morale a much-needed boost.

I even managed to get in an hour when a student, scheduled for a solo flight, cancelled. Once back in the air, the Blue Bird seemed to fly even more smoothly than it had before landing in the tree. As I practiced my maneuvers the motor hummed in the clear morning air. I had to give Jim credit; he was one hell of a mechanic.

Carl had been too busy with other students to fly with me for some time, and although it would take me forever to qualify for a commercial license at the rate I was going, I *was* making headway.

At day's end, tired but happy to be flying on a regular basis again, we fell wearily into bed.

Flying Breakfast Enjoyed by Air-minded Citizens

# Mother Nature Versus Ungerer Flying Service

Early in April, E.M. Watham, a CAA inspector from Wichita, flew to Marysville to give flight checks to six of our GI students and, later in the month, two more received their licenses. Fortunately, however, we were signing up GI students as fast as they "graduated."

"Now if the weather will only continue to cooperate," Carl said.

But this was not to be; the April rains, though late in coming, again brought student training to a halt. The runways were bogs. Once a plane rolled off the ramp, it was mired deep in mud.

We now had twenty-five students; fifteen, our limit allowed on the GI training program, and ten civilian students. So much inclement weather made it difficult to keep them all on schedule.

Then the rains stopped, and the wind began to blow. No sooner were the runways dry enough to fly off, however, then the rains began again.

I began to wonder if Mother Nature had it in for us.

"Damn it to hell!" Carl exclaimed as he stood at the bedroom window in his undershorts watching the downpour.

We dressed and ate a leisurely breakfast. Hoping it would clear up later in the day, we drove to the airport. By noon, the rain had slackened to a heavy mist, alternating with showers.

Inclement weather hampered charter flights as well as student training. If it was possible to get an airplane off the ground, however, Carl never turned down a request. Although I trusted his judgment, I suffered many an anxious moment.

We spent the morning catching up on odds and ends and had just returned from lunch when a local manufacturer called and asked if Carl could deliver a piece of equipment to Kansas City. I was about to explain that the visibility was practically zero; that it would be impossible to take off on the water-soaked runways, much less fly in this kind of weather, when Carl took the phone from my hand.

"Sure," he said. "Bring it out."

"Now how do you expect to get a plane off the ground in this mess?" I asked.

"I'll take off from the ramp," he replied.

"You can't do that!"

"Just watch."

I stood inside the hangar door and looked out at the heavy skies and drizzling rain while Carl flight-checked the Ace. A lighter plane, it would be airborne faster than any of the heavier planes. I crossed my fingers hoping he would change his mind.

"Remember when you took off at the Woden's?" he asked, coming to stand beside me.

I nodded.

"The wind is in the northeast—about forty miles an hour," he said. "I'll rev up the motor before I release the brake and, by the time I reached the end of the ramp, I should have enough airspeed to carry me until I reach flying speed."

"But look how foggy it is!" I exclaimed. "The clouds are practically down on the ground!"

"That's no problem. I can fly the highway until I get out of it."

"It's too dangerous," I said flatly.

A car drove up. The driver got out and handed Carl a foot-long package.

"You planning to fly in *this*?" he asked incredulously.

When Carl said yes, he looked up at the lowering sky and shook his head.

"Good luck!" he said and headed back to his car.

Carl grinned at me and shrugged his shoulders.

"Now don't worry your pretty little head about me and flying," he said. "We wouldn't be in this business if we didn't know what we were doing—now would we?"

He stowed the package in the baggage department, got into the plane, and I spun the prop.

Standing to one side, I watched as he warmed up the Ace then gave it full power, holding the brakes until the tail of the plane rose into the air. When he released the brakes, the Ace shot across the ramp, lifted slightly, then settled, skimming the ground until it disappeared into the fog.

I strained to hear the engine as it gradually faded into the distance then walked slowly to the office. A few minutes later, the phone rang.

"I thought I heard a plane," Dad said.

"You did. Carl just left for Kansas City."

"How the devil did he get off the ground?"

"He took off from the ramp."

"The dumb bastard!" Dad said.

I could picture him chomping furiously on his cigar.

While I fumed about his flying in these conditions, the townspeople admired Carl's flying ability. There were times when, though both furious and scared, I gritted my teeth and laughed along with them. I'd learned that a certain amount of showmanship went a long way toward inspiring confidence in the public, keeping prospective clients interested.

"The important thing in this business is to instill public confidence in the safety of flying," Carl said. "Everyone enjoys the thrill of watching a maneuver that appears a might dangerous—as long as it turns out all right."

When someone asked if I wasn't worried when Carl flew under less than amiable weather conditions, I replied: "Of course not. Carl is one of the best pilots you'll find anywhere; if *he* thinks it's all right to fly, it is."

Unable to concentrate on the books, I turned on the radio and paced nervously around the office. "In a speech given at the South Carolina statehouse," the reporter said, "Bernard Baruch announced today: 'Let us not be deceived. We *are* in the midst of Cold War.'"

That didn't help; I turned the radio off.

An hour and a half after he took off, the phone rang.

It was Carl.

I breathed a sigh of relief.

"I'm at the Kansas City airport," he said. "Delivered the part and getting ready to take off for home. How's the weather there?"

"Still raining but the fog's lifted a little. I can see the poor farm."

"Okay. I'll see you in an hour or so. It's clearing here so will probably continue lifting there. I'll land on the grass strip. Keep your fingers crossed that I don't get mired down."

"You be careful now!"

"I'm gonna do that—just for my Honey," he laughed, and with a smack-smack into the phone, he hung up.

I breathed a sigh of relief when, exactly fifty-eight minutes later, I heard the sound of a plane and looked out to see the Ace flying at about 300 feet circling for a south landing. When he touched down, Carl revved the motor. The plane shot forward, the wheels barely skimming the ground until, on reaching the hard surface of the ramp, he hit the brakes and spun it around only a few feet from the hangar door.

We wasted no time closing up and heading for home. I didn't know about Carl, but I needed a drink.

The latter part of the month, the weather cleared and, again, the students were scrambling for time in order to catch up on their flying.

I was busy at my desk, as usual, when the Blue Bird taxied onto the ramp, and Carl got out. He'd been checking out Mark Nichols, one of our GI students who'd logged more than enough dual hours to solo.

He came into the office, filled a disposable paper cup with water, downed it, and filled it again.

I looked up from my work to see a scowl on his face.

"You go watch," he said. "I can't."

"What can't you watch?" I asked.

"I just soloed Mark."

"He *should* be ready to solo," I said. "He has seventeen hours dual."

"Right! More than the usual. I probably should have washed him out."

He sighed.

"At times like this, I think I'm in the wrong business."

"Well," I said consolingly. "All he has to do is make three take-offs and landings."

"Right! But he's so damned inconsistent! He continually goofs up! I never know if he's going to do it right or not. After seventeen hours, I still have to recover for him occasionally. Well—it's done—I'd better go see how he does."

I followed him out. Mark was making the approach for his first landing; he was too high.

"Don't try to land!" Carl yelled (as though Mark could hear), giving him the crossed arm signal for aborting the maneuver.

He stood, mouth agape, arms still in the air as Mark continued. Two-thirds of the way down the runway he saw his error and pulled up just in time to clear the telephone lines.

Carl paced back and forth as Mark flew the flight pattern and made his next approach. This time he made a perfect landing on the designated spot.

"I can't believe it," Carl said, shaking his head. "If he gets through this without cracking up, I swear, I'll never let him fly again!"

We watched as Mark turned the plane and taxied back to the north end of the runway.

"Maybe I should stop him now," Carl said. "Can you think up a good reason—?"

"I *will* say he has plenty of guts," I said.

"Guts is all he *has* got. He certainly can't fly."

We waited nervously for the next approach.

"I'll be damned!" Carl said when Mark made two more perfect landings.

When he taxied in after the third landing, Carl waved him onto the ramp and stood aside as he climbed out of the cockpit.

"Good job, Mark!" he said. "Although you had me worried that first time around."

"I came out of it okay though, didn't I?" Mark asked.

"That you did," Carl replied as Mark followed me into the office to schedule his next flight. I put him down for the next morning, wondering if Carl would be up to handling it by then.

We had scheduled a flight breakfast to Lincoln for the last Sunday in the month. Thankfully, the day was beautiful—sunny and with hardly any wind. Eight planes participated.

To lure the public back to the airport, we had dropped tiny parachutes over town on Saturday promising a free ride to those who presented them at the airport Sunday. This brought a nice crowd Sunday afternoon; we gave more rides than we'd given since the fall.

Throughout the spring and summer season and well into the fall, our Sunday flight breakfasts were looked forward to as "the Sunday thing" to do. Almost all our newly licensed pilots participated at one time or another. Each time, we flew to a different city—or town. If the airport didn't boast a restaurant, airport personnel, or members of one organization or another, either fed us or drove us into town. Occasionally, we hosted flight breakfasts from other towns, making reservations and driving the guests to a local restaurant.

The breakfasts not only provided additional income, they also familiarized a few skeptics with flying, and promoted good will throughout the community.

# Bookwork

When the month of May brought gale-like winds, Carl lost his patience.

"This has been one hell of a year," he said. "First it snowed and then it blowed and then it rained and then it blew some more."

"It's sure to stop soon," I consoled. "This can't keep up forever."

"We seem to be backing up instead of moving forward," Jim sighed.

"Maybe this is meant to teach us what civilian flying business is like," I said optimistically. "After all, these planes aren't like the B-24s and B-29s—they could get up and out of the weather."

Carl laughed.

"Remember when we were flying out of Liberal and they stacked B-24s five hundred feet apart to fly out a blizzard over Kansas?" he said.

"And what about the time they sent you to fly one out over Alaska?"

He laughed again.

"I guess we should be thankful. We *are* making a living—*and* growing the business; albeit slowly. The weather will settle down eventually."

Sure enough, as Kansas weather is prone to do, the rains stopped and the winds moderated. Once again, all the planes were in the air!

Mid-month several hundred people gathered at the airport when The Kansas Flying Farmers,[9] flying fifteen planes, each carrying two farmers, landed at the airport. They were on a state-wide tour to promote the Flying Farmers and the convention to be held in Hutchinson on May 20.

While the planes were being fueled and serviced, photos were taken, and Al Ward Johnson, Flying Farmers president, gave a short speech about the importance of the airplane to the farmer and the upcoming convention. Two Marshall County members joined them when they took off.

Carl was on a dual cross-country, and Jim had gone to the post office. I was alone in the office when I heard a plane skim low over the telephone lines. That would be Jim Walsh. I went to the door and watched as the Blue Bird made a perfect three-point landing.

I met him as he taxied in and motioned him toward the gas pump.

"Good landing, Jim!" I said as he cut the switch and jumped to the ground.

"Thanks," he said. "It's a beautiful morning. You oughta go out."

"I'd like to, but I can't leave the office unattended."

"Too bad," he said. "Can I help tie the plane down?"

"No thanks, Jim. Just leave it here. Wiley should be here any time."

"Okay. I'll see you tomorrow at the same time!"

I went back to the office and entered his name on the appointment calendar for Tuesday, posted his time in his logbook and the airplane log, and went out to fill the plane with gasoline.

Placing the step ladder where the wing strut joined the fuselage, I filled that wing tank then moved to the other side and checked the other. I was filling the tank in front of the cockpit when Wiley, who was also a GI student, drove in.

"I was so busy at the store, I almost called and cancelled," he said. "But it's such a nice day, I said 'Hell, I oughta be able to take off for an hour!'"

"Jim Walsh just came in. He said the air is nice—calm—no turbulence."

"Considering all the wind we've been having, I guess we'd better take advantage of every break we get," he said, taking the hose and hanging it in place while I climbed down. Together, we moved the plane away from the pump and switched off the wing tanks.

I waited as he climbed into the cockpit and fastened his seat belt.

"Switch off, throttle closed!" I called out.

"Switch off, throttle closed."

I grasped the propeller with both hands and pulled it through a couple of times.

"Contact!"

"Contact!"

I gave the prop a sharp snap. The motor caught, and I stepped back to avoid the spinning prop.

I watched him taxi out for takeoff then stood for a moment, enjoying the warm sun before returning to the office. I should have had an uninterrupted hour for work providing, of course, I had no visitors or phone calls. *I can get a lot done in an hour,* I thought. Today was the third of the month; if I didn't complete the reports before closing time, I'd have to burn the midnight oil. I wanted to attend the monthly Cessna meeting in Wichita with Carl tomorrow; that wouldn't be possible if I didn't complete the bookwork.

I sat down at my desk and looked at the forms stacked before me. Bookwork was tedious. Though it commanded most of my time, it was definitely not my favorite part of the job. I had learned, however, that if I tackled it resolutely and had no interruptions, it went smoothly. On the other hand, frequent interruptions prolonged the work, making it a seemingly never-ending task. I'd also learned that if I kept the logs and journals up on a daily basis, the monthly reports went much easier.

"I'm learning!" I'd remarked to Carl only yesterday. "Someday I'll have it down to a routine job—I hope!"

The hour went smoothly; I accomplished a great deal. If the afternoon went as well, I would finish by sundown.

Carl returned in time for lunch. Mrs. Jones had prepared chicken sandwiches and a salad.

"Isn't it nice that we can take time to relax and have a leisurely lunch instead of eating on the run as we used to?" I said as we ate.

With Mrs. Jones, Jim, and George here to help, life was much easier and more pleasant.

"That first year was pretty rough," Carl agreed. "But we made it, didn't we, Babe?"

Back at the airport, Carl looked at the schedule.

"I have only two hours dual this afternoon, so I can run interference for you while you work on the reports," he said.

Grateful, I attacked the work with gusto.

Jim had rolled the L-2 onto the ramp, washed it, and had began the lengthy task of waxing and polishing the fuselage and wings. Carl joined him. As I worked, I could hear them laughing and joking as they shined up the plane.

Mid afternoon, I took a short break.

"I'd much rather be out here helping you guys," I said, "It's too nice to be inside."

As solo students came and went, Carl stopped his polishing job long enough to prop the plane and send them on their way, then service the plane when they returned. As a rule, they would come inside for a brief chat, but they had learned that I wasn't to be disturbed at the first of the month. As they called their "hello's" from the door, I marked their time, and they continued on their way.

It was five-thirty when I looked at the clock. Carl was flying with a student, and Jim was still working with the L-2. With no interruptions, I would complete the forms by the time all the planes landed for the day.

At exactly 6:30, I made the final entry, breathed a sigh of relief, and arranged the forms in neat stacks for Carl to sign.

I went outside, watched the last two planes land, then helped Carl and Jim service and hangar them for the night.

Jim left and Carl and I went back to the office. One more job to do before we quit for the day. As he signed each form, I folded it, placed it in the proper envelope, already stamped, and sealed it.

That done, we made a quick run to the post office and headed home for dinner.

I always enjoyed the monthly trips to Wichita, and the Cessna business meetings were always pleasant and informative. Even though it was a "busman's holiday," it was good to get away from work for a while. Since I was flying the plane, I also got a rare taste of negotiating heavy air traffic.

We were just rolling the planes out of the hangar Sunday morning, tying them down on the flight line, when the first student arrived. The day had dawned bright and clear. A few minutes later, three others arrived and by the time the sun was thirty minutes into the day, all the planes were in the air.

Carl took off to fly dual with Ron White, who would soon be taking his flight check, and George was flying with Mark Carter.

"Looks like we'll make up for some back time today," Jim said as we watched the last plane take off.

"Yes," I replied. "I hope this weather holds for a while."

"According to the weatherman, it should."

The morning passed rapidly. We had several spectators out and students, trying to make up for lost time, kept the planes in the air most of the day.

Late in the afternoon, Dr. Randall, Fred Burris, George McAnany, and a few students lingered at the hangar door exchanging news and opinions.

Carl and I were going over the schedule when we heard the roar of airplane engines.

Jim burst through the office door, his face white.

"You've no idea what those damned fools are doing!" he exclaimed.

Carl was at the door in a bound.

There, flying formation over the field, were three of the planes. I looked at Carl. His face was pale. He needn't say a word; I'd never seen him so angry.

One by one they broke away. When the distance between them was safe, he sighed with relief. Two of the students had less than five hours solo time! He dropped into his chair, his hands clenched. Jim joined the other men who had stopped talking to watch the exhibition.

"What are you going to do?" I asked. "You can't ground all of them."

"Right now, I just don't know," Carl replied.

A few minutes later, we heard one of the planes approaching for a landing. He rose from his chair and went outside.

As the plane taxied toward the hangar, he motioned the student to the flight line.

"Go into the office," he said calmly after tying the plane down. "Wait for me there."

As the others came in, they received the same instructions. Ignoring me at my desk in back, they were laughing and joking about their escapade. When Carl entered, the chatter ceased. For a long minute, not a sound could be heard.

He stood inside the door looking at one first and then another, his face expressionless. The boys stole a few sheepish looks at each other, then down at the floor. To coin a phrase, I'd never heard so loud a silence.

It was several minutes before Carl spoke.

"Do you have any idea what would have happened if any one of you had goofed the slightest bit?" he asked then.

They avoided his eyes and cast furtive glances at one another. His standing there quietly—looking at them with that intent gaze, speaking quietly—was worse than if he had yelled and cursed.

"Just think about it for a minute," he continued. "Try to picture what would have happened if just one of you had flubbed."

He hesitated, giving them time for his words to penetrate. "Not one of you would have had a chance in hell."

Their expressions grew serious. Obviously, it didn't seem as funny now.

"I won't ground you this time," Carl continued in the same soft voice. "But if you pull a stunt like that again—if you don't kill yourselves first—I will, not only ground you, I promise you will never fly again."

"That's all," Carl said. "Now schedule your next appointments with Edna and get the hell out of here."

Without a word, they moved to my desk to schedule their next flights.

"Remind me to have a discussion on safety and common sense at the next ground school session," Carl said after they left.

---

[9] Conceived as a state organization in 1944 on the campus of Oklahoma A&M, The Flying Farmers went national the next year. Machinery was taking over on the farm and farmers embraced flying machines as a new implement. (The Flying Farmers became international in 1961 with the addition of Canadian chapters).

Kansas Flying Farmers

# The Advent of Summer

I t was the first Sunday of the month, and a group of unhappy pilots and their passengers sat in the office, and milled around outside, hoping for a dense fog to lift so they could fly to Lincoln for the previously scheduled flight breakfast. At nine o'clock the fog had shown no sign of lifting, so the flight was postponed until the following Sunday.

It was well worth the wait; eight planes took off for Lincoln on one of the most beautiful mornings we'd had for some time.

"We couldn't have asked for a more perfect day," said Dr. Randall once we arrived at our destination.

Following breakfast, we headed back to Marysville in time for everyone to attend church services.

Everyone, that is, except the Ungerers.

We had dropped handbills, some marked as "free tickets," over Frankfort and Vermillion so our afternoon was spent flying with students, giving rides, and enjoying one of the busiest days of the season.

It was 100 degrees in the shade. The windsock stood straight out before a fifty-mile-an-hour southwest wind, and dust devils danced gleefully up and down the runway. Jim had gone home, and Carl was struggling to secure the heavy hangar doors, whipping and banging in the strong wind while I, sweltering at my desk and sipping a cold drink, laboriously added figures to the pile of government forms before me.

Dad and Lillian drove into the parking lot.

"Close 'er up!" Dad yelled without cutting the motor. "Let's go fishin'!"

Carl walked to the car and leaned in the window.

"I don't think we should," he said. "Jim took the afternoon off.

We should be here in case someone wants to go somewhere."

"Shit!" Dad said. "Anybody'd be a damned fool to wanna fly in *this* weather!"

"We brought some old clothes for you to change into and some fishing poles," Lillian said.

"Come on—lock up," Dad ordered. Let's go fishin'."

I looked hopefully at Carl. The thought of being near water sounded heavenly.

"All right," Carl said doubtfully. "I guess it won't hurt to take a few hours off—long as we're back by the time the wind goes down."

"*If* it goes down," I interjected.

While Carl closed and locked the hangar doors, I left a note on the office door.

We got into the back seat, a shorn Blackie, not to be left behind, close at Carl's heels.

Blackie's fur had been so thick that, with the coming of hot weather, Carl had decided best leave him at home where he could find a cool spot to escape heat. That lasted only one day. Blackie, who had appointed himself airport mascot was, apparently, serious about his job. When we returned home that evening, he growled fiercely when Carl started to pet him, snapped at his hand, and marched away, head high. He would have nothing to do with him—until the next morning when we were leaving for the airport. As we walked to the car, Blackie, tail wagging the dog, stuck firmly to Carl's heels until he gave in and held the car door open for him to get in.

The result was a close haircut which, though not becoming, was cooler than the thick fur. Blackie seemed not to care how he looked, as long as he was allowed to take his rightful place at the hangar doors.

On the way to Dad's favorite fishing hole, he sat happily upright, his butt between Carl and me, his head out the open window, ears blowing in the wind as we drove down the hot, dusty road.

Twenty minutes out of town, we arrived at a clear, slow-moving stream. Sheltered from the wind, it was secluded and seldom used by others.

As I sat on the bank, fishing pole in hand, bobber bouncing in the water, I considered going wading, but dared not spoil Dad's fishing by stirring up the waters.

Lillian unpacked a picnic lunch, and I munched on a chicken leg as I waited for a strike.

Sitting in the shade of a tree beside the cool stream, I felt refreshed. I put the thought of the work waiting for me back at the airport out of my mind.

Feeling a tug on my line, I watched the bobber pop playfully up and down in the stream. Soon, however, it stopped. The fish had either lost interest or had taken the worm. I lifted the line. The bait intact, I cast it further upstream.

The others were having no better luck. Then, a few minutes later, Carl brought in a nice crappie. I got up and went to admire his catch and when I returned, my bobber had disappeared. By the time I reeled it in, the fish had disappeared—and so had the bait.

Although we caught few fish, the afternoon passed pleasantly. By the time we returned to the airport feeling refreshed, Jim was back, the wind had gone down, and students were beginning to arrive for their evening appointments.

"The most frustrating part about this business," Carl said the next day, identical weather-wise to the day before, "is having the planes sit idle for most of the day, then not having enough planes for the students who want to fly during the morning and evening hours."

# Disaster Strikes

I t was a pleasant Friday evening. The wind had settled to a slight breeze, the windsock wavering from north to north-west. All the planes were in the air.

More than the usual number of spectators were out to enjoy a balmy evening while watching the planes take off and land. Some sat in their cars; others stood around in groups, visiting.

Red Andrews, who had soloed earlier in the month and already had flown ten hours solo, was flying the Blue Bird, shooting landings on the northwest/southeast runway.

"He's doing exceptionally well," Carl remarked as he turned to wave to Fred Burris and Bob Craven who were just driving into the parking lot.

"Fred has been promising me a ride in his new plane," Bob said, joining Carl and I and Jack Williams.

"You couldn't have chosen a more perfect evening," Carl replied.

"Come on! Let's get that plane in the air!" Fred called out.

We watched as they walked toward the 120 sitting on the flight line.

"Fred's really proud of that plane," Jack said. "Says it's the best buy he ever made."

As Carl turned to answer, he saw that Red was approaching for another landing. The 120 was pulling out onto the north/south runway, heading for what he presumed was the northwest/southeast runway for takeoff.

Carl spun around when he heard Fred advance the throttle, but it was too late to stop him. The plane hurtled down the runway for a takeoff to the north.

The crowd stared agape as the two planes reached the intersection at the same instant. I thought for a second they had missed, then there was a sharp, clicking sound as the 120 clipped the tail of the Blue Bird.

Horrified, I rushed to Carl's side.

"Cut the throttle! Damn it! Cut the throttle!" he said under his breath.

Red, however, apparently froze at the controls. As we watched, the plane shot fifty feet into the air, flipped and fell with a thud, the nose buried in the ground, the tail section protruding grotesquely into the air.

As in one breath, the crowd gasped. For an instant, everyone stood, petrified. Then a woman screamed, and we all ran toward the fallen plane.

Carl was first to reach the scene. Red was crumpled over the wheel, blood gushing from his mouth while Fred, covered with blood and sobbing hysterically, tried to pull him from the cockpit.

Carl pried Fred's hands free and led him away from the plane.

"Come on, Fred. You can't do Red any good." Carl said as he tried to break free,

A few minutes later, an ambulance arrived, and Carl called the CAA. Instructions were to leave the plane where it was until an investigation could be held.

There was very little sleep for the Ungerers that night, and the next day the heavy veil of death hung heavily over the airport.

Carl and Jim had gone into town when a Civil Aeronautics plane arrived mid-morning. I watched from the office door as they landed and taxied to where the Blue Bird stood. Two men got out and milled around for some time studying the accident scene.

They surveyed the layout of the runways, and walked around the plane, taking pictures. Stepping around the pool of blood, they looked inside the cockpit.

Then they taxied to the ramp and came into the office. I answered their questions with a strange feeling of guilt—as though I could, in some way, have prevented what had happened.

They asked for the names of those involved and others who had seen the accident.

"May we borrow your car to go into town?" one of them asked.

Without speaking, I handed him the keys.

Carl and Jim arrived just as they were leaving. Carl stopped to exchange a few words with them.

Jim took refuge in his workshop; Carl and I waited in the office—Carl pacing, while I tried to work on reports, finding it difficult to concentrate.

"What do you think?" I asked. "Will we have to stop flying?"

"They may suspend flying for a while. I don't know," he replied. His face was drawn.

Throughout the day, the curious came; some walked up the hill to gape at the plane, still on its nose, the pool of blood congealed at its side, while others sat in their cars, talking in hushed voices.

I answered questions as briefly as possible without seeming rude.

"They're like vultures!" I said resentfully.

"Will they let you fly again?" some asked.

"Of course," I replied. "It was tragic, but accidents do happen—in airplanes as well as automobiles. We've been very lucky up to now."

Nevertheless, I wondered.

"What if they *don't* let us fly again?" I asked again.

"I'm sure they will," Carl replied. "It *was* just an accident. Although it happened on our airport, we weren't responsible. There was nothing we could have done to prevent it."

The time dragged slowly. I called Mrs. Jones to prepare sandwiches then drove home to fetch them. Jim came into the office and we ate silently, each thinking our own thoughts.

When the CAA officials returned, Carl and Jim walked with them to the site of the accident where they looked at the plane again, then walked up and down the runway, stopping often, looking in all directions, studying the scene.

At last they returned to their plane and took off. Carl came into the office.

"We're not allowed to fly until they've completed their investigation," he said. "If you want, you can go home."

"I'd rather stay with you," I said, and turned back to my desk.

Three days later, the inspectors returned. They didn't come into the office, but stood outside, talking with Carl.

I waited nervously at my desk. What would the verdict be? Even if we *were* allowed to fly, what affect would the accident have on the business? How many students would we lose?

As the roar of their AT faded into the distance, Carl came into the office, Jim on his heels.

Carl was carrying a sheet of paper. He looked grim.

"Can we fly?" I asked.

"Yes," he replied. "We can fly. We'll just have to make a few modifications before we resume student training."

"What kind of modifications?" Jim asked.

He handed Jim the paper. Jim looked it over then passed it to me.

I read it and looked up. Carl was staring out the window, slumped as if the accident had sapped all the energy and enthusiasm from his body.

"Well," he said, "best we go move that plane; get it out of sight. No one's going to want to fly as long as it sits there with its tail in the air."

It didn't take long. Once the tail had been lowered to the ground, it towed easily. Together they moved it into the shop.

That done, they returned to the scene and shoveled dirt over the dried pool of blood.

That week's headline in *The Marysville Advocate* read:

## PLANE CRASH TAKES LIFE OF STUDENT PILOT CLINTON ANDREWS

The accident was the first plane fatality in more than 2,000 flying hours logged by student pilots in the seventeen months the flying school has been in operation.

Andrews, who made his solo flight on June third, and had logged ten hours since that date, had made a spot landing—

The question uppermost in everyone's mind now was how the accident would affect Ungerer Flying Service, a firm the townspeople had considered an important addition to the Marshall County business community.

One of the modifications specified by the CAA was that we erect a wind tee[10] at the intersection of the two runways.

"Well," Carl said the next morning, "the first thing on the agenda for today is to buy the material and start building that wind tee."

"I'll go along," Jim said.

I watched them drive away, turned to go back into the office, but changed my mind. Bookwork was the last thing I wanted to do.

I sat down in the doorway and sighed. The sun was shining; the air was calm, a perfect morning for flying. It was strange not to see any planes in the air.

I wondered how the accident would affect the students. How many would continue to fly?

For that matter, what about me? After what happened, how did *I* feel about flying? I thought about that for a minute. Was I afraid? I expected a stab of fear, but it didn't come. I stood and walked to the hangar. The Ace, looking peaceful and friendly, sat just inside the open door. I thought of what Carl had said—about always sending a rooky pilot back up after an incident—or accident. "It's like the old maxim 'get back on the horse'," he'd said. And this was what he'd insisted Dan Brungardt do after he landed the Blue Bird in the tree.

The CAA had given us permission to resume flying; nothing was preventing me from flying right now. Did I have the nerve?

I decided to find out.

I pushed the Ace out onto the ramp, gave her a pre-flight check and chocked the wheels.

I hesitated.

*I don't* have *to do this,* I thought.

I pulled the prop through several times then went to the cockpit, turned on the switch and pulled the prop through again. The motor started easily. I pulled the chocks, got in, fastened the seat belt, and eased the throttle forward.

The Ace rolled smoothly to the center of the runway. I sat for a moment, evaluating a slight hollow sensation in the pit of my stomach, then gave it full throttle. The plane surged forward. As we soared into the air, my spirits lifted. I patted the control panel. Perhaps there would be moments of fear and doubt, but I had won. I *would* fly.

I made a circle over town then decided that, with both Carl and Jim away, I best not leave the airport unattended too long. When I taxied up to the hangar they were just driving into the parking lot.

"That was a damned fool thing to do!" Carl exclaimed, getting out of the car.

His voice sounded angry, but he didn't look angry.

"Why?" I asked. "The CAA said we could fly—just not with students."

He didn't reply.

"One thing *you* don't lack is guts, girl," Jim said.

Carl told me later that they were standing in front of the post office, discussing the effect the accident would have on the flying business, with Dr. Randall and a couple of businessmen when the Ace flew over.

"I just did what you teach," I said. "You sent Dan Brungardt back up after he crashed the Blue Bird—remember?"

Carl nodded, his face grim.

"You don't stop driving just because someone is killed in a car wreck," I added defensively. "Why is it any different flying airplanes?"

The tragedy of Red's death would never be forgotten but, hopefully, it would eventually be accepted for what it was—an accident.

The CAA approved our return to flight training and gave us two months to complete the requested improvements which, in addition to installing the wind tee, included widening both runways. Though not one of the requirements, we decided to install a concrete floor in the large hangar while we were at it. This would make it easier to move the planes around.

The GI students were the first to resume flying. Although several were nervous at first, they all drifted back except two—both civilians.

The accident had a stabilizing effect. No longer were hangar flying discussions about stunts and "hot pilots." The students treated their plane with more respect; valuing it for what it was—a safe and dependable means of transportation.

So ended the month of June, the most tragic month in the history of the Ungerer Flying Service.

But we *had* survived.

---

[10]A Wind Tee is a large weather vane shaped like a T, located at an airfield to indicate the wind direction. A mechanical device attached to an elevated structure, the wind tee rotates freely to show the direction of the wind.

# A Day of Leisure

Heavy rains to the north in the last of June caused severe flooding to the Big Blue River which, at points a mile wide, inundated lowlands and overran Highway 36. As the threat to the city grew, Carl was kept busy flying reporters and others wanting to see the flooded area from the air.

We'd had very little rain locally, but that suddenly changed.

I turned off the alarm, got up, and stood at the window for a minute watching the rain falling in sheets so dense only a shadowy outline of Frederick and Viola's house was visible.

I climbed back into bed and snuggled close to Carl.

"This is nice. Let's stay in bed all day."

"I'm hungry."

"You're always hungry."

"Like I said—I'm just a growing boy."

"What are we going to do today?"

"We certainly can't fly. Are you caught up at the office?"

"Almost. Actually, I'd like nothing more than to spend the day sitting around home."

The tempting odor of fresh-made coffee drifted up the stairs.

"Mmmmmm—that smells good," Carl said.

"Tell Mrs. Jones to make a big breakfast!" he called out as I headed down the stairs.

The coffee was percolating cheerfully on the stove, and Mrs. Jones was just layering two slabs of ham in the frying pan.

"We're being lazy this morning, but we'll be ready for breakfast in twenty minutes or so," I said as I poured two mugs of coffee.

"If any two youngsters ever earned the right to be lazy, it's you two," she retorted. "You just take your sweet time. Breakfast will be ready when you are."

Twenty minutes later, we sat down at the table to fresh mugs of coffee and a large glass of freshly squeezed orange juice. Mrs. Jones served us hotcakes, ham and eggs, and fresh fried potatoes—Carl's favorite breakfast.

We had almost finished eating when the phone rang. I refilled our coffee cups while Carl went to answer.

"It was Dad," he said when he returned. "He wanted us to know that we're to come over there for dinner this evening."

"What did you tell him?"

"Yes, of course. He said Lillian's been cooking all morning, and if she keeps it up, she'll have enough to feed an army by dinner time."

"I wonder why she goes on a cooking spree when the weather's bad," I said.

"Dunno," Carl said, shaking his head. "She always has."

"Would that I'd live long enough to be the cook she is!" I said.

He took a sip of coffee, leaned back in his chair, and sighed with pleasure.

"This is the life," he said. "Mrs. Jones, that breakfast was super!"

Mrs. Jones's face glowed with pride.

I stood and picked up our plates.

"I'm going back upstairs to take a nap," he said, giving me a kiss on the cheek.

"Good," I said, glad that he was willing to take the day off. The accident had been an enormous strain.

"What time are we expected at the folks'?" I asked.

"Dad said to come over any time, but that we'd probably eat about five. Why don't we go over around four?"

"I'm going to visit with Mrs. Jones for a while," I said as he headed up the stairs. "I'll join you in a bit."

Spending as much time alone as she did, I knew she must grow lonely at times. I'd encouraged her to invite friends over, but she seldom did. I doubted, at her age, she had many friends left. She *did* seem happy with us, however, and I was grateful for all she did.

When I went up, Carl was fast asleep. When I lay down beside him, he put his arm around me, kissed me on the neck, and snored.

I lay awake thinking about the business. Worrying a little. Ours wasn't the only flying business suffering. One couple we knew were even thinking of closing down.

The lines on Carl's forehead were getting deeper with each passing day.

It was almost four when he woke.

"Did you have a good nap?" I asked. He looked more refreshed than I'd seen him for some time.

"We should compliment Mrs. Jones more often," I said as we dressed. "She's a good cook, and we're lucky to have her. Sometimes—especially on days like this—I feel positively spoiled."

"You have a right to be spoiled once in a while," he said, patting my hand.

"Perhaps the rain won't last long," I said. "If it stops, and we can fly as much the last half of the month as we did the first half, we'll get by."

"Yeah," he said. "That would be great."

We were fortunate that we were selling planes. In addition to Dr. Randall, we had sold planes to three area businessmen—Earl Craven, Fred Burris, and Bus Vincent.

"The rain might cool down the atmosphere, so we'll have less turbulence for a while," I said encouragingly. "That would be good."

He nodded in agreement.

"What are we celebrating anyway?" Carl asked, standing in the center of Lillian's kitchen, hands on hips, surveying the fruits of her labor. "This looks like a damned banquet!"

"I just felt like cooking," Lillian smiled.

"It smells delicious," I said, lifting the lid off first one pot then another. "What can I do to help?"

"You can start dishing it up," she replied. "The other kids are coming over too. They should be here any minute. Would you like to carve the duck, Carl?"

The table had been set, and serving bowls were ready on the sideboard. I began dishing up food—scalloped potatoes with cheese, home-canned green beans, dandelion greens, and corn on the cob. There was also a Jell-O salad and apple sauce and, in addition to the duck, a baked ham. Not only had she made home-baked bread, there was cornbread, raisin cookies, mince and apple pie, and a chocolate one—Carl's favorite—on the sidebar.

"What a feast!" I exclaimed. "You don't expect us to eat all this, do you?"

"I'll freeze what we don't eat for later," Lillian said. "It'll save me having to cook for a few days."

Jim and Nelda and Frederick and Viola arrived at the same time, oh-ing and ah-ing over the food.

"Lillian, if you keep feeding us like this," I said as we gobbled up our dessert, "I'll have to go on a diet."

"Listen to that girl!" Dad said, talking around a mouthful of mince pie, smothered in whipped cream. "Always worrying about her figure. You've got him now, so eat up and enjoy yourself!"

"I've got him, Dad," I retorted, "but I still have to worry about keeping him. There are a lot of girls who'd like to take him away from me."

"Hell," Carl said. "As long as I've got you to sleep with and Mrs. Jones and Lillian to feed me, you don't have anything to worry about."

"That's right," Dad said. "You never have to worry about keeping a man as long as he's happy and contented."

Carl leaned back in his chair and winked at me and patted his stomach.

"And boy, oh boy—am I happy and contented!"

Amid the laughter that followed, Lillian and I stood and began clearing the table, and Dad went to get the cards.

With three girls to help, the dishes were washed, the kitchen spotless, in short order. We joined the men at the dining table where a game of pinochle was in progress.

The time passed swiftly.

"Lands sakes, it's almost midnight," Lillian exclaimed. "How about a cup of coffee and some cookies before we call it a night?"

"Sounds great to me," Carl said, dealing the men a poker hand.

I poured coffee while Nelda and Viola set out cookies and cinnamon rolls. The moon was shining brightly through the kitchen window.

"It's stopped raining, fellas!" I called out. "Looks like we'll be able to fly in the morning!"

Although the CAA had given us two months to complete requested improvements for continued GI flight training, the heavy rains complicated the process. Carl and Jim spent every possible minute widening the runways, mowing, dragging, rolling, leveling, and filling in ditches.

Big Blue Inundates Lowlands

# Wheat Harvest

The view from the air of wheat fields turning from green to gold, almost overnight, was a beautiful sight to see; and now the wheat harvest was getting underway.

As combines began moving into the fields on the first of July, they looked, from the air, like a great patchwork quilt with bugs crawling over the blocks.

Farmers prayed for hot, dry weather and, although a shower on the morning of the fourth caused a brief delay in some fields, most of the combines kept going.

Little did we know that Ungerer Flying Service would turn out to be a valuable asset to Marshall County wheat farmers until a local farmer called, asking if it would be possible for Carl to deliver a machinery part to the field.

Of course, Carl said "of course."

So it was that we added a new service.

"Broken-down machinery at harvest time can cost the farmer thousands of dollars if there's considerable delay," Carl explained to the *Marysville Advocate* reporter who was doing an article on the subject. "If the part needed isn't available in Marysville, I can go for it—save the farmer hours—days sometimes. It might even save the crop if there's a threat of rain. If inclement weather is threatening, speed is essential"

"Is it safe to land in the field?" the reporter asked.

"If the field is dry enough to accommodate the harvesting equipment, it's dry enough to land on," Carl replied. "I've landed on worse. However, the part must weigh under 250 pounds.

"In an emergency, the farmer calls his supplier in Marysville," Carl explained. "If the part is in stock, the dealer delivers it to the airport and we fly it to the field. If the part isn't available locally, the dealer will call suppliers in other cities. Once the part is located, whether in Kansas City, Topeka, Lincoln, or elsewhere, it will be delivered to the airport there where we'll pick it up and fly it directly to the field."

If the part was available locally, we promised to deliver it, anywhere in a range of twenty-five miles, within fifteen minutes after we received it, at a cost of only four dollars. If we had to go out of town, the cost depended on where we had to go for it.

Five local machinery companies joined us in the venture. An advertisement in both Marysville newspapers announced *Operation Repair Parts*.

As the harvest progressed, Carl flew a couple of area farmers to check on the status of their fields in South Dakota.

"They'll be moving equipment up there as soon as they finish here," he reported when they returned.

Bob Craven, one of our first students, and son of Earl Craven who owned the Craven Implement Company, an International Harvester dealer, had convinced his dad that a plane would be a valuable piece of equipment in the business. He'd purchased a Cessna 140, and Bob kept the plane busy during the harvest delivering parts to the company's customers. After harvest season was over, Bob convinced his dad to learn to fly.

"I think Nadine is going to start taking flying lessons!" I said. "I just talked to her, and she said that Bill has finally agreed it would be all right."

"Great! When is she going to start?"

"Perhaps next week. She has to wait until her mother gets back from Canada to sit with the kids."

I had been trying to get Nadine to take lessons from the time we went into business.

She called again the next day.

"If Carl can fit me in Sunday afternoon, Bill said he would sit with the kids."

"Will two o'clock be all right?" I asked, checking the schedule.

"That'll be perfect!"

I was enthusiastic. I'd been the only female pilot in town long enough. Nadine being my best friend in Marysville made it all the more exciting.

Farmers were still hard at work harvesting the remains of the wheat. The season had proved to be hectic as harvesters rushed to salvage the precious crop, keeping their eyes on the skies for signs of rain. Luckily, the crop hadn't suffered as much damage as it might have.

Thursday afternoon, we received a request to pick up a part in Lincoln—a round-trip flight of about an hour and a half including take-off and landing.

"I hate to cancel my appointment with Gene," Carl said. "Where's Jim?

"He's busy doing a major on the L-2," I said. "Why don't I go?"

"Okay. I guess Jim can keep an eye out and answer the phone."

"Can I call Nadine and ask her to go with me?"

"Good idea," he nodded. "But she'll have to get out here right away."

"Joan Allen is here; she'll watch the kids. I'll be there in a jiffy," Nadine said.

Fifteen minutes after the call came in, we were in the air.

When we took off, a strong, stifling hot wind was blowing out of the southwest. The Ace pitched and tossed so that I wondered if I'd been wise to ask Nadine to come along. As I climbed to a less turbulent altitude, I kept an eye on her, watching for any sign of air sickness. However, talking excitedly about learning to fly, she seemed not to mind the turbulence. By the time I leveled off at 3,000 feet, the air was calm. The wind was less severe when we landed at the Lincoln airport.

The parts were waiting when we arrived. We lingered only long enough to have a cold drink then, storing the part in the luggage compartment, we took off.

The southwest wind had been an advantage on the flight to Lincoln but now, flying directly into it, we were traveling at a crawl, even at 3,000 feet. Telling myself that the rough air hadn't bothered Nadine early on, I headed down, leveling off at 300 feet. Although the air was rougher, we made better time.

"Do you feel all right?" I asked as we neared the airport.

"Sure," she replied. "I'm fine. Thank God, rough air doesn't seem to bother me."

"You'll make a good pilot then."

We were only five minutes out, when Nadine suddenly covered her mouth with her hand and reached for the ice cream container.

I thought it strange that she should get sick on the landing approach, after having done so well during almost an hour of turbulence.

I kept an eye on her as I taxied to the hangar. Though pale, she seemed to feel better. There were several waiting customers, so she gave me a wave, called out "I'll talk to you later," and went to her car.

"She was fine the entire trip then, just as we were getting ready to land, she got sick," I told Carl later.

"It's not unusual," he replied. "She wasn't used to flying and the air was pretty rough—even for a weathered pilot."

When I hadn't heard from her the next day, I called.

"I don't know why I feel so rotten," she said weakly. "If I don't feel better by tomorrow, I'm going to see Dr. Randall. There's no reason that flight should have made me sick."

"Maybe it's a touch of the summer flu," I volunteered.

"Could be," she said. "I'll call you tomorrow and let you know what the doctor said."

She called back Saturday afternoon.

"It wasn't the flying," she said.

"Well, that's a good thing—I guess. What was it?"

She giggled.

"I'm pregnant!"

"Oh, no! That means you'll have to cancel your flight training!"

"I guess so."

"Darn it," I said when I told Carl the news. "We just lost our prospective lady pilot."

Later in the month, Ungerer Flying Service "added spice" to the Blue Valley Ranch rodeo. A reported twelve thousand people attended the event. Carl was kept busy throughout the weekend giving rides.

"It was a strange contrast," the newspaper reported: "the airplane and the rodeo both providing entertainment for the spectators."

It was about this time that flying discs—or "flying saucers"—were making headlines nationally. Theories about the phenomena floated through the airwaves and via newsprint both locally and nationally. They were a popular topic of controversy at Ungerer Flying Service. Hangar flyers' discussions consisted of a great deal of speculation. The more imaginative insisted they must be alien invaders. Another theory was that they were a part of a secret government project.

# Lake McConaughy

I looked at the clock. It was almost ten. I'd been working on government reports since six o'clock. Still a long way from completing them, I was so absorbed in my work that I didn't hear Carl's approach until he rapped loudly on the door.

He had returned a short time before from an airport operator's meeting in Salina.

"You've had your head burrowed in those books long enough," he said. "How about taking a break? Let's take a little walk."

Where are we going?"

"Just up the hill to check the runways.

"It *is* nice to get out for a while," I said as we walked the north/ south runway watching for foreign objects such as sticks or rocks that might damage a propeller, a wheel, or the fabric of a plane.

Carl carried a shovel and stopped once or twice to fill in a rut with dirt, tamping it tight with his boot.

"What with all the rain we've had, we're going to have to mow again," Carl said.

The alfalfa was lush and green. Although he mowed the runway often, he let the alfalfa strip, parallel to the runway, grow until it could be cut for hay.

"We should get a pretty good crop. I told Dad that if he'd pay for having it cut, he could have it for his cow."

"I thought he was going to get rid of the cow."

Carl laughed.

"He's been going to get rid of the cow for years. He complains about having to milk her every day and threatens to sell her. Every time he does get rid of one, he says 'that's it!' But before long, he has another cow. They'll have a cow as long as he's able to milk. They like that milk and cream and cheese too much."

"So do we," I laughed. They practically kept us in dairy products.

I picked up a stick and hurled it off the runway.

"What did Floyd Cos have to say?" I asked, referring to the Seneca airport manager who'd stopped in earlier in the morning.

"Not much," he replied. "They're busy too. Like you, his wife is trying to catch up on the bookwork."

"How's the baby?"

"He has a little sniffle, Floyd said. Otherwise, he's okay."

"I don't know if I'd want a baby of mine crawling around on that dirty floor, picking up cigarette butts and anything else lying around. It's a wonder he isn't sick all the time."

"Aw, come on now," Carl joshed. "We could set up a washing machine in the back hangar, and you could dry the diapers on the wing struts."

I smacked his butt with a stick I'd picked up.

"How many students do they have now?"

"Fifteen. He was flying a dual cross country."

"You have a charter to Wichita this afternoon."

"I'd almost forgot. Ron Cook has a business meeting in Wichita; he wants to take his wife along."

"Talked to Ed Fisher lately?"

Ed Fisher had returned home from the service recently and started an airport and flying service in Summerville.

"I stopped in a few days ago. Seems to be doing okay. Six students; not bad for no longer than he's been in business."

A few days later, we awoke to the sound of wind howling around the eves. Carl was strangely quiet as we ate breakfast.

"What say we take the day off?" he said suddenly.

I looked up, startled by this sudden radical suggestion. I couldn't remember when we'd last had a day off.

"Great!" I said. "What shall we do?"

"Let's go fishing."

"Go fishing? In this?"

"Sure," he said. "According to the weather report, the wind isn't blowing as hard up north. It'll only take a couple of hours to get to Lake McConaughy."

Lake McConaughy, in western Nebraska, was one of the best fishing lakes within a two or three-hour radius. It boasted a landing strip and cabins for overnight trips.

"It does sound like fun!"

"Good! I'll call Jim and see if he can keep an eye out here."

By the time we'd cancelled all Carl's dual appointments and apprised Jim as to who was to fly what if the wind settled, the sun was high overhead.

When we took off the Blue Bird rocked and tossed in the rough air. Carl kept the nose pointed heaven-ward and climbed steadily leveling off at 4,000 feet in smooth, calm air. We set down on the landing strip paralleling the lake just after two o'clock. Although a breeze rumpled the waters of the lake, it was nothing compared to what we'd left behind.

We rented a cabin and tied the plane down outside the door. When we went to the café for lunch, a group of men were sitting around talking fishing.

"If you came here hoping to catch fish," said a tall, grey-haired man, "you came at the wrong time. They aren't biting worth a darn today."

"Oh, well," Carl replied. "It'll feel good to be out on the lake. Where we came from, the wind was blowing like the devil, and it was as hot as hell!"

By three o'clock, fishing equipment at ready, we were motoring toward the center of the lake.

An hour later, we'd caught only three small fish. The occupants of other boats didn't seem to be faring much better.

"You were right," I said. "Whether the fish are biting or not, it feels good just to be here—together."

He was thoughtful for a while.

"I guess I haven't been very good company," he said then. "We may work together, but we never have enough fun together."

"Don't worry about it," I said. "You and I have a good thing going."

"One of these days we'll take a real holiday—do anything you want to do," he promised.

A cool breeze ruffled our hair, and a fine mist cooled our faces and bodies as we trolled. Voices from fishermen drifted across the lake and other boats began moving out from shore.

Sitting lazily back in the seat, watching my line trailing in the slight wake, I felt at peace, not particularly caring whether the hook was baited or not.

"Why don't we go in and take a nap," I suggested an hour later. "Maybe they'll be biting better closer to sundown?"

"Let's wait a little longer," Carl said.

He'd come to fish. I knew from experience that we would sit there all night if necessary.

"That's another thing I like about you," I laughed. "You're always optimistic—especially when it comes to fishing."

Carl smiled at me indulgently. We were doing what he loved to do. Fishing and boredom were opposites as far as he was concerned.

Then, without warning, a black cloud, which had drifted in unnoticed, darkened the sky, and we could hear rumbles of thunder. Flashes of lightening crisscrossed the sky.

Other fishermen were reeling in their lines, revving up their motors, and heading for shore. Carl turned the boat toward the dock, and we trolled slowly toward the landing.

As the wind increased in velocity, huge waves began to toss the boat about, but Carl's eyes were focused on his line, now taut in his hand. It slackened and he let it out again.

One clap of thunder now followed another, and lightening flashed across the sky. The waves were getting high and spilling water into the boat. Other fishermen were heading to shore at top speed. Not the Ungerers! We puttered slowly toward the dock.

I grew increasingly nervous as the boat tossed wildly in the white-tipped waves. Huge drops of rain splattered the lake as Carl sat slouched in the prow, silhouetted against the stormy sky, his eyes glued to the line, his body rocking with the tossing boat like a cowboy riding a bucking horse.

Then I felt a strong tug on my line.

"I've got a bite!" I squealed above the roar of a thunderclap.

"Reel him in!" Carl shouted. "I've got one too!"

I was fighting to reel in the fish when Carl landed a huge wall-eyed pike. He turned to help me and together we got mine into the boat. He was larger than the one Carl had caught.

The rain was pouring in buckets by now, and we were both drenched. Rather than head for the shore, Carl turned the boat back toward the center of the lake.

"Let's go in!" I shouted.

I could have been talking to the wind.

I looked anxiously toward the plane. Though it rocked from side to side in the gusting wind, it seemed to be in no danger.

My clothing clung to my body and water flowed down my neck in tiny rivulets from strands of my hair and clung to my lashes so that I could hardly see.

I glared at Carl who sat, the rain pelting his face and running from the brim of his hat, rocking back and forth with the boat as though he didn't have a care in the world. Suddenly, another fish struck his line. I watched, fascinated as he reeled it in.

I slumped back in the seat.

*Well, if I'm going to drown*, I thought, letting the line back into the water, *I might as well drown fishing!*

No sooner was the line out than I had a strike.

We trolled until we had our limit.

Carl and I, the lone fishers on the lake, must have been quite a sight to the people watching from the shore.

As the storm slowly moved on, Carl headed for the dock.

Carl was in good spirits. After we changed into dry clothes, a crowd of onlookers gathered around, admiring our catch.

"I'd never have believed it if I hadn't seen it myself!" remarked one onlooker.

When we went to the lodge to eat, the air was calm, the sun shining, and the lake as smooth as glass. The only sign of the storm was a retreating black cloud, drifting before a slight breeze on the western horizon.

Our catch was the topic of conversation in the bustling dining room. As we ate, we ignored varied opinions such as "utter stupidity" to admiration bordering on heroism.

"At least we know there's fish in the lake," said one.

Dinner over, we walked down to the water's edge. Several boats were heading back out. The sun, now low on the horizon, left a silver path across the darkening lake, silhouetting half a dozen hopeful fishermen.

Occasionally a fish leaped into the air, leaving a widening circle as it disappeared back into the shadowy depths.

"Let's go," Carl said.

"But we've already caught our limit!"

"Not of crappie and perch," he replied, pushing the boat away from the dock.

For an hour, we drifted lazily over the calm water of the lake, but we didn't catch another fish.

# A Wedding Announcement

The morning was warm and sunny. A gentle breeze from the south-southwest barely stirred the windsock. All the planes were in flight.

Carl was flying with a student, and I was working on the reports when Jim arrived somewhat later than usual. He and Nelda had been out almost every night, and both families were expecting an engagement announcement. Even though they had been dating for almost six months, no such announcement had been forthcoming.

Rather than come to the office to chat and look at the mail as he usually did, Jim went directly to the work hangar.

*Strange*, I thought.

Flyers from surrounding airports had been bringing their planes to Jim to service and, although Tom Arganbright from Waterville had left his plane the day before for a carburetor adjustment, it wasn't *that* urgent.

Carl and his student came in at nine-thirty. After briefing him and dismissing him, Carl sat down at his desk and picked up the mail.

"Something's wrong with Jim," I said. "He didn't even come into the office to say 'hello.'"

Carl got up from the desk.

"I'll check on him. Can't be anything important."

He was back in a few minutes with a serious expression on his face.

"What's wrong?" I asked.

"He and Nelda broke up last night."

"It's probably only a lover's quarrel."

"It's worse than that. She stepped out on him."

His ten o'clock appointment arrived, and he left. A few minutes later, Jim came into the office and, without a word, sat down and picked up the mail.

"I hear you and Nelda had a little spat last night," I said.

"Spat hell!" He exploded. "I'm through with that woman for good. No damned woman is going to step out on me!"

"Well, after all, Jim, it isn't as if you were engaged or anything."

He spun around in his chair and glared at me. Then, suddenly, his expression changed. He gave me an odd look and, without another word, got up and went back to the hangar. He didn't return to the office all day and left early.

"I hope Jim isn't angry with me for saying what I did," I said as we drove home.

"Aw, he'll be all right. It's just something he's going to have to work out for himself."

As the days passed, Jim remained unusually quiet. Although he usually took an occasional break and laughed and clowned around with those who came by, he now said hardly a word and, although polite, avoided people as much as possible. He hadn't gone out since his spat with Nelda.

One Saturday evening, he came into the office early.

"Think you guys can handle it if I take off early?" he asked.

"Sure," I said. "We'll see you at the folks' for dinner."

He left without replying.

Dinner was on the table when we arrived. A plate was set for Jim, but he was nowhere to be seen. We had just started to eat when he came to the table dressed to go out.

"Got a new girl?" Dad asked, studying him from under his brows as he passed the platter of pork chops.

"Nope," Jim replied shortly, spearing a chop with his fork. "I'm taking Nelda out."

"I thought you two had split up," Lillian said.

"We have!" Jim said indignantly. "But that doesn't mean we can't go out once in a while.

"We have a new arrangement," he added. "We can both go out with anyone we choose."

The next morning, he arrived at the airport, once again his happy, go-lucky self, whistling as he went about his work and kidding around with the students.

Late in the evening, Nelda drove into the parking lot and went directly to the work hangar.

She left without coming to the office. I waved to her as she drove away.

A few minutes later, Jim stuck his head in.

"Can you—?" he was about to say when Carl spoke up.

"Yeah, go on. We'll finish up here."

"It's good to see them together again," I said.

"It looks like they've patched things up," Carl agreed.

"You're invited to the folks' for supper tonight," Jim announced the following Sunday.

During a lull in the activities, I called Lillian.

"Jim tells us we're invited to dinner," I said.

"Indeed, you are," Lillian laughed. "It's his party, so he wanted to ask you himself. He's also invited Nelda—and her parents!"

"Oh. Oh. Sounds like we're finally going to hear an engagement announcement!"

She laughed.

"It's about time."

Jim left the airport early to dress and pick up Nelda. Carl and I closed up, went home, and dressed. We were the last to arrive. As we took our places at the table, I noticed a small diamond engagement ring glistening on Nelda's finger.

"Nelda and I are going to get married!" Jim announced abruptly, without ceremony, once everyone was seated.

Dad, as usual, rose to the occasion. He had served his best wine, and now stood and lifted his glass.

"That's the best news I've heard for a long time," he said.

"Here's to the new bride—my future daughter-in-law—the third and last."

As everyone stood to toast the happy couple, I stole a look at Dad in time to see two big tears roll slowly down his cheeks.

After the toast, I blew Nelda a kiss. She winked slyly, confirming my suspicions as to why she had "stepped out" on Jim. Obviously six months was long enough to date a man in this day and age—especially if you'd known all along that you were going to marry him.

The wedding date was set for December 14.

# Moving Ahead

Although local farmers needed moisture badly, Ungerer Flying Service was enjoying the longest stretch of good flying weather we'd seen since going into business.

With the coming of cooler weather, clear skies, and calm air, enthusiasm ran high.

Students were enjoying cross country solos and taking flight checks; as fast as they finished the course, we signed up new students.

Flight breakfasts continued to be a popular Sunday event.

On Tuesday, I stopped in at the Summerville airport to talk to Ed Fisher about the breakfast planned for the following Sunday. Not having been there for a while, I hardly recognized the field. One of the many improvements included a new 50- by 60-foot hangar.

The following Sunday there was a great deal of grumbling when a severe thunderstorm delayed our take-off. However, the storm passed and fourteen planes—eight from Marysville, four from Seneca, and two from Summerville—flew to Lincoln through clear skies and calm air, landing at the Union Airport where thirty pilots and passengers had breakfast at the airport café.

As an increasing number of businesses and corporations now utilized planes, we were beginning to see new innovations in aircraft from all the manufacturers.

Cessna luncheon and business meetings, which had been suspended during the busy summer months, were resumed in October. Carl and I flew to Wichita to attend the conference. There was much discussion about the Cessna 170, the new four-place Cessna. We were told that it would be rolling off the production line soon.

The highlight of the meeting was a demonstration of the new Cessna 195, dubbed the "Businessliner." Sporting a Jacobs R-755-A2 300 hp radial engine, it was the first Cessna airplane completely constructed of aluminum. Carl and I were allowed to fly it cross-country. We flew to Liberal, spent the night and returned to Wichita the next morning.

"That's quite a plane," Carl said as we flew back to Marysville that afternoon, "but I don't think we'll be needing one for some time."

A couple of our GI students had signed up for the commercial course, but the 170 would suffice for the present.

The following week, the Cessna Corporation treated area-wide Cessna dealers and owners to a three-day fishing trip—destination Otis Lodge, in Itasca County, near Grand Rapids, Minnesota. Carl, with Earl Craven as his passenger, flew one of seven planes, carrying fourteen pilots and passengers, which took off from Marysville to fly the 560-mile trip together.

Although the two CAA representatives, impressed by the progress we had made and how smooth our operation was running, had given Ungerer Flying Service a clean slate, we still faced the city's airport improvement plans which had not yet gotten underway.

Despite the council's earlier expectations for an immediate start, there was no indication as to how soon improvements and modifications would get underway or how long they would take. Nor did we have any idea to what extent it would disrupt our activities while construction was underway.

Meanwhile, Chuck Yeager—a former United States Air Force officer, flying ace, and record-setting test pilot—became the first pilot to exceed the speed of sound in level flight. Flying the experimental Bell X-1 at Mach 1 at an altitude of 45,000 feet over the Mojave Desert, Yeager was the first to break the sound barrier—at 660 miles per hour.

Back on earth, however, things were not boding as well for corn farmers. According to Ben Breeding, an implement dealer, and Virgil Curtis, a farmer of Malvern, Iowa, who stopped in while Carl was on the Cessna fishing trip, some farm machinery items were becoming increasingly hard to find. After checking— unsuccessfully—to find a local dealer who could sell them a corn picker, they continued on.

They stopped in again on their return trip. They had flown west as far as Dodge City, they said, stopping at dealers along the way, but had been unable to find a single available corn picker.

Dr. Randall, one of Ungerer Flying Service's first three students, whom we called our "star student," was in the news again when he tried his hand at night flying. Since Marysville had no landing lights, he took off after dark from Kansas City, where he had attended the Fall Clinical Conferences, and flew to St. Joseph, spent the night with friends, and flew on to Marysville the next morning.

A few days later, thanks to his granddad, Dennis Waren Jones took to the air before he was born when Dr. Randall flew his daughter, Betty, to Marysville. The baby made his second flight when Dr. Randall flew the young mother and her twelve-day-old son back to Hutchinson.

"I guess Dr. Randall might be called a 'youngster' when it comes to flying," I said. Carl had just come into the office with the mail and I was looking over the *Topeka Daily Capital.*

"How's that?"

"Says here that Senator Capper has started taking flying lessons at the age of eighty-two."

To my consternation, almost two years had passed and, in spite of my efforts to interest other women in flying, I was still the only woman flying out of Marysville.

"Do you think Nelda might want to learn to fly?" I asked Jim hopefully.

"I'll ask her," Jim replied.

Nelda, however, flatly refused to take flying lessons.

"You can do the flying," she said, tossing her head. "I'll just be a housewife and raise our six kids!"

Jim slapped his hand to his forehead in mock desperation.

"My God!" he exclaimed. "How am I going to support a family like that?"

"In many ways, flying is still in the infant stage," Carl said. "Most women just don't relate to flying an airplane."

"I can't help but think that there's *someone* in the area who's interested!" I said.

"Women have a different sense of values than men. Little boys grow up dreaming of flying an airplane. Little girls—or most little girls—dream of romance and raising a family. Those who think they want to fly do so because it sounds glamorous. When it comes down to the actual mechanics, they lose interest."

I was sitting at my desk, filling out forms, as usual, when Carl returned from the post office.

"Looks like Howard Hughes finally launched the wooden monster," he said, tossing a copy of the *Kansas City Star* on my desk. "I never thought he'd get it off the ground—or off the water, rather."

I picked up the newspaper. The headline read:

HOWARD HUGHES' SPRUCE GOOSE TAKES FLIGHT

November 2, 1947: From aboard the world's largest aircraft, Los Angeles KLAC REPORTER, James McNamara described the first and only flight of Hughes' Flying Boat. Dubbed the 'Spruce Goose' because it was constructed entirely of wood, McNamara, who thought the plane would only be running taxi tests, expressed surprise when the craft briefly became airborne.

"I heard it took him three runs to get it in the air, and it only flew about a mile," Jim said, coming in from his workshop.

"Not much for twenty-five million dollars. It'll be interesting to see if he ever gets any kind of service out of it," Carl said.

"The article says it weighs two hundred tons!" I exclaimed. "The wingspread is as wide as a city block and the tail as tall as an eight-story building!"

"Whoever dreamed that up certainly thinks big," Carl said. "Boy! What a waste of money!"

Cessna Plane Dealers and Owners Leave for Minnesota

# Jim Takes His Flight Check

It was a beautiful day. Carl had spent hardly any time on the ground all morning. When Jim came in from a late lunch, the Ace was just landing.

"Since no one is scheduled to fly the Ace in the next hour," I said. "I think I'll go out for a while."

"Go ahead," Jim said. "I'll listen for the phone."

Due to the pleasant weather, I'd been getting in an hour almost every day of late.

I took off and flew the flight pattern. Off to the northeast, I could see the Blue Bird leisurely flying lazy eights. The air was smooth, the sun shining, not a cloud in the clear azure blue sky. Below, the patchwork of emerald green fields glistened in the sun. I could see farmers busy at their chores—mowing hay, building fences, and driving cattle to pasture. Occasionally, I rocked the wings of the Ace to and fro as one of our neighbors looked up and waved.

As I climbed higher to practice stalls and spins, a huge flock of white geese appeared off my left wing, flying in perfect formation, parallel to the plane. It was a beautiful sight. Fascinated, I flew along beside them for several minutes before initiating a stall and going into a spin.

"Congratulate Jim," Carl said as we sat at the folk's dinner table a few days later. "He took his flight check today, which makes four Ungerers who are licensed pilots."

"Took me long enough," Jim said. "Like Edna, I've been dragging my feet."

"Well, it isn't as though you haven't had enough to keep you busy, Son," Dad said. "Congratulations."

After dinner, Jim left for his date with Nelda. Their wedding date was approaching rapidly.

**228**

Lillian was bustling around in the kitchen, and Carl, Dad, and I sat at the table, lingering over coffee.

Carl was bragging about the progress I was making toward my commercial license.

"She's determined, that's for sure," he said. "I think she's going to turn out to be one hell of a pilot."

Dad shook his head doubtfully.

"You can preach all you want, but I don't think I'd want a wife of mine flying," he said.

"Dad, I couldn't keep Edna on the ground if I wanted to," Carl laughed.

"Hey guys! Don't forget—I'm here!" I broke in.

They both looked at me. Carl winked and said:

"Edna's a good pilot, Dad. One of the best!"

"I guess you're gonna do whatever you want," Dad said. Taking a swig of coffee, he said no more.

"Ungerer airport will be two years old in January," read *The Marysville Advocate* caption over a photo of the four "Flying Ungerers." We were all wearing the military flying suits—khaki colored, wool and warm, with nine zippered pockets—I'd ordered from an army surplus store.

The photo was followed by an article which read:

> "Two years ago, we had one runway, one airplane, and Carl was the only Ungerer who had a pilot license," Mrs. Ungerer told the *Advocate* this week.

> "We are all now licensed—Carl commercial and instructor; Frederick, Jim, and I private. We have four runways, three T-hangars, in addition to the five-place hangar, and an office building—all built by the Ungerer brothers—and six planes. Also based at the airport are planes owned by Fred Burris, Dr. Randall, Elmer Anderson and Robert Craven."

"In the past two years, thirty students have earned private pilot's licenses," Mrs. Ungerer continued, "and an additional fifteen are under training and will soon become licensed as well."

Carl Ungerer

# Wedding

Excitement ran high as the date for Jim and Nelda's wedding drew near.

"I don't know why she has to have a big church wedding," Jim complained. "Why can't we just get married at home with a few members of the family present? I feel like I'm on exhibition."

"I guess most girls want to have a big wedding," Carl said. "I happened to be lucky. My girl and I just went to the Justice of the Peace, and he said a few words, and it was over."

"Not that I wouldn't have liked a big wedding," I said. "But what with the war and all—"

"I just wish it was over," Jim grumbled.

"You'll live through it," Carl promised, slapping him on the back.

The day arrived, sunny and relatively warm for December. I had decided to wear the dress I'd been married in. I hadn't worn it since my own wedding. It was A-line in soft, off-white wool, and it seemed appropriate. I was almost ready when Carl came home. He had flown with a couple of morning students but had no more appointments until evening. George had scheduled his appointments to leave time open to man the office in our absence.

"You look just like my bride!" Carl said. "It doesn't seem like it's been over two years!"

"It's been an interesting two years," I said. "And I love you as much now as I did then!"

"Even though I work you to death?"

"You do not!" I said, shoving him playfully away. "I do it because I love our business, and I like what I do. Now go get dressed. Your clothes are laid out."

After he had bathed and dressed in the navy-blue suit—the only suit he'd bought since we returned home—he came to where I was standing before the mirror, adding a few last-minute touches to my hair. He rested his chin on top of my head.

"We *do* make a pretty good-looking couple, don't we?" he said.

I agreed.

The church was already crowded when we arrived a few minutes before the ceremony was to begin.

"I hope it's short!" Carl whispered in my ear as we were being ushered to our seat.

Dad and Lillian and Frederick and Viola had already been seated.

The wedding was charming; the church was magnificently decorated, the ceremony was impressive, and the bride glowed in her floor-length satin gown and lace veil. Jim looked ill at ease, but very handsome in his tuxedo, which had been a gift from Dad.

Neither Carl nor I had a drink at the reception, and after we'd joined the crowd, waving the bride and groom off on their honeymoon, we rushed home to change then hurried to the airport. Carl's first student for the evening was waiting when we arrived.

"Did Jim tell you where they were going on their honeymoon?" I asked as we hangared the planes at dusk.

"I don't know why he needed to keep it a secret, but I think Dad is the only one he told. They'll only be gone a week; he promised to be back in time to help out next Sunday."

Jim had made sure all the planes were in top shape before the wedding.

"He'll need time off to get settled in their new home," I said.

Dad had readied the house just up the street from us for the new married couple. He spent their honeymoon week putting on the final touches, making sure it was ready for them to move into when they returned. All four Ungerer families now lived in the same neighborhood.

"We should call it Ungererville," I joked.

"Getting settled in shouldn't be a problem," Carl said now.

"You always find things that need done after you move in," I said. "Think of all the wedding gifts that have to either be put in use or put away."

Carl was flying, and I was alone in the office when Jim and Nelda drove in late Saturday evening—radiantly happy and acting like two playful children.

"We just got in," Jim said. "We haven't even been to the house yet. Decided to stop here first, and let you know we're back."

"From the looks of you, you had a good time," I said. "When you get settled in, you'll have to tell us all about it."

"We'll do that," Jim said. "Tell Carl I'll see him first thing in the morning."

Sunday was a beautiful day; it was good to have Jim back to help with the crowd.

"Reminded me of last summer," I said after the last car drove away and the three of us rolled the last plane into the hangar.

"If you two'll finish closing up, I think I'll mosey along," Jim said. "I've got other things to do besides talk flying."

"Go ahead," Carl laughed. "You'll get back down to earth soon enough."

Jim started toward his car then turned back.

"Can you manage if I take a couple of days off later this week?" he asked.

"Sure!" Carl replied. "If we get in a bind, we know where to find you."

"I'll call tomorrow and ask Nelda if there's anything I can do to help," I said as we drove home.

"Everything is fine," Nelda said when I called. "We opened our gifts last night, and Lillian is coming over this afternoon to help me put them away. We need more closet space so Dad is going to help Jim with that. It's great that you can manage without him for a few days."

"Call me if there's anything I can do," I said.

Jim took three days off instead of two, but even though we were busy, everything flowed smoothly.

"Thanks for being patient this week," he said when he arrived at the airport Saturday morning. "Dad and Lillian helped, and we got a lot done. We had to put in another closet and build more shelves in the bathroom and kitchen."

"Does Nelda plan to keep working?" I asked.

"For a while anyway. We sure as hell can't afford all the things she's planning to do on my salary. She says if Edna can work as many hours as she does, she ought to be able to keep house for two while holding down a nine-to-five job."

"Good for her," I said. "As long as she enjoys it. As many hours as we spend out here though, I couldn't manage without Mrs. Jones."

"Hell, we couldn't get along without you!" Jim said. "You do the work of two people!"

"Yeah—she makes a pretty good flunky," Carl teased.

"Flunky, hell!" Jim said. "This whole operation would fall apart if she wasn't here to keep it together!"

"You're going to give me a big head if you don't stop talking like that," I broke in. "First thing you know, I'll be asking for higher wages."

"If we could afford it, we'd all be asking for higher wages," Jim laughed.

Even though it was December, we had been flying regularly and looking forward to the day when, hopefully, everything would be paid for, we would have money in the bank, and a day off now and then—when the sun was shining.

I called Nelda.

"I'm glad you're getting settled in your new home," I said. "You're to come to dinner at our house Sunday night. I've asked Mrs. Jones to plan a big feast. We're having a party for the bride and groom; everybody will be there."

Jim & Nelda Wedding Picture

# Happy Holidays

S aturday evening, I left early to dress for the Country Club dance. After I'd bathed and dressed, I stood before the mirror and studied the results. I had chosen a red dress— my favorite color—for the occasion.

I looked at the clock. If Carl didn't come soon, he'd have to rush to dress. I ran his bath, then went downstairs to mix drinks.

The house seemed strangely silent. Mrs. Jones had gone to spend Christmas with her daughter and family. It was the first time she'd been away for more than a day since she came to live with us. She had left prepared meals in the freezer and enough cookies, cakes, and pies to feed an army.

"I'd certainly hate to have to do without her permanently," I had said the second day she was gone.

"You're getting spoiled," Carl had laughed, then added, "in spite of everything, we got through this year without having to let her go, and I think everything will go fine—as long as she's happy and comfortable here."

I was measuring bourbon into short fat glasses when Carl arrived home from the airport.

"Hmmmm—you look good," he said. Kissing me on the cheek, he rushed up the stairs.

I added Coke and two cubes of ice to each glass and held them at arm's length as I negotiated the stairs. Carl was out of the tub, drying himself on a huge white towel when I entered the bathroom. I gave a low whistle.

He took the drink.

"Here's to the sexiest man in Marshall County," I said, clinking my glass to his.

"Thank you, Ma-am," he said, grinning, as he tied a towel around his waist. "And here's to my equally sexy wife!"

I leaned against the bathroom door and sipped my drink as I watched him shave.

"How many hours did we fly today?" he asked.

"Dual and solo—sixteen and a half," I replied. "Not bad considering it was barely above freezing out there."

"Great for this time of year," he agreed. "If we could fly as much every week as we have this week, we might get ahead a little."

"What made you so late?" I asked, taking his suit from the hanger.

"George hadn't returned from Kansas City. There wasn't any use for both of us to stay, so I sent Jim home. We didn't even service the plane—just rolled it into the hangar and closed the doors."

"So what if we're a little late," I said. Laying his suit out on the bed, I unbuttoned the starched, white shirt and selected a blue tie to match the suit. I loved him in blue. It matched his eyes.

The drink sent a warm glow coursing through my body, and I felt extremely happy as I sat on the edge of the bed watching him dress. He always did everything in the same order: First the boxer shorts, then the undershirt, then the right sock, then the left.

He was buttoning his shirt when he turned to me and grinned.

"I'll give you a penny for your thoughts," he said.

"The usual," I retorted. "Too bad we're running late."

When we arrived at the country club, the cocktail hour was well underway. The room was buzzing with the hum of merry makers.

Nadine waved from across the hall, and she and Bill began weaving their way through the crowd toward us. Nadine looked very pregnant and glowing with health.

"Pregnancy agrees with you," I said when they reached us. "You look wonderful."

"Thank you—I think," Nadine laughed.

The next hour was a whirlwind of introductions.

"Don't let all this popularity go to your head," Carl whispered as we filed into the dining room. "Tomorrow it's back to the grind-stone."

The band was just starting up when we finished dinner and moved into the ballroom.

We had hardly circled the room when someone cut in, and we spent the rest of the evening dancing with first one partner then another.

When the band struck up "Auld Lang Syne," Carl took my arm and swung me onto the floor.

"Do you know this is the first chance I've had to dance a whole dance with you this evening?" he asked.

For once, no one cut in.

We met Nadine and Bill in the parking lot and stopped to chat.

"Carl, what do you think of that new plane Beechcraft is putting out?" Bill asked.

"Pretty nifty," Carl replied. "The next time I'm in Wichita, think I'll check it out."

"If I can get away, maybe I'll go with you—unless you're loaded," Bill said.

"Now don't you be getting any ideas about buying an airplane!" Nadine chimed in. "With two kids now, and another on the way, I certainly don't want you taking any chances."

Bill winked at Carl.

"Would you listen to that? There she was—ready to start flying herself; then she comes up pregnant and suddenly gets protective."

"With my insurance, Babe, you'd be a hell of a lot better off without me than you are with me," he teased.

She punched him in the arm.

I snuggled close to Carl as we drove home. It was bitter cold—what we Kansans call a "sharp" night. The street lamps gleamed on a blanket of white snow while, overhead, the moon and stars glittered brightly in a clear sky.

"Another good flying day tomorrow," Carl said.

And a busy one. It was also going to be a short night.

The weather held for the next several days. An occasional snow during the night didn't prevent our flying through to Christmas.

The Saturday morning before Christmas the airport was crowded with children and their parents. The newspapers had reported that Santa Claus would arrive by plane this year and, sure enough, at ten o'clock, a red plane circled the field, landed, and out stepped St. Nick himself!

The crowd soon dispersed, however, following a car which whisked Santa to Eighth and Broadway, where he passed out 1500 sacks of candy, nuts, and oranges.

Mrs. Jones returned from her daughter's home early to help prepare for the open-house party. More attended than the year before, and the house was crowded with merry makers until well after midnight.

"These parties are expensive," Carl said after the last guest had said 'Good night! Merry Christmas!' "But I have to admit, it *is* good for business."

The day after Christmas, it snowed heavily, suspending all flying for the rest of the year.

Santa Arrives in Marysville by Plane

# New Year's Eve

Carl and I had planned to spend New Year's Eve quietly at home—enjoying the luxury of a relaxing evening—then the telephone rang.

"You kids get over here," Dad shouted. "We're going to have a New Year's Party!"

Jim and Nelda and Frederick and Viola had received similar messages. Everyone was in high spirits. Lillian had cooked up a dinner equal to the occasion, and we spent a festive evening eating, laughing, talking.

Five minutes into the New Year, Dad held up his hand to silence the shouts and cheers and well-wishing that began when the Grandfather clock in the living room struck twelve.

"I want to make a toast," he said when the noise subsided. "But first, I want to say that, even though I'm getting to be an old man, I'm happier than I've ever been in my life. Right here in this room is everything I ever dreamed of—three good boys, happily married and successful businessmen; a good wife of my own—though she does give me a bad time now and then."

He winked slyly at Lillian.

"Before the end of this next year," he continued, "I'll have a grandchild or two—maybe three." He paused and looked at each of us in turn as if he expected verification. His eyes came to rest on me. I gazed steadily back.

Viola blushed and looked down at her protruding stomach. I saw Nelda look knowingly at Jim.

"Yes," Dad continued. "Thanks to all of you, this past year has been a good one for me—and I'm looking forward to an even better year coming up."

His voice broke and tears came to his eyes as he blurted out:

"And I want to drink a toast to the best God-damned family a man ever had!"

Everyone was so quiet you could hear a pin drop.

Then Carl stood.

"Thanks, Dad," he said: "I also have a toast. I want to drink to the best Dad any three boys ever had. If it wasn't for Dad, none of us would be where we are today!"

Dad left his seat and hugged each of the boys and kissed us girls with tears streaming down his cheeks.

Then he turned toward the corner of the room, pulled his handkerchief out of his hip pocket, blew his nose loudly, and returned to his seat.

"Okay everybody," he said gruffly. "Let's cut this damned sentimental stuff and have some fun!"

"I think Dad is a little disappointed in me," I said as Carl and I trudged home through the snow an hour later.

"How's that?"

"Well, both Nelda and Viola are being nice little wives—keeping house, preparing to have babies—did you see the way Nelda looked at Jim when Dad mentioned grandbabies? And here I am—I don't keep house, let alone have babies."

"You're still his favorite."

"No way! Why do you think so?"

"I just know so."

"But he'd be a lot happier if I stayed at home and—"

"But *I'm* happier having you with me—and that's what's important."

# Year Three

"**I** hope the weather isn't going to be a repeat of 1947," Carl said.

He, Jim, and I were huddled in the office around the pot-bellied stove on a snowy January morning.

Now into the second week of 1948, heavy snow and strong winds had kept the planes on the ground since Christmas. Not only student training but flying in general had come to a complete halt.

"It can't get any worse," Jim countered.

"Not only did we have every kind of weather imaginable last year," Carl said. "We had a fatal plane crash, three minor accidents, and some pretty scary moments."

We all thought that over.

"We *did* learn a lot though," he said. "And, in spite of everything that happened, we came through—and we actually made progress financially."

"Yeah," Jim said. "I guess we shouldn't complain. After we got the VA contract, we did pretty darned good. *And* we've got a stable full of students to start the New Year."

"You're right," Carl said, adding, "the weather service predicts a break in the weather later in the week. Let's hope they're right."

The next day, Jim, Nelda, Carl, and I attended the wedding of George McAnany, the first student to sign up with Ungerer Flying Service in December 1945. He and Ruth Benda were married at St. John's Catholic Church in Hanover.

As Jim had predicted, five days later the snow ended, the city cleared the runways, and the students, glad for a break, kept the planes in the air for most of the day on Saturday.

Although cold, the skies remained clear, and flying conditions were, shall we say, endurable. Scheduling remained a problem. Alt-
**242**

hough weather-wise we didn't have to depend on early morning and late evening hours only, most of the students worked during the day. Morning and evening hours continued to be most in demand.

However, enthusiasm ran high as students, nearing the completion of the course, anticipated receiving their private pilot's licenses. In spite of the cold, they took an occasional hour off from work when possible, or skipped lunch, to get in extra time.

A few charter trips added to our income for the month. Despite our high overhead, we more than covered the bills.

"I wonder if there's any other business so completely controlled by the weather," I said.

"Weather will always influence flying to a certain extent," Carl said. "Oh, the big planes will fly up and out of it, and we'll have instruments in the small planes one of these days. That will make a difference, but I doubt a light plane will ever be manufactured capable of flying anywhere, anytime, regardless of the weather."

"I guess there are problems with any business you go into," Jim said. "Ours just happen to be the weather. However, there are a lotta good things about it. I, for one, can't think of anything I'd rather do."

"I feel the same way," Carl said.

"Me too," I said. They both turned to look at me as if what I had said startled them.

"This should be a national holiday," I said. Carl was just coming in from sending a student out solo. I handed him the newspaper. "Orville Wright just died," I said.

He sat down to read the news item. "Wilbur died early on," he said. "Of typhoid."

"Orville was seventy-six years old," I mused. "It's mind-boggling—the progress made in aviation in only forty-five years."

The weather broke early in February. With the appearance of spring-like days, new faces began to show up at the airport.

We couldn't have asked for business to be better for this time of year; students soloed, flew cross-countries, one GI trainee obtained his private pilot license, and another took his place. Visitors came and went, and pilots were discovering new uses for airplanes.

Then, just when things were going so well, we had another blizzard.

# A Flight Through a Snow Storm

Jim had gone home hours ago. I was alone. Sitting at my desk, I was growing increasingly nervous as the clock ticked away. I got up and paced the floor, pausing from time to time to stare out the window. It was almost four o'clock and darkness was approaching. Carl should have been back an hour ago.

I hadn't heard from him since he left early this morning to fly a charter passenger to Oklahoma City. A few flakes were falling when they took off, but not enough to be concerned about. Now, however, the snow, flying by the office window in vertical waves, diminished the visibility so that I could barely make out the wind tee a hundred yards away.

I turned on the radio.

"Heavy snow covers the entire area from northern Kansas, as far south as Oklahoma City," the reporter said.

I switched it off.

If Carl was still in Oklahoma City—or had landed somewhere between here and there—he should have called by now. I had the utmost confidence in his judgment and his ability to handle any situation, but flying in weather like this was hazardous—even for an expert pilot.

Waiting alone, the snow swirling about outside, I was frightened to think what might be happening. I could only hope that if he *was* in the air, he was flying over the storm. Knowing Carl, however, I could picture him, visibility practically zero, flying just off the ground to make out landmarks.

Perhaps the passenger hadn't completed his business, and they were staying overnight. Then why hadn't he called? It wasn't like him not to call if he was staying over.

I turned on the desk lamp and continued pacing the floor. It would be dark soon. What if the passenger had decided not to make the return trip with Carl? What if he'd taken off for Marysville alone, and been caught in the storm? If so, it would be like him to try to make it home.

The hangar doors, left open anticipating Carl's return, were banging in the wind, so I put on my coat and went out to close them. They were heavy—almost more than I could manage—but I finally succeeded.

Once back inside, I sat down at my desk without removing my coat and turned on the radio, straining to hear the weather report over the crackle and pop of static. The storm was increasing in velocity throughout the central United States, the reporter said.

I began pacing again, my mind whirling. Did he leave Oklahoma City? Was he flying in the storm? Had he landed somewhere? Or had he…? A sob caught in my throat.

I started when the telephone rang. "Hello?" I said, grabbing the receiver. But it was Mrs. Jones, calling about dinner.

"Don't go to any trouble," I said. "If Carl comes in, we'll make do with what's there."

"You mean he isn't back yet?"

"Not yet," I replied.

"Lord a mercy! And in this storm!"

"He's probably spending the night in Oklahoma City," I said. "I'll call when I hear from him."

A few minutes later, it rang again. But it was Dad.

"What's going on?" he asked.

A typical greeting, the question encompassed everything.

"I'm waiting to hear from Carl," I said, fighting to keep my voice as normal as possible.

"You mean he hasn't come in yet?"

"No," I replied, trying to keep my voice calm. "He probably decided to stay over. I should hear from him any time now."

There was a brief silence as though he was trying to digest the implications of what I had just told him.

"Well, I'm sure he's all right!" he said loudly as if the volume of his voice would make it so. "Don't worry about it and come on home. Lillian's just getting dinner on the table."

Suddenly, I heard a faint roar. I held the receiver away from my ear and listened. It was growing louder. It couldn't be—but it was—an airplane!

"Dad, I've got to go. I think he's coming in now," I said.

"He can't be!" Dad exclaimed. "You can't see a damned thing out there!"

"Yes, it's him," I said. "I've got to go." I hung up and ran outside just in time to see the ghost of a silver plane fly low over the telephone wires.

Carl's head was out the window, the better to see to land.

The snow stinging my face and eyes, I held my breath until the plane touched down. I was struggling to open the hangar doors when he taxied onto the ramp.

He was alone.

"Hold onto the right wing!" he called, jumping out of the plane. "I'll get the doors."

I did as he said, then together we rolled the plane into the hangar and closed the doors.

When we reached the office, I was sobbing. He took me in his arms and held me close.

"Now—now," he soothed. "What's this all about?"

"I was scared to death! I was afraid something had happened."

"Well, I'm all right," he said, "so stop this and let's go home. I'm cold and I'm starved."

The phone rang. He picked up the receiver. Whoever it was must have started talking before he could say hello.

He listened for a minute then shouted into the phone: "Hell yes—I know it ain't flying weather, but—"

He was silent for a minute.

"Sure thing, Dad. We'll be right there. Tell Lillian I haven't had anything to eat all day."

"I'd better call Mrs. Jones," I said.

"Call her from Dad's. Let's get out of here."

"Why *did* you fly in this kind of weather," I asked as we headed into town.

"I was disgusted," he said. "I cooled my heels until one o'clock, waiting for Martin, then he calls to tell me he's decided to stay in Oklahoma City for a few days. I could have been back home by noon had I known that. The weather was okay when I took off. When I ran into the snow, it wasn't too bad; so I kept flying. This could last for a long time, and I knew if I landed and we had a heavy snow, it was no telling when I'd be able to fly the plane home. The worse it got, the lower I flew. Remember the trip we made to Colorado—when we were flying right off the ground? That's what I did the last few miles. I settled over Highway 77 and followed it in."

"Well, I hope it never happens again," I said, moving close and putting my arms around him.

When we arrived, Dad was mixing us all hot toddies. He neither looked up or spoke.

When we were seated at the table, he picked up the bread knife and began slicing the hot, homemade bread into thick slices. An air of expectancy permeated the silence.

"Well," he said finally. "I certainly didn't know I'd raised a damned idiot for a son!"

Carl looked at me and winked knowingly.

"Here's a man—over thirty years old," he continued, "who doesn't even have sense enough to come in out of a storm. His poor wife sits at home and worries—and don't tell me you weren't worried, young lady," he said, looking up at me. "I never heard such a scared voice in my life as I heard over that telephone." He turned back to Carl. "What do you plan to do? Make a widow out of her? And how do you expect a poor widow to run an airport? No money. No husband. No nothin'. I'm tellin' you, I never saw anybody act so stupid! NOW—FOR CHRIST'S SAKE, TELL ME WHAT HAPPENED!"

Carl slowly laid his fork down on his plate and repeated, almost word for word what he'd told me.

The Old Man continued eating without taking his eyes from his plate.

"Don't let it happen again," he grumbled when Carl finished.

"Now," Carl said indignantly, "is it all right if I continue eating?"

Dad nodded his head and, after a few minutes of silence, the conversation turned to hunting.

# Student Antics

The weather moderated again the latter ten days of February, allowing students to maintain their schedules. We continued to have occasional snow but, all in all, weather conditions were seldom severe enough to keep us on the ground for long. The outlook for the year was optimistic.

I was looking forward to the Saturday night dance at the American Legion hall.

A beautiful day for flying, all the planes were in the air until dusk and, by the time we hangared the planes, ate, and dressed, the party was in full swing.

"Here they are!" Bill shouted, greeting us at the door. He slapped Carl on the shoulder. "I thought you'd never get here."

"You gotta get 'em while the gettin's good," Carl said.

"Good flying, eh?"

"Great!"

"How's the new C of C going?" Nadine asked.

I had joined a group of women to form a Chamber of Commerce auxiliary and had been elected president. In anticipation of the busy months ahead, however, I'd agreed to serve only on a temporary basis.

"We've only had the one meeting," I said. "Hopefully, they'll find a new president by the next time we meet.

We turned as the men, standing to one side, laughed uproariously. Someone had told a joke, no doubt. Carl went to the bar and came back with our drinks. A few minutes later, the music started, and we all headed for the dance floor.

Because of our work schedule, nights out like this were rare. It would be hard to get up in the morning, but tonight we were having fun.

"We saw the new Cessna 170," Carl said when he and Jim returned from the business meeting in Wichita Monday afternoon. "It's quite a plane—looks good and handles great; should sell well. After they get into production—we'll have one over for a demonstration."

One thing about the flying business: it was never dull. Something was always happening, was about to happen, or had happened. Some of the antics the students pulled would have been funny had they not been so frightening.

I was working on the books one afternoon when Carl entered the office just as the phone rang. He picked it up, his face growing red with anger as he listened. He slammed it furiously back on the hook and turned to me.

"You would never in your wildest imagination, guess what Jimmy Ronson is doing right now!" he exclaimed.

"Acrobatics?" I guessed.

"No! He's taking his relatives for a ride—from his uncle's pasture!"

Jimmy had only ten hours solo.

Carl picked up the phone again. There was no answer at the Ronson farm.

"Evidently they're all out at the pasture," he said. "All the planes are out; there's not a single damned plane for me to fly. He'd be back here before we could drive that far—unless he kills his damned fool self."

We could do nothing but wait and hope for the best.

"Believe me," Carl fumed, "if he doesn't kill himself out there, I'll kill him when he gets back here!"

He looked at his watch. Jimmy's one-hour practice session would be up in ten minutes. He went to the door, searching the skies to the northwest.

"Who called?" I asked. "Could they be mistaken—or joking perhaps?"

"Hell no! It was Martin Clowsky. Jimmy flies over his house every time he takes off. Martin thought it was me and drove over to the Ronson pasture."

I was standing at the window when I saw the Blue Bird approaching, still a mile out.

"Here he comes now," I said, turning to Carl, now pacing the floor.

Without breaking his stride, he headed for the door.

"Please don't do anything foolish, Carl," I said, picturing him knocking the daylights out of his wayward student. But he was already halfway across the ramp.

I couldn't bear to watch; I returned to my desk.

Jimmy landed and a couple of minutes later I saw him hurry to his car, head down. He drove off. A few minutes later, Carl returned to the office.

"You can cross Jimmy off the list," he said. "He won't be flying anymore—at least not from this airport."

Incidents like this were rare, although students often gathered in the office—before or after flying—to enjoy a session of "hangar flying." I smiled as I listened to the stories they told of their flying adventures, seemingly oblivious of my presence. If some of the accounts I heard were true, the skies over Marshall County were much more dangerous than Carl and I were aware. I knew, however, that most of the stories evolved from minor incidents enhanced in the telling by vivid imaginations.

If I heard anything that might bear investigation, I passed it along to Carl.

Often a student stopped by my desk just to talk. It wasn't unusual for them to discuss personal problems—as though I was "one of the boys." I appreciated that.

Their friendship made up in a small way for my lack of female companionship. Since we had common interests, I related to them better than I did to women. Because of our work schedule, opportunities to meet other women were almost always under business or professional circumstances—or when they visited the airport; then the conversations were, predictably, about aviation.

The only women I could consider friends close enough to confide in were Nadine and Lillian. For the most part I saw Nelda and Viola only at dinners with the folks. Having no interest in flying, they seldom came to the airport.

If, on a rare occasion, I found myself with a group of women socially, I felt out of place; the conversation foreign to me as they talked of their children, housework, homes, and gardens—all beyond my ken.

On the other hand, I could converse knowledgeably with the boys about activities of uppermost priority in my life—flying, hunting, fishing—and the weather.

The students got a kick out of the "Pilot's Motto" which hung on the wall at the end of the counter:

NEVER WORRY BECAUSE...
When you take off you have only two things to worry about;
Whether the airplane will fly or whether it won't.
If it flies, you don't have anything to worry about.
If it doesn't, you have only two things to worry about;
Whether it will crash or whether it won't.
If it doesn't, you don't have anything to worry about;
If it does, you have only two things to worry about;
Whether you'll be killed or whether you won't.
If you're not, you don't have anything to worry about.
If you are, you won't be able to worry anyway.
So why worry?

# The Cessna 170

T he sun, midway in the morning sky, reflected off the snow, casting a cheerful brightness over my desk. Carl and George were flying with students, Jim had gone into town for the mail and, as usual, I was hard at work on government forms.

Spring was just around the corner and, so far, the weather had been rather pleasant—for March. Between flying and ground school, we'd been kept busy from dawn until well after dark. This was a good thing, typical of the two years we'd been in business, during which, to borrow a maxim, we had "kept our noses to the grindstone."

Several students, nearing completion of the course, were nervously looking forward to their private pilot check. Luckily for Ungerer Flying Service, as rapidly as one completed the course, another was waiting to take his place.

With the coming of April showers, winter was definitely over. Spring flowers burst into bloom almost overnight.

The first streak of light was just appearing on the eastern horizon as Carl and I pushed the first plane out of the hangar. The sky was a clear cerulean blue, the air warm and moist, and the windsock hung limply on its pole. By sunrise, the first student would arrive.

Balmy spring days were luring people out, and the airport buzzed with activity.

Our days were long and strenuous, but we were proud of what we had accomplished. So far, we had graduated thirty students and, not only was flight training going well, charter service, rentals, and sales had increased exponentially with the passage of time.

Students, catching up with their schedules, were taking solo flights and flight checks, while recently licensed students demonstrated their skills to families and friends. Carl and George spent most of their time in the air.

When the new four-place Cessna 170 began rolling off the production line, Ungerer Flying Service was privileged to play host to the eighth plane off the line—sent over by the company for a demonstration.

Like the 140, the 170's sleek silver metal fuselage and fabric covered wings glittered in the sunlight. The plane boasted a 145-horsepower engine, as opposed to the 140's 85-horsepower. With a fuel capacity of forty-five gallons, and cruise speed at 120, we could not only take more than one passenger on charter trips, we could do so in less time.

We would also be able to use it to train commercial students.

A large crowd showed up for the demonstration. Several businessmen, including Fred Burris and Earl Craven, showed interest, as did a couple of farmers.

"Come on, let's go for a quick ride," Carl said during a break. I'd ridden in the plane at the factory but was eager to try it at home base.

George and another student, Tom Best, were standing nearby.

"You two come along," Carl said.

Once in the air, he turned the controls over to me.

"It's more quiet than the 140," I said as we circled over town, the motor humming smoothly.

"That'll be to our advantage with charter trips," Carl said. "Passengers who haven't flown much will feel more comfortable and safer."

The demonstration was not only a huge success; both newspapers had been tremendously supportive, giving us generous publicity.

Two weeks later, Carl and Jim flew to Wichita to bring our own 170 to Marysville.

# A Little R and R

I was busy at my desk when Carl came in after a dual flight. I logged the time, and he sent the student on his way just as another arrived. He propped the Blue Bird and sent the student out for a solo. I looked up when he came back into the office. He sat down, sighed, leaned back, and crossed his legs.

From the look on his face, we were both feeling the need of a bit of R and R.

"I've been thinking, Honey," he said cheerfully. "Hasn't Oren Black chartered a trip to St. Louis next week?"

I nodded.

"Why don't I take the 170, and you and I will both go; stay for a couple of days and have ourselves a little fun for a change—what do you think?"

"What about the airport?"

"No problem—we won't schedule any dual for any of my students for the two days we're away. We both need to get away for a few days."

"All right," I said listlessly. "Whatever you think."

"You don't sound very excited. I thought you'd like a little vacation."

"It's just that it's been so long since we've had one, I don't think I'd know how to act."

"Think of the bright lights, the great restaurants. We'll see a show or two, go dancing—"

I perked up; that *did* sound exciting!

"It's all set then. We're to leave Tuesday morning, so don't schedule any dual for Tuesday or Wednesday. Might as well leave Thursday open too, just in case—"

Tuesday dawned clear and calm—perfect for a cross-country trip. With students having kept the planes in the air every flyable

**256**

minute of late, I hadn't had a chance to go out. It felt good to be flying again—even as a passenger.

Oren sat up front with Carl, so I had the back seat to myself. The sound of their voices, blending with the hum of the motor was soothing and peaceful.

We set down in St. Louis just before noon. While Carl arranged for the plane, Oren summoned a cab, and we headed into the city. Carl had made reservations at a downtown hotel.

"So we'll be right in the middle of everything!" he said.

"Let's eat before we go up," he said once we reached the hotel.

"Good idea," I said, realizing for the first time that I was hungry.

Our room was on the tenth floor facing the street. As I looked down at the throng of people on the street swarming with traffic, I felt a thrill of excitement.

"Isn't it…" I started to say, turning toward Carl who was at the mirror combing his hair. He looked so tired, I stopped, mid-sentence, and went to him and put my arms around his waist. He turned and rested his chin on top of my head.

"Have I told you lately that I love you very much?" I said.

"No," he said. "Tell me."

"I love you very much," I said, smiling at him in the mirror.

"What do you want to do now?" he asked.

"Go to bed."

We awoke several hours later, refreshed, but hungry.

"We'll ask the bellhop to recommend a good place to eat," Carl said as we dressed.

The café suggested was eight blocks away.

"The best food in town!" the bellhop promised.

"Let's walk!" I coaxed. "It's a beautiful evening; the walk will be good for us."

"Okay," he agreed. "But I'm as hungry as a bear, so there'll be no loitering to window shop along the way."

"I promise," I laughed.

"We'll window shop a little after dinner," Carl said, laughing as I craned my neck, eager to see everything. "If you're nice to me, I might take you shopping for a new dress tomorrow."

The restaurant was beautiful: dim lighting, candlelight reflecting off the white table covering, sparkling glassware, and gleaming silver.

"This is awfully expensive," I said once we'd been seated and were scanning our menus. "Shall we go somewhere else?"

"Nope," Carl said. "We're on vacation, remember? I'm going to have a T-bone steak."

"Okay," I said. "I'll have the sirloin."

The dinner, served with stuffed baked potatoes and a salad, was as delicious as the bellhop had promised it would be.

"What now?" Carl asked as we ventured out onto the street. A billboard down the street advertised "The best floor show in town!" There was also a dance band.

"Want to go in?" Carl asked.

"Let's!"

"Mmmm—this tastes better than the ones I make," I said, sipping my Collins once we were seated.

The show was uproariously funny then, as the band began to play, the strains of "Moonlight Serenade" drifted over the room.

"That's the first song we danced to," I said.

"By gosh, you're right," Carl said, standing and holding out his arms. "Shall we?"

It was midnight when we left the club. When Carl started to hail a cab, I stopped him.

"You promised!" I said.

"You and your walking," he laughed.

"I notice you don't complain when we're hunting," I teased.

"Oh, but that's different—entirely different!" he laughed.

"Ah-ha!" I retorted.

We walked slowly, stopping often to look at the elaborately decorated shop windows.

"I can't believe we have two whole days to do anything we like," I said as we were dressing for bed. "We don't even have to get out of bed in the morning if we don't want to!"

"Maybe we won't. Maybe we'll just order up our meals and lay around all day."

"We can pretend it's our honeymoon!"

"Right!" he agreed. "We never did have a proper one, did we?"

It was noon, and the sun was streaming through the window when I awoke.

"Well, good morning!" Carl said, turning to look at the clock on the bedside table. "I was just joking when I said we might sleep all day."

"You needed the rest," I said. "We both did."

"I wonder if they'll still serve us breakfast," he said. "I'm starved."

"So am I."

"I'm going to have steak, three eggs, potatoes, and lots of toast and coffee," he said, picking up the phone. "How about you?"

"A big slice of ham, scrambled eggs, and toast."

We were just getting out of the shower when our breakfast arrived.

As we ate, I noted that much of the drawn look was gone from Carl's face.

"Which would you rather do; go shopping for that new dress now or put it off until tomorrow and go back to bed?"

"Go back to bed; we still have another day to shop."

The following morning, we ordered up breakfast, then, as Carl promised, went in search of a new dress. I also bought a pair of inch-high platform pumps. Then we shopped for a new shirt and tie for Carl.

We spent the rest of the day strolling through the zoo, then we went back to our hotel and dressed for dinner. I wore my new dress and shoes; Carl wore his new shirt and tie.

"Aren't we the handsome couple?" I said admiring our reflection in the mirror.

We chose a Chinese restaurant we'd spotted earlier in the day.

"This has been a wonderful vacation," I said as we ate.

"What shall we do now?" Carl asked.

"Let's go to that night club where you can look out over the whole city!"

It was only a short distance by cab.

"It's beautiful!" I said as we sat at a table by the window, looking out over miles and miles of sparkling lights.

"Would you like to live in a city?" Carl asked.

I thought for a minute. "No," I said. "I don't think so. As I've heard you say: 'It's fun to visit, but it would be a hell of a place to live.'"

"I'm glad you feel that way," he said. "I only asked because you seem to enjoy our trips to the city so much, I've often wondered."

"I've had a wonderful time, but I'm ready to go home," I said, then added: "I'm really happy there, you know."

We left the night club and strolled through a near-by park. It was two o'clock when Carl hailed a cab.

The next morning we had a late breakfast in the coffee shop.

"We have four hours," Carl said, looking at his watch. "What would you like to do?"

"I'd like to browse through one or two of the big department stores then, if there's time, I'd like to go to the airport and watch the big planes take off and land."

"That's what they call a 'postman's holiday,'" Carl laughed.

"I never saw so much merchandise in one store," I exclaimed as we strolled from clothing to china to housewares to bedding to furniture and lawn equipment in Macy's. "You could shop here for days and never leave the store."

Carl looked at his watch. "It's about time we headed to the airport."

We didn't have time to watch the big planes, and when we reached the area where the 170 was parked, Oren Black was waiting.

"I never saw so many airplanes," he said as we waited for take-off instructions.

"That's why radios are becoming increasingly necessary when flying off a busy field like this one," Carl said.

Sitting in the back seat, I watched the buzzing activity of the airport with interest. Once in the air, however, I settled back and watched the landscape fall away beneath the plane.

The holiday had been very enjoyable, but I was ready to go home.

I'd almost drifted off to sleep when I became aware of clouds forming, like wisps of cotton, beneath the wings. As they became more dense, it seemed as if we were floating on a soft white pillow. The sun formed a rainbow on the billowing sea of white and I felt as if I were dreaming.

"It isn't going to last long," Carl announced, checking his radio. "We'll be in the clear by the time we reach home."

And so we were; landing well before dark with clear skies and a light southwest wind.

**Edna Bell-Pearson**

# It's Later Than You Think

Jim and George had gone home, and I was waiting for Carl to return from a charter trip to Kansas City. Hearing a plane in the traffic pattern, I went out to watch the last student of the day land.

Up on the hill, the new administration building was nearing completion. Two years after the city applied for the government airport improvement grant, work was finally getting underway. It had been a long delay.

The new red gas pump with a white crown, installed by the oil company a few days previously, stood out in the late afternoon sun.

The student flying the Blue Bird had soloed only a few days before and, although his approach was perfect, I was interested in seeing how his landing went.

The plane touched down—smooth and on the spot.

I signaled him to the gas pump.

"Very good!" I said as he climbed out of the plane.

Headlines predicting the possibility of World War III caused all the Ungerer boys a great deal of concern as to what the future would bring, as did an article in the spring issue of the *Aeronautical Journal* entitled "The Shocking Truth":

> Whether or not we like it, we must fact the fact that the United States is virtually without an Air Force.
>
> This is not startling news to those who have noted the disintegration of the once mighty WWII armada of some 80,000 planes and 2,411,294 officers

and men; and the slashes and cutbacks that reduced this force to a mere 300,000 officers and men and, at most, 2,900 combat planes many of which are now virtually obsolete.

The article continued:

Take a look at these figures, then at the $12,000,000,000 (Ours is a full billion less) and the 14,000 planes included in Russia's proposed military budget.

The only possible defense against the Atomic bomb and guided missiles is a well-equipped Air Force. Considering these facts, one would be inclined to believe that the United States is as vulnerable today as it was December 7, 1941.

The article ended with the admonition: *It is later than you think!*

The fact that we were seeing military planes fly over with increasing frequency was also a constant reminder of the possibility of impending war, which meant that Carl and Jim, as well as Frederick, could be called back into service at any time. A world-wide conflict would have drastic effect on our plans.

*Airport Office Nearing Completion*

# Farewell to Blackie

May brought clear skies and a great deal of enthusiasm. Several students soloed; others flew cross-countries, both dual and solo. Three students took—and passed—their flight checks.

We had numerous fly-in visitors. As they came and went; we were encouraged by the increasing number of companies using planes for business purposes.

As civilian aviation continued to thrive, *The Civil Aeronautics Journal* reported that 7,499 more student and private pilot licenses were granted in 1947 than in 1946. The state of Kansas alone now boasted a total of 179 airports—seventy-three commercial, sixty-nine municipal, three FFA Intermediate, twenty-six Military, and eight categorized as "all others."

The Industrial Development Commission reported that twenty-five Kansas airports were undergoing improvement and expansion under the Federal Aid Program and that, among states, Kansas was in the lead in aviation in airplane production, number of airports, number of Flying Farmers and ideal flying weather. They also reported that 12,815 hours were flown during the month of April by seventy-four airport operators with 637 planes. This included training, charter, and sight-seeing trips. Yingling Brothers, Kansas's leading airplane distributor, announced "The Flying Farm Car of the Year"—the Cessna—in five models: the 120, 140, 170, 190, and the 195.

Early in the month, pilots from a wide area were invited to the Union airport in Lincoln for breakfast at which time we would be introduced to a new plane—a post-war innovation—being built there.

Over 100 planes and 224 people had responded to the event, and it was a clear, calm morning—one of the most beautiful mornings we'd seen—when, at 6:30 AM, eight planes took off from Marysville. We were among the first to arrive in Lincoln, and the eighteen pilots and passengers were in an exuberant mood.

Once breakfast was over, Thomas Umberger, operator of the flying school, led us to the mechanics school where work on the Doran, a new pusher-type plane, was in progress. The Doran was different in that propellers were mounted behind, rather than in front of the engine. The advantage of this, Umberger explained, was that this position of the propeller increased the efficiency by reducing the drag, making the plane easier to maneuver.

A week later, a new use for the flying machine was introduced to our area when six planes equipped with spray equipment arrived at the Marysville airport, offering Marshall County farmers a more efficient form of weed control.

*"A Special War-On-Weeds,"* read the ad in *The Marysville Advocate.* *"Yes! At only $3 dollars per acre, weeds can be conquered with 2-4D!"*[11] The ad listed more than seven weeds that would succumb to the weed killer.

When Carl suggested we buy spray equipment and offer this service ourselves, I vehemently vetoed the idea. "We're doing well enough," I argued. "It's too dangerous. You have all you can handle and there's no need taking unnecessary chances."


It was a hot, windy day. The sun beat down on the dry earth; and whirlwinds danced across the runways. Our early morning students had come and gone. George was on a cross-country, Jim was piddling in his workshop, and the heat was building up in the office where Carl and I sat, finishing up the weekly forms.

"Let's go fishing," Carl said out of the blue. Since he had no charter trips and no students scheduled until five-thirty, I agreed.

We headed for the Country Club Lake just across the way.

Once on the lake, Carl's spirits lifted. We soon had our limit, but still he fished, throwing the smaller ones back, keeping the larger ones. Then he hooked the big one of the day—a three and a half pound bass. He was elated.

"Let's run these by Dad's," he said, looking at his watch. "It's almost time we got back to the airport."

"I think now would be a good time to schedule that weekend fishing flight to Lake of the Ozarks," he said on the drive back to the airport.

I agreed.

Two days later, three planes took off for a weekend of fishing at the Lake of the Ozarks. We had signed up three passengers, so Carl took the 170. Jim, George, and I stayed behind, and I supervised what solo flying Carl had scheduled.

When we went to the car for the trip to the airport Tuesday morning after Carl's return, Blackie, who was always waiting for us at the car door to begin his day as airport mascot, was nowhere to be seen. That was very unlike Blackie; he would never take a chance on being left at home. Carl whistled and called to no avail. Finally, we backed out of the driveway and headed for the airport. Halfway up the block, Carl slammed on the brakes; Blackie's body was lying by the side of the road. We knew he liked to take little sojourns around the neighborhood, but Marysville was a friendly town, so we hadn't been concerned. Carl was devastated. We never knew who ran him over.

---

[11] 2,4-D  an organic compound a systemic herbicide which selectively kills most broadleaf weeds was first used in the United States in the 1940s. 2,4-D is still used in many products to control weeds, often mixed with other herbicides. It was one of the primary chemicals used in Agent Orange notorious Vietnam War defoliant, named so because the canisters they were transported in were painted with bright orange stripes.

Spray Plane

# Construction Begins

Heavy rains the latter part of June and the first of July brought the harvest, which had just gotten underway, to a halt. Over the Fourth, however, the rains stopped and harvesting resumed.

As the skies cleared and the winds came, the runways dried out, and we were able to take to the skies again. Out of town pilots dropped in, and local pilots took advantage of good flying weather to take trips of their own.

Everything was going smoothly when the July heat set in with a vengeance; 100-degree temperatures parched the earth, and strong, gusty winds out of the southwest brought turbulent air which began at sunup and lingered through the evening hours. Charter flights and student training had practically come to a stand-still. With no indication of change, Carl was getting grumpy.

Meanwhile, thousands of feet overhead, military planes were flying over with increasing frequency.

The administration building was nearing completion; the adjoining concrete apron installed when, on the first of August, heavy equipment moved onto the runways to transform the old runways into new. Grosshan and Peterson, contractors, brought in tractors, graders, and huge earth moving machines. At the north end of the field, three gigantic Corbas, with 18-yard capacities, together with Carry-alls and Caterpillars, began breaking ground, chewing away at the surface of the field.

Although rains frequently disrupted progress, reconstruction moved assiduously forward.

Spectators now came, not to watch airplanes take off and land, but to watch the heavy equipment at work.

Since plans included three runways to replace the existing two, the city announced that, due to high costs and a miscalculation in funds, the runways would be planted to grass rather than hardtop surfaces as previously planned.

We had originally been promised that one runway would be left open for our use. Limited to using only the north/south runway for take-off and landing, business continued much as usual. For a while. However, due to the cross sections which, of course, was unavoidable, we ultimately reached the point of limited access.

In spite of construction on the runways, plus intermittent heavy rains, we continued to have an occasional visitor, and some of our own local pilots flew out—usually on business.

Student training, however, proceeded cautiously, ultimately coming to a halt. Not only were the problems caused by the construction a contributing factor, but the number of students was falling off as students completed the course, and the CAA tightened down on approval.

For several months hot and heavy controversy had been underway between aviation enthusiasts and the Veteran's Administration as to whether veterans should receive flight training on the GI Bill of Rights. Although several applications had been made by local GI's, few had been approved on the basis that flying was recreational, rather than educational, which had been the original purpose of the bill.

Construction Equipment

# Bad Medicine Lake

"Since we're not doing anything else, why don't we fly up and visit Bill and Nadine?" Carl asked one morning as we sat at breakfast.

Planning to spend their summers there, Bill and Nadine had bought a fishing camp on Bad Medicine Lake in southern Minnesota. Their letters enthusiastically expounded on what a wonderful place it was, how great the fishing, the cool nights, and on and on.

"The fish practically snap up the bait as soon as it hits the water!" Bill wrote.

"That sounds nice," I said. "When?"

"How about this afternoon?"

"*This afternoon?*"

He nodded.

"Can't we ever plan anything in advance?"

"Sure, but that would take all the fun out of it."

I had to admit, the timing was right.

"We've been talking about taking a vacation," he said. "Since flying is practically at a stand-still, we couldn't pick a better time to go. Jim can take care of anything that comes up, and we can always be home in a few hours if there are any changes."

"What time to you want to leave?"

"I can be ready about noon. After breakfast, I'll call to be sure they can have us, and while I go to the airport and get the plane ready, you can pack a bag and get the fishing gear together."

Mrs. Jones had lunch on the table when Carl returned shortly before noon.

"You young'uns have yourselves a good time and be careful." Mrs. Jones said. "Some a them lakes are pretty deep!"

I laughed. Bad Medicine Lake, Bill had said, was almost a hundred feet deep in spots.

By 12:30, everything was tucked away in the baggage compartment of the Blue Bird. Carl had decided that it would be more maneuverable if the condition of the field we'd be landing on was not good.

I was in the plane, ready to go, while Carl took a last-minute pit stop. Then he climbed in beside me. Before he had his safety-belt fastened, I was taxiing down the runway to the north end for a take-off.

"Let's go fishing!" he said, slapping me on the shoulder. "Minnesota, here we come!"

As the plane climbed into the air, the wind caught at her wings, tossing the small plane violently about.

"Good God, it's rough!" Carl said. "If it's this turbulent higher up, it's gonna be a mighty rough ride!"

I flew the traffic pattern and headed north by northeast, still climbing, heading toward the big blue yonder. Seventy miles out at three thousand feet, the air was still rough; we had a strong tailwind, however, and we were making good time. At five thousand feet, the air was as smooth as glass. I leveled out. We were sailing along at about a hundred and fifty miles an hour—or so we calculated after getting the winds aloft report from the tower at Omaha.

Carl, who could sleep anywhere, anytime, leaned back in his seat and dozed off.

I adjusted the trim tab until the attitude of the plane was on a straight and level course, then relaxed and sat back in my seat to enjoy the trip, keeping my eye on the instrument panel, occasionally checking the map to be sure the wind hadn't shifted and we were still on course.

Somewhere over Iowa, Carl woke, rubbed his eyes, and yawned.

"Have a nice nap?" I asked.

He nodded. "About time to land for gas, isn't it?"

"We've still got quite a bit," I said. "I thought we'd land at Des Moines."

He took the controls, and I leaned back in my seat. I didn't wake until I felt the wheels touch and the plane settle to the ground.

"I don't know how you slept through that descent," Carl said. "The wind was as turbulent as when we took off."

After filling with gas, Carl took the controls, again reaching smooth air at 5,000 feet. The earth below slowly changed into varied shades of green, interspersed with blue lakes.

"The land of a thousand lakes," I said. "It's like a picture postcard,"

Dreamily watching soft, white fluffy clouds float by in a background of azure blue sky, I drifted off again.

I awoke when Carl patted my knee.

"We're almost there," he said.

"What time is it?

"Almost five.

"Start looking for Bad Medicine Lake and Bill's camp," he said, easing back on the throttle. "Hopefully, the air has smoothed out down below."

"I don't see anything but trees and lakes," I said as we slowly descended.

"According to Bill, we have only to locate the lake, follow the west bank half way down, and look to the west for the field we're to land in. He said we couldn't miss it."

He leveled out at a thousand feet. Bad Medicine Lake should be only a few miles ahead.

"There it is!" I said. Sure enough, the long, narrow lake stood out in the vast forest of trees just as Bill had described it.

Descending to 500 feet, we began looking for the field in which we were to land. It, too, was easy to spot. Bill had said to land near the east fence-line to avoid tree stumps located toward the center.

Carl buzzed the area checking for holes, rocks, stumps, anything that would prevent a smooth landing.

"Look! Our windsock!" I exclaimed, pointing to a pole from which a pair of panty hose waved gently in the wind.

"Looks all right to me," Carl said, pulling up.

"Okay. Let's find the camp and let them know we've arrived," he said, heading for the west shore of Bad Medicine Lake.

They had heard the plane, and when we flew over, Bill, Nadine and the baby, and her brother Rich, who was visiting them over the summer, were standing on the boat dock waving.

Carl waved the wings to and fro; Bill responded by waving his arms, crisscrossing them over his head indicating that everything was copacetic.

Carl did a 180 and headed for our landing field. Bill, already in his jeep, was speeding down the trail in a cloud of dust. By the time we landed and taxied back to the north end of the field, he had arrived.

"It's great to see you!" he exclaimed, pumping our hands excitedly.

"It's good to be here," Carl said. "This is a whole different world than the one we left behind."

"Compared to the weather at home, this is paradise," I said breathing in cool, fresh air.

Bill talked a blue streak as he helped Carl tie down the plane and get our bags and fishing tackle into the jeep.

When we arrived at the cabin, Nadine had supper on the table.

As we ate, we brought them up to date on the news at home. After we finished, Bill announced that the rock bass were biting and asked if we would like to go out for a while.

"That's what we're here for, buddy!" Carl said.

Leaving Rich in charge of the baby, the four of us headed for the dock.

The sun had set and, as we motored up the lake, the water looked like a clear, blue mirror in the fading light. The surrounding trees cast dark shadows along the bank and fireflies flickered over the water like thousands of tiny stars.

"What a beautiful night!" I exclaimed as the moon, a huge golden ball, rose over the horizon. "What a beautiful place to live!"

A few minutes later, Bill cut the motor and showed us how to weight our hooks and let them down until they touched bottom then reel up until the bait rested just off the bottom of the lake.

The night was still—peaceful and quiet and, as we waited for the first bite, Carl looked as though he was in seventh heaven. We didn't have long to wait. Carl was first, then I felt a tug on my line. In the next hour, we reeled in fish after fish. Finally, Bill said, "Let's call it a night!"

As we reeled in our lines, he asked, "How about a nice cold beer?"

As the boat skimmed lightly over the smooth water of the lake to the opposite shore, where bright lights from a rustic beer tavern sparkled across the water, a soft breeze ruffled our hair, and the motor stirred up a fine mist cooling our faces.

Back at camp, Carl and Bill stored the fish in the ice shed.

"We'll clean them in the morning," Bill said.

Nadine made a pot of coffee then gave me a tour of her home while Bill and Carl talked of home, flying, and fishing.

Though rustic, the cabin was comfortable and conveniently arranged.

"It must be heavenly to live in such beautiful surroundings with nary a worry or a care," I said as we moved from room to room.

"It gets lonely at times," Nadine said. "You'd never be satisfied here for long, Edna. "You'd be bored to death."

I thought about that for a moment.

"I've always envied you and the exciting, adventurous life you lead," she added.

"I guess we mortals are never satisfied," I laughed, and we went to join the men.

Carl insisted we spend every minute fishing. At times we trolled for walleyed pike; at other times we fished for bass. But we never failed to bring in a line of fish, which, after cleaning, Carl and Bill packed down in the icehouse.

The icehouse was an interesting novelty to me. I listened, fascinated, as Bill explained how, during the winter months, all the men who lived around the lake worked together, chipping huge blocks of ice from the lake and storing them between layers of saw dust from the saw mill in sheds such as this one. Stored this way, Bill said, the ice lasted all summer.

The lake was also the source of their water supply, he said. It was so pure, it needed no treatment.

Our week was almost up when Bill asked if we hadn't had enough fishing for a while and suggested we drive up to Itasca National Forest for an outing.

"I think you'll both enjoy it," he said.

The air was crisp and clear, the immense shadowy forest so dense the sun hardly penetrated the foliage. I was spell-bound by the huge, centuries-old trees.

"This is a nice break for me too," Nadine said as the jeep bounced over the rough dirt road. "With the baby and guests to see after, I don't often get away from camp."

"You are now in the Itasca National Park," Bill announced, parking the jeep near a small trickling stream only a couple feet across. "And this is the Mississippi River."

It was hard to imagine that this tiny rivulet, which I could easily step across, was the beginning of the sprawling Mississippi River I had seen in the south.

Nadine had packed a lunch, and we ate in a cool arbor, after which we continued to explore the forest. It was well after dark when we got back to the camp.

The next day was Saturday. Carl decided to fish during the morning and leave shortly after noon which would get us home before dark. After a good night's rest, we would be ready for what we hoped would be flyable conditions on Sunday.

"I'm going to stay and visit with Nadine," I said as they prepared to leave.

"Are you sure?" Carl asked dubiously.

"He can't understand why anyone who has a chance to fish—or

hunt—would want to do anything else," I said, laughing, once we'd seen them off.

"I'm glad you stayed," Nadine said. "We've still got a lot to catch up on."

Carl and I took off at one o'clock, the two portable ice chests packed with fish. With a tailwind, provided by a brisk northeast breeze, we arrived home well before dark.

Sunday was a beautiful day; the first in over a week, Jim said. Though hampered by runway conditions, Carl flew with two of our advanced students, and we gave several rides.

As unsettled conditions in Europe and the Middle East continued to escalate, rumors of the possibility of World War III dominated the news.

"The statement that America would vaporize its enemies quickly and accurately, without hesitation, if the need arose, is correct," Major General William Hix said in a newspaper interview. "I absolutely agree. There is NO doubt about the tremendous powers of Russia, China and Iran, et cetera, and of the lunacy of North Korea but they MUST realize and accept that WWIII would be the END of their existence in lightning time should they push the US too far!"

The Air Force was reported to have grown from 311,000 officers and enlisted men to over 400,000 in the past year. If a war did start, we knew that, considering their military background, Carl and Jim would be among the first to be called up.

In August, sixty-eight men and four officers of the Marysville's National Guard unit, Battery B, 154th Field Artillery Battalion, were dispatched to Fort Leonard Wood, Missouri for two weeks combat training during which they would be acquainted with new army equipment.

Since Carl, Jim, and Frederick were all members of the National Guard, this left me to see that all ran smoothly with Ungerer Flying Service.

One runway had been completed and opened for use, which made it possible for a few advanced solo students to fly. But other than the weekly ground school session and seeing to the needs of incoming and outgoing planes, there wasn't a lot for me to do.

Carl & Edna with String of Fish

# Plane Crash

With Carl and Jim back on the job, September started off pleasantly. Work on the runways forged ahead, but with calm, sunny weather and one runway made available, flying resumed, albeit on a limited basis. Then, on September 9, disaster struck again!

Dusk was deepening into night when we closed the hangar doors and locked up. It was dark by the time Carl and I reached home, and we were just heading into the house when we heard a light engine plane. We paused to listen. It was circling the airport.

"Damn!" Carl said. We jumped back into the car. By the time we reached the airport, the plane had turned on its landing lights and was making an approach to land to the south on the north/south runway.

Letting me out at the office door, Carl yelled "Call Dad! Tell him to get out here!" Then, stomping on the accelerator, he veered onto the runway, headlights illuminating the spot where the plane should land.

Seeing that he was overshooting the runway, the pilot pulled up. He was still circling ten minutes later when Dad's car tore into the parking a lot. He parked alongside Carl, the lights of both cars shining up the runway. The light was inadequate, but all we could do was hope it was enough.

As a crowd gathered, two more cars joined Carl and Dad shining lights on the runway.

Holding our breath, we watched as the plane did a 180 and head in for another attempt at landing.

"You're too low, damn it!" Carl yelled as if the pilot could hear. "Pull up!"

Fifty feet north of the runway, the plane stalled out. We heard a crash, and the plane burst into flames.

"Oh God, *no*!" Carl moaned.

Leaping into the car, we sped to the north end of the runway. Several vehicles had already reached the scene via the county road. We got as close as we could, but the plane was an inferno. Four figures were visible in the flames. A man, presumably a fire-fighter, had tried to get close enough to pull them out but it had been an impossible endeavor. When we arrived, men were drawing him toward an ambulance, his arms severely burned.

We learned later that the pilot, Walter B. Zimmerman, was a Methodist minister. His passengers were his wife and daughter and an orphan girl. He was flying a Stinson from Crete, Nebraska, where he had performed dedication ceremonies at a Methodist church, to Manhattan, Kansas, to visit with family before returning home to Broken Bow, Nebraska.

The newspaper reported that Reverend Zimmerman had obtained his private pilot license only two weeks previously.

Again, a veil of gloom settled over the airport. For several days, government inspectors came and went. Eventually, we were cleared to resume operation, and construction work on the runways resumed.

The Marysville Municipal Airport was rapidly on its way to becoming a reality. As we watched "our airport" being transformed, we could only accept the inevitable and hope that the improvements, as well as our new status, would prove to be to our advantage.

Though runway lights were included in the reconstruction plan, it would be some time before they were installed. After the Zimmerman crash, we ordered portable landing lights from war surplus.

# Recovery—or Not

Weather conditions and airport construction—then the accident—had sharply curtailed flying for the past two months. When graders began working on the north/south runway the last of September, access was opened to the northwest/southeast runway, now complete except for seeding.

We'd had a few visiting planes in, and a few planes had flown out, but conditions being as they were, in general, student training had virtually come to a halt. Our student list had diminished dramatically due, not only to airport construction, but also because of the government's crackdown on private pilot training.

The situation being what it was, George Wirth decided to move to more lucrative pastures early on.

Construction equipment had moved north—away from the hangar area—when, shortly after the first of October, Carl and Jim and I rolled the planes out of the big hangar. Armed with rags, brooms, and elbow grease, we preceded to remove the dust that had collected on the unused planes.

We were a sorry mess when we finished, but it was good to see them shining and polished again, ready to take to the skies.

The three of us attended the 4th State Airport Conference in Manhattan. The exhibitions included a demonstration of the crosswind landing gear and the Rawdon plane, manufactured in Wichita, exhibiting fast take-offs, slow landings, and acrobatics. A helicopter from Fort Riley, used by the army for search and rescue work, gave an exhibition of vertical take-offs and landings, hovering and backward and sidewise maneuvers.

As time passed, the public was finding numerous new and unusual uses for small aircraft. We were seeing companies using planes for advertising—employing loudspeakers, dropping handbills, banner towing, and sky-writing. A plane, blaring an advertisement for Jones-Mack of Topeka, had flown over Marysville the previous week, dropping handbills.

November started out with sunny skies and calm air and, after waiting out an early morning fog on Sunday, three planes carrying eight people took off for Lincoln for the first flight breakfast we'd had for some time.

That afternoon, a larger crowd than usual turned out after church, and three area businessmen got their planes out to try the new Marysville Municipal Airport. It was the busiest Sunday we'd had for some time. Sort of like old times.

The fair weather didn't last long. The following week the rains came, turning the runways into slush.

"Good weather for the ducks," Carl growled after the third day.

A staunch Republican, Dad was furious when Harry Truman won the election.

"You just watch; the son of a bitch is going to have us back in a war in six months!" he fumed.

Thrust into the presidency by Franklin Roosevelt's death in 1945, Truman's chances of winning the election were thought to be slim. Dad thought Dewey's campaign had summed up the nation's needs perfectly. He was one of many doubtful that Truman was capable of effective leadership, as well as Truman's proclaimed solution to a confused postwar world. Even Democratic voters viewed him as an ineffectual shadow of his four-term predecessor.

It appeared that no one—except Truman himself—thought he could pull it off.

But he did.

# An Emergency Flight

It was several minutes before I realized that the ringing telephone was not part of my dream. Startled, I sat up, turned on the light, then jumped out of bed, pulling on my robe as I ran down the stairs.

"Hello?" I said sleepily.

"Edna, can I talk to Carl?" Dr. Randall's voice sounded urgent.

I turned to call Carl, but he was standing at the head of the stairs, his eyes dazed with sleep. I looked at the clock; 3:00 AM.

"It's Dr. Randall," I said.

He came down the stairs, took the phone, and listened thoughtfully.

"I think so," he said. "We'll figure out something. Since it's a baby I don't think it'll be a problem."

He listened again.

"It's three hours until sunup, but I can take off as soon as I can see the outline of the runway. Let's plan on around five—five-thirty."

A minute later he said; "Okay, I'll see you then."

"What is it?" I asked after he hung up.

"He wanted to know if we could make up a bed in the Cessna 170 to take a patient—a baby—to St Louis," he replied. "It's an emergency; he needs to get there as soon as possible."

"Whose baby is it?"

"I didn't ask."

Thirty minutes later we were at the airport. I'd brought pillows and blankets which I used to prepare a make-shift bed. Since the baby was only eighteen days old, it would take up only one seat.

"It looks comfortable enough," I said when I finished.

We were ready when the ambulance arrived. Dr. Randall had followed in his car.

283

Carl motioned the ambulance to pull up to the plane. While the attendants transferred the patient, the baby's father, Herbert Balmer, and Katherine Calkins, an R.N., got out of Dr. Randall's car and came to the plane.

"Balmer and Katherine will go along," Dr. Randall said, adding, "Mrs. Balmer is in the hospital."

The windsock, dimly visible above the lights of the hangar, indicated a slight northwest wind.

"They have a tailwind, so they should be there in a couple of hours," I said.

Once the baby was strapped into his make-shift bed, I helped Katherine into the remaining back seat and buckled her seat belt. Balmer got into the front.

"You did a good job on the bed," Dr. Randall said then turned to Carl. "I wish I could go, but Katherine knows what to do."

It was barely light enough for Carl to see the runway when they took off. I knew, however, that as they climbed eastward, the sun would appear over the horizon and they would be flying in light with the earth appearing as a dark shadow below.

"They have a tailwind, so they should land in St. Louis easily by eight o'clock," I said, mentally calculating the distance against the airspeed of the plane and the wind velocity.

"Good," Dr. Randall said. "I'll call the hospital to make sure an ambulance is waiting at the airport when they arrive."

As we watched the 170 disappear, I breathed a sigh of relief and said a prayer for the Balmers and their baby.

After Dr. Randall and the ambulance drove away, I walked slowly to the office and sat down in the doorway to wait for the sunrise. The first student was due in less than an hour, so it would be foolish to drive home and back. We could go for breakfast when Carl returned.

I pondered on this—our first mission of mercy—as I watched the cool, white sun creep slowly over the horizon. Occupied as we were with the mechanics of the business, it felt good to know that, in addition to teaching people to fly, we were in a position to contribute a bit of good to this old world.

A slight breeze stirred the windsock. The air, though cool, was refreshing.

I was still sitting on the step when Jim arrived.

"You're here awfully early!" he said. "Where's Carl?"

"He had an emergency flight to St. Louis," I said, and filled him in.

"I know the Balmers," he said. "What was wrong with the baby?"

"I don't know," I replied.

I helped Jim roll the airplanes out of the hangar and tie them down on the flight line. By the time we finished, Wiley Lewis, now a solo student, arrived.

"Switch off!" I heard Jim call out as I walked toward the office. Another student drove into the parking lot. I sat down at my desk, called Carl's nine o'clock dual student to reschedule his lesson for the next morning, got out my books, and went to work.

Bored with the monotony of bookwork, I soon became drowsy. I was tempted to put my head down on my desk and take a nap. Instead, I got up and went to the door and breathed in the fresh air.

Carl would have a headwind on the return trip, so he wouldn't be coming in until close to noon. I went back to my desk, looked at the schedule, and cancelled an early afternoon dual. When we went home for breakfast, perhaps we could nap for an hour or two.

I returned to my work.

Over time, my ears had learned to detect each plane from the sound. At a quarter to twelve, I heard the 170 in the flight pattern and jumped up from my desk.

I called Mrs. Jones and told her we'd be home for breakfast shortly, then went out to meet Carl when he landed. Katherine Calkins had returned with him.

"How did it go?" I asked as he stepped out and stretched.

"Good. The ambulance was waiting. It took no time to get the baby switched over, and I took off immediately."

"Is the air rough?"

"A little. The wind is getting stronger and I hit a few rough spots coming in."

"I called Mrs. Jones so breakfast should be on the table by the time we get home."

"Good! I'm starved. We'll take Katherine home first."

"I postponed your one o'clock dual till three o'clock so we can take a couple of hours and catch a nap."

He sighed. "Great! I'll tell Jim to take care of things."

Carl's dual was waiting when we returned, still groggy from our ninety-minute nap. They were out only a few minutes.

"Come out tomorrow morning at seven," he said, dismissing the student.

"The air's too rough," he said and headed for the hangar to work with Jim while I returned to my bookwork.

Late in the afternoon, Dr. Randall drove in and came into the office.

"Thanks to the Ungerer Flying Service, the Balmer baby is in good hands," he said. "I talked to the doctor, and he said he had given the baby a blood transfusion and would go from there."

I breathed a sigh of relief.

"Thanks for letting us know," I said. "I hate to think what losing him would do to the Balmers."

He nodded gravely.

"Where's Carl?"

"Out in the work hangar with Jim."

"I'll go give him the news." At the door he stopped. "I just wanted to thank you kids for what you did."

"It's our job," I said.

A week later, Dr. Randall reported that Davie Balmer was "over the hump." The doctor at the children's hospital had reported that he was suffering from anemia which, they thought, might be caused by an RH Negative blood factor. As soon as his mother was released from the Marysville hospital, she would go to St. Louis for a blood test to ascertain her blood type.

A few days later, Dr. Randall showed up again at the airport.

"I think it's about time for me to upgrade," he said. "I figure it will be a good idea for me to have enough plane in case we have another case like the Balmer's. What if you hadn't been available when that happened? Let's see what kind of a deal you can get me on the 170."

A week later, Carl flew the doctor to Wichita and checked him out in a brand-new Cessna 170.

Except for the installation of electricity, the administration building was ready for occupation. As work on the runways neared completion, a work crew installed orange and white runway markers which could be seen for miles.

Soon, according to city officials, the Marysville Municipal Airport would be "one of Northeast Kansas's outstanding airports."

The best news for the Ungerer family, however, was the arrival of Frederick and Viola's first baby—a boy—born on November 4.

Dad was ecstatic.

# Transition

The administration building had been completed for some time; but still I hadn't moved.

Even though it possessed conveniences my "hen house" office didn't have, I faced the transition reluctantly. Despite our attempt at optimism, this meant the end of an era. Although we had "worked our asses off" (to quote Dad), the past three years had been exciting. We had built the airport and flying service from the ground up, feeling that we were doing something worthwhile; that we were contributing to the community.

True, we would continue to operate our own business. Ungerer Flying Service would carry on, but it just didn't seem the same.

Other changes were happening simultaneously—changes which drastically affected our business. Most importantly, the Veterans Administration continued to cut back on approvals for flight training under the GI Bill of Rights. In the past two months, only three of the applications submitted had been approved. The argument was that the purpose of the program was to train GIs for employment, and that private pilot flight training alone did not fit the bill. Most of the GIs, they argued, were taking the training for pleasure; not for commercial use. We had to admit that, in many cases their assertion was true; our argument was that several of our students had purchased planes for business purposes, and that future sales to students who were business owners, or farmers, were expected. Also, other students now in training were looking to continue with the commercial and/or the instructional course.

"Except for an occasional commercial student, looks like we may have to rely on civilians for most of our student training from now on," Carl said as one after another our GI students completed the course.

I was reading the morning newspaper when Carl entered the office.

"Here," I said, passing it to him, "read the story on page two."

He turned to page two and read aloud: "Eighty-three-year-old Starr Nelson led the flight of 200 Flying Farmers from Gainesville, Texas, the starting point of the Chisholm Trail, to Dodge City where they attended the Chisholm Flight Festival.

"Nelson had made the cattle drive over the Chisholm Trail sixty-four years previously at the age of nineteen. The four-hour flight, he said, was quite a contrast to the four months it took to make the drive (to Abilene) in 1884."

"I guess it was!" Carl said, adding: "Are we all set for Sunday's flight breakfast?"

This was a special event. What with the construction, and winter setting in, it could be our last flight breakfast before spring.

I nodded. "And it looks as if the weather is going to cooperate."

Sunday morning, eight planes carrying eighteen passengers headed west at 7:00 AM to attend the invitational flight breakfast and air show in Belleville.

Since the airport didn't sport a restaurant, members of the Chamber of Commerce, sponsors of the event met us when we landed and drove us to the restaurant in town where breakfast was served. After breakfast, they drove us back to the airport for the ceremonies.

By this time, the early morning cloud cover had dissipated, and several hundred attendees enjoyed a splendid air performance.

When the air show was over, we took off, one by one, for the return flight to Marysville.

To our surprise, we were just over Washington, halfway to Marysville, when we flew into a heavy snowstorm blowing out of the north.

As we all knew, a Kansas pilot never knows what he might encounter on a cross-country flight. Due to fronts, barometric pressure, air masses, and other phenomena, weather can change in a heartbeat.

One thing Carl prided himself on was making sure his students were given thorough, in depth, ground school training in meteorology, including safety measures encompassing incidents of all kinds. Thanking the powers that be for Highway 36 connecting the two towns, everyone arrived home safely by keeping the highway in sight.

To celebrate my birthday the following Thursday, I accompanied Carl on a charter flight to St. Louis. We spent the night, had dinner out, and attended the Sonia Henie Ice Follies—a rare treat; one I'd been promised and had been looking forward to, praying the weather would give us a break.

The next day when we took off from the Ross Airport for the return home, the sun shone dimly through a heavy fog of smoke hanging over the city. However, once beyond the city, the skies were clear. We were in the vicinity of Columbia, Missouri, when we flew into a dark mass of clouds, and it began to snow. The further west we flew, the more severe the storm. We were flying low but still could hardly see the ground, which was already covered by a heavy blanket of snow. Cattle huddled with their tails to the wind and cars crept slowly along the icy highways.

Thirty minutes later, breaks began to appear in the sky ahead. Although it was still snowing, we could see occasional patches of blue, so Carl pointed the nose of the plane toward one of the breaks and climbed. Flying over the clouds, the sky was a brilliant blue. The sun, shining brightly, cast tiny rainbows on the white, billowy clouds floating beneath us. It was hard to believe that a storm was raging below.

Gradually the clouds thinned out. When we landed at Marysville, the sky was almost clear. A strong wind was blowing out of the north, and the ground was white from the storm which had passed through the area earlier.

That weekend, we had a heavy ice storm. The wreckage could be seen from the air the following morning. Huge branches had split from the trees, telephone poles had broken off at the bases, cars were stalled in ditches, and the fields looked like great sheets of glass. A marvelous sight but immense destruction. Fortunately, no one had been injured.

The second week in December, the Riddle Engineering Company of St. Joseph, Missouri, overseers of airport and runway improvements, completed their inspection and recommended that the city accept the work so far completed, which included the administration building and ramp, the access road, fencing, grading, boundary markers, and the nylon wind cone which had been added to the segment marker at the runway intersection.

To be completed in the spring was the fertilizing and seeding of the runways. Installation of electrical fixtures for runway lights had been put on hold.

The following day, two CAA officials flew in to inspect and approve the airport for flight training. They pronounced everything in order.

Considering the vagaries of the weather and airport construction, the flying business proceeded as smoothly as could be expected. A few planes flew in, a few out, and two more students passed their flight checks.

Jim and Nelda, Frederick and Viola with their new son, and Carl and I celebrated a marvelous Christmas with Dad and Lillian.

And so ended our third year in the flying business—on a happy, slightly optimistic note with just a touch of angst about the future of Ungerer Flying Service.

James Ungerer, Mrs. Carl Ungerer, and Carl Ungerer

# Merry Christmas

FROM THE
CESSNA FAMILY

# 1949 - Year Four

As moderate weather continued into January, folks from town and the surrounding area dropped by to admire Marysville's new municipal airport. A squadron of fighter planes had flown over, resulting in curiosity and a barrage of questions for which we had no answer.

Fly-in visitors came and went, checking out Marysville's new airport. Although the number of students was falling off, student activity was strong, as those remaining, preparing for their private pilot flight checks, took advantage of pleasant flying weather. Our three commercial students, nearing the end of their course, were flying "day and night" to fulfill the requirements necessary.

Although I should have moved my office up on the hill after the improvements were approved in December, I postponed it as long as possible. Finally, I had no more excuses. Reluctantly, I transferred my files to the new administration building.

As I feared, it was lonely. It had to be manned, of course but, other than an occasional visitor out to see the new airport, all the action was down below. Carl brought the day's reports on students and airplane time each evening, and I still scheduled the flights—plane, student, and charter—and kept the records, but I was accustomed to being where the action was.

With not enough to do to fill the hours, I spent a lot of time eating M&M's from the machine that had been installed and staring out the windows, hoping, wishing for something to restore my life to normal.

I had to admit that the view from the administration building's wide windows was, indeed, beautiful. I could watch the planes taking off and landing from all the runways.

A new year and a new Marysville Municipal Airport required new field rules. The city posted:

> After takeoff, climb straight ahead to 400 feet. Level off then make a left hand 90 degree turn and climb to 500 feet.

> In leaving the pattern, make a 45 degree right-hand turn and fly straight ahead until clear of the field.
> If wind is 5 miles per hour or less, traffic will be on the southeast/ northwest runway to whichever direction the prevailing wind is closest. If no choice, landing will be to the southeast.

> After landing, all planes will make a left-hand turn and taxi back on that side of the runway except when landing to the southeast and returning to the hangar area. Then taxi straight ahead after landing and taxi straight ahead to end of runway.

> If landing to the southeast and returning to the new administration building or taxiing back for another take-off, then make a left-hand turn after landing.

# Marysville's Municipal Airport

As winter progressed, things were not going well for Marysville's Municipal Airport, which meant that things were not going well for Ungerer Flying Service. With the return of winter storms, the newly reconstructed runways waiting seeding in the spring were a quagmire of mud from melting snows. The condition remained critical through the early spring rains. Grosshan and Peterson had done a great job, but newly worked ground took much longer to recover from heavy rains and snows.

However, Carl's flying proficiency allowed him to take off and land on sodded areas paralleling the runway—as he always had under adverse conditions. This, of course, was not advisable for less experienced flyers.

The strips proved a life saver in that we could still accommodate an occasional charter passenger.

The bulk of our flights early in the year consisted of flying sightseers to the devastated areas to the north where seventy inches of snow had fallen since December 19. According to news reports, wind-driven blizzards had piled snow as high as forty feet in some areas. Roads were blocked, isolating a vast area, marooning farm families and leaving livestock without food or shelter.

The Army had dispatched equipment to the area to help reach the snowed-in farmers, and "Operation Haylift" flew planes from Fort Riley and other bases to drop hay to stranded livestock.

J.D. Rogers, Chairman of the Marysville Industrial Development Committee, was one of the charter passengers Carl flew to the northwest. The week following the flight, we were astonished by an article which appeared in both Marysville newspapers.

> "Marysville [Rogers wrote], is the owner of a very
> big, heavy eating WHITE ELEPHANT in the
> form of the Municipal Airport. As this now stands,
> and no prospects for it being anything else seem to
> be shaping up, this will never be anything but a
> WHITE ELEPHANT for the tax payers to sup-
> port."

Mr. Rogers strongly recommended that, rather than seeding the runways in the spring, they be hard topped, or covered with crushed rock.

The article was lengthy. Disconsolate, I stopped reading half way through. This had been Carl's and my baby for three years. We had worked hard to build our business and were proud of what we had accomplished, and now—

Although the condition—or the future—of the airport was no longer our responsibility, it saddened me to read what Rogers had written.

Late one morning, Carl drove up to the new office. He had just returned from driving John Haverfield, a Scott City cattleman, into town.

Haverfield, whom Carl had instructed where to land, had flown in to check on his cattle, part of a herd marooned by the blizzard. They had been hauled in and were being fed out at the Marysville stockyards before shipping to the St. Joseph stockyards to sell.

"How did the cattle look?" I asked.

"They're looking good considering what they've been through," Carl replied.

"Haverfield said his plane has been the best investment he ever made—a valuable asset to his business," he added. "After the storm, he used it to drop supplies to families and stranded cattle, and later to estimate cattle loss."

He stood and stretched then kissed me on the cheek.

"Guess I'd better get back down below. Just thought I'd stop in and say hello to my sweetie."

In spite of high hopes, the weather continued to be unpredictable well into March. Construction, rain, snow, sleet, and now mud had played havoc with flying.

Because of the poor runway conditions, alternating days of high winds and frequent rain showers, student training was practically at a standstill. Only the more experienced flyers dared brave the soggy runways.

In addition to that, the VA had approved only two GIs for commercial flight training.

After checking out his proficiency on a soft north/south runway, Carl allowed one of his students to fly to Salina to take his private pilot check.

He returned exuberant.

"If you're still in business," he said, "I'll be sending my son out for you to teach how to fly in a few years." He was a prospective father.

While flying lagged in Marysville, records were being broken nationwide. Bill Odom flew non-stop from Honolulu to New York in a single engine commercial aircraft, a distance of over 5,000 miles. A Boeing B-50 Superfortress (a revision of the B-29) flew around the world, a distance of 23,452 miles without stopping, and a Convair B-36—the largest mass-produced, piston-engined aircraft ever built—set a non-stop record of forty-three and $1/2$ hours without refueling, covering a distance of 9,600 miles.

During and after the war, I had prided myself on being good at aircraft recognition; however, as new planes continued to appear on the market, the planes I knew and recognized grew fewer. Records were being set in all phases of aviation including production and design. No sooner did a manufacturer come out with a "new, startling, and revolutionary" model than we read that it had been junked for something even more "new, startling, and revolutionary."

Now, only twenty-two years after Charles Lindbergh landed *The Spirit of St. Louis* at Le Bourget airport in Paris, France, at the time a doubtful accomplishment, we were hearing talk about man flying to the moon! To date, we had reached an altitude of almost fourteen miles, which left only 238,846 miles to go!

# Spring

With the coming of spring, the runways were fertilized and seeded with a mixture of grasses, reputed to be an ideal landing surface. Hopefully, with the warm spring weather, they would set in quickly.

Activity at Marysville Municipal Airport, however, was slower than it had been when Ungerer Flying Service went into business three and a half years ago. The excitement was gone, and the three of us had little to do to keep us busy. Because the condition of the runways was still undependable more often than not, pilots avoided Marysville except when necessary. Only a few planes flew in and out, and student training often came to a virtual halt.

Having little to do, Jim enrolled in the liaison pilot training school in Waco, Texas; once again, Carl and I were sole operators of the airport.

As business lagged, and with flying at a minimum, my newspaper column suffered. What does one write about when there is no flying?

During the latter part of April, flying began picking up, albeit slowly, and in early May five planes flew to Concordia for an invitational breakfast at the new Skyliner Motel, a marvelous prototype of what we might look forward to in the future.

After a delicious breakfast we were treated to a tour of the motel. In addition to the dining room and thirty-six beautifully decorated bedrooms, a broad lounge provided a view of both the highway and the rolling hills to the west, and the airport to the east. An apron surrounding the building made parking space available for both cars and planes.

Later in the week, an ever-hopeful representative of the Civil Air Patrol visited Marysville to meet with a group interested in organizing a Marysville unit. Although I was no longer a member, I was asked to act as captain of the unit. In hopes that a CAP unit would boost local interest in flying, I accepted on a temporary basis.

Dr. Randall, one of our most enthusiastic students when we first went into business, was still one of our most active pilots. Although boggy runways often kept him on the ground, he took to the air as often as weather and runway conditions allowed. Proud of his new Cessna 170, he used it for both business and pleasure trips, often combining the two.

Once he obtained his private pilot license, Mrs. Randall had been his first passenger. After he purchased the 170, she accompanied him on most of his trips.

In March, the newspaper reported:

> Dr. Randall, accompanied by Mrs. Randall flew to Kansas City this week, and from there to Chicago, where he attended a medical society meeting. They then flew to Evanston, Indiana, to visit their youngest daughter. After attending a medical conference in Wichita the following week, Dr. and Mrs. Randall flew to Hutchinson to spend a couple of days with their eldest daughter and family.

In May a photographer from *Plane News Magazine*, published by the Kamas Industrial Development Commission, flew to Marysville to take the doctor's photo with his new 170 in front of the new administration building,

Dr. Randall, manager of Western Auto, Fred Burris, Bob and Earl Craven of Craven Equipment Company, and Bus Vincent—the first of thirty-three students to obtain private pilot licenses through Ungerer Flying Service—were also among the most active. All four had purchased planes and used them consistently in their businesses.

The latter part of May, Carl took an overnight charter trip to Siloam Springs, Arkansas. After his return, he had very little to say about the trip and was unusually thoughtful for several days. When I asked him if anything was wrong, he said no.

His mood lasted until Sunday when, in spite of threatening skies and occasional showers, we had a burst of activity. I spent the day at the old office and a larger than usual crowd showed up. Dad and Lillian came out; we gave several rides and it was almost like the old days. Almost.

The rains began again in June. With no encouragement of any change in the foreseeable future, Carl decided it was time for a fishing trip to Lake McConaughy.

We took off during a brief break in the weather and an hour and a half later circled Johnson Lake south of Lexington, Nebraska, in a driving rain. The lake boasted a landing strip, so we set down to wait out the storm.

The rain let up after landing, and thirty minutes later we were on the water and had netted our first fish—a two-and-a-half-pound walleyed pike. Leaving the work and worry behind, our spirits lifted.

We fished until dark, tucked delicious steak dinners under our belts, and were off to bed.

The next morning, under clear skies, we packed up our tackle and took off for Lake McConaughy. We caught our limit in both walleye and crappie before nightfall and returned to Marysville the next morning feeling refreshed and in much better spirits.

The ringing of the alarm seemed a long way off, but when Carl reached over me to turn it off, I awoke with a start.

Four o'clock! If I lived to be a hundred, I'd never become accustomed to rising at such an ungodly hour.

I could hear Mrs. Jones's slippered feet shuffling down the stairs. She would have breakfast on the table by the time we dressed.

"Wish I was as organized as she is," I mumbled and swung my feet out of bed.

Grumbling, Carl stood and pulled on his trousers.

"Might as well go down and see what the weather's like this morning," he said.

We took our time dressing and, once down the stairs, went out onto the front porch. The sky was beginning to lighten in the east, and the stars sparkled brightly in the sky overhead. There was hardly any wind.

"Looks like it's going to be a good day for flying," Carl said.

When we entered the kitchen, the table was set, and Mrs. Jones had a dish of scrambled eggs, a platter of crisp bacon strips, and toast on the table. I gave her a hug and poured two mugs of coffee while Carl switched on the radio.

The news was just coming on. The headliner was a report that two gunmen, sought over a five-state area, were suspected of heading for northeast Kansas. They were, the reporter said, possibly already in the area.

The sun was just peeking over the horizon when we arrived at the airport. Together, we rolled the planes out of the hangar and tied them down on the flight line, then walked up the hill to the administration building. Carl read the paper before going down to wait for his first student, due to arrive at seven. The only one scheduled for the morning, he arrived promptly. After sending him on his way for a solo flight in the 120, Carl walked back up the hill.

We had settled down for a slow day when, at a quarter to ten, the first plane flew in. By eleven o'clock the airport was swarming with reporters and photographers from major city newspapers, pursuing the story of the two gunmen we'd heard about on the news.

I drove the reporter and photographer from Kansas City to the site where the suspects had last been seen and we arrived just before the arrest was made. The day had started out gloomy, but turned out to be one of the most exciting days Ungerer Flying Service had seen for some time.

On Sunday, four planes flew to Belleville to attend a flight breakfast sponsored by the pilots of Belleville and their wives. The ladies prepared and served a delicious breakfast at the country club across the road from the airport. As we ate, the topic of conversation was the manhunt earlier in the week and the Lockheed F-80 "Shooting Star" which had crossed the United States—2,445 miles in four hours and thirteen minutes—thereby setting a record.

The Belleville ladies listened in, entranced, and invited us back—anytime.

With the wheat harvest approaching, the spray planes returned. They did a lively business as the abundance of rain in recent months had caused weeds to flourish in ripening fields causing possible harvest difficulties. Grasshoppers, which were thriving in the weedy grain fields, were also a problem the spray planes would address.

A meadowlark, perched precariously on a strand of barbed wire outside my window, warbled loudly as if his mission was to entice me out into the fresh, morning air.

I rose from my desk and rested my chin on the window sill, watching him hop from strand to strand bursting forth in fresh song each time he changed positions.

"You've got a great life, little bird," I said. "You can fly, and you can sing—but you don't have to work. I'd come out and join you, but I have to man the phone."

I went back to entering figures in the six log books lying on my desk. An hour later, I heard the whirring sound of a plane coming in to land.

I watched from the door as Carl, flying the Blue Bird, landed and taxied toward the administration building.

I went out to meet him.

"How did it go?" I asked as he cut the motor and swung his long legs out of the cockpit.

"Could be something out there—eventually," he replied, as we returned to the office.

Drawing himself a cup of water from the dispenser, he added: "If any farm family could make good use of an airplane, it's the Daley's."

With the runways firming up, the charter business had picked up a little but, even so, with the few students we had, that wasn't enough to cover expenses. We were selling off an occasional training plane, and Carl had been looking for sales of new planes as a way to replenish our dwindling income. He had taken to "dropping in" on a couple of the farm families who, he felt, would benefit from adding a plane to their farm equipment.

The Daley's, one of a number of area farmers who relied on us to fly parts into their various fields, owned several hundred acres of wheat land, as well as corn, barley, maize, hay, and a large herd of cattle, in Oklahoma, Kansas, and Nebraska. An airplane would be a huge asset in helping them keep in touch with their holdings—especially during harvest and planting time.

Their Marshall County farm was one of several Carl visited occasionally.

"Roy and Guy are in Oklahoma getting machinery lined up for the harvest there," he continued. "Mama's the one I've got to sell anyway; she controls the pocketbook. I had a cup of coffee with her while we chatted—while *she* chatted, anyway—you should have heard her." His voice rose to a high falsetto. "Those boys! Always have to have some new-fangled piece of machinery. They're going to send me to the poor house yet with their wild spending. An airplane yet! Humph! Why in my day…"

I couldn't help laughing.

"Anyway, I listened for twenty minutes or so, thanked her for the coffee and that was that."

"It's still possible you can sell Roy and Guy."

"Yeah," he said. "But with farms in three different states, they're so busy, it's almost impossible to catch them when they're in the area." He stood.

"I've invited the Rotary Club members to come out for a tour of Marysville Municipal Airport now that it's completed," he said, heading for the door to return the Blue Bird to the hangar.

"When?"

"After the meeting tomorrow."

Dr. and Mrs. Randall and Daughter with New Cessna 170

# Rethinking

Carl had flown with three students early in the day. Around noon, the wind had increased to gale proportions and flying came to a stand-still; no one had flown—in or out.

Hopefully, it would calm down by seven when another student was scheduled to fly.

Carl was unusually thoughtful at lunch and when we returned to the airport, he leaned back in the chair, put his feet up on the desk, crossed his arms over his head, and stared out the window.

"You know," he said finally. "The longer I'm in this business, the more I wonder where it's going to end."

I was busily polishing the furniture, a never-ending task what with the broad windows and the dust stirred up by the wind. I turned to face him.

"What do you mean?"

"When I was at Salina the other day, Red and I got to discussing the flying business. You know—since the war, hundreds of small-town airports just like ours have cropped up all over the country. And do you know what's happening?"

I shook my head.

"Throughout the United States, these operations are training students, just as we are. Private, commercial, and instructors' ratings are being issued daily. Now take the private pilots: most of them will seldom, if ever, fly after they complete the training. Why? Because they can't afford to. Most of them are starting families, buying homes, establishing businesses. Even if they're working at a regular job and have no family to support, there's seldom enough money to put into something as expensive as flying.

"At first, they'll fly once in a while, to keep their hand in, but after the new wears off they'll fly little—if any. It'll make a lot of difference when the money has to come from their own pocket. Oh, we'll always rent a few planes; the charter service will hold up and, although there won't be as many, we'll continue to sign up an occasional new student.

"In spite of our sales talk, about flying being an easy, economical way to travel, flying is *not* a convenient or an inexpensive way to travel for the average John Doe. It is in some cases—sure—but not for everyone. Take us—we own all these planes—and we think nothing of going when and where we choose. We don't have a nine-to-five job we have to report to. But if we had to rent a plane to fly somewhere for the weekend, just how often would we do that?"

I began to understand what he was thinking.

"Not very damned often," he continued. "Maybe once a month—if we had a good job—and it would have to be a really good job. Why? Well in addition to the expense of renting a plane, there's the weather. How often can we depend on having two or three days of good flying weather? Not all that often. And most of these guys can't take a chance on getting weathered in somewhere and not being able to get back to work on Monday morning.

"Suppose you really wanted to continue flying and decided to buy a plane. Then you have, in addition to the cost of fuel, payments on the plane, hangar rent, insurance, upkeep, yearly inspections—more expenses than you have on a car, and you can use it only a percentage of the time—all dependent on the need, the convenience, *and* the weather.

"Then, when you do fly somewhere, you have to rent a car or take a cab to complete the trip to your destination."

"And, back at home, the wife is objecting because she's scared you might crash and get killed or injured; so you increase your accident insurance," I interjected.

Carl sat for a minute staring at the toes of his shoes.

"And—for those who want to make a career out of flying," he continued, "there are already thousands of well-trained pilots out there—trained by the Air Corps during the war who, if they didn't start an airport," he laughed, "are looking for a job. New pilots won't be able to compete for those jobs for years—not until the war-trained pilots begin to die off or get too old."

He slumped back in his chair.

"Do you see what I mean? Just where are we going? We're training pilots, but for what?"

"This isn't like you, Carl," I said. "You've been so enthusiastic about our business ever since you got out of the Air Corps. I don't understand your concern now. Even if what you say *is* true, we're opening up a whole new world to a lot of people. And, from a personal point of view, we have a good business and are making a fairly decent living. We just have to make a few adjustments, that's all."

"That's another thing I've been thinking about," he said, swinging his legs down off the desk. "*Are* we making a good living? We both work like hell—twelve to fifteen hours a day—and every cent we make goes back into the business. We started out great; we built an airport! We laid out runways, put up hangars, bought airplanes, and built a business. And where do we stand now? We're still paying for airplanes, the city owns the airport, and student flying has fallen off. We trained a lot of students, but we've skimmed the cream off the top and, with the government tightening down on GI training, we're going to be left with only a few GIs and an occasional civilian or commercial student."

I hesitated. I'd never seen Carl in such a mood. But, perhaps he was right; what did the future hold? Perhaps it *was* time we sat down and took a good hard look at where we were going. What he said was true; we had worked hard to make our dream come true. We *had* built an airport—and a business—and it had turned out pretty much as we'd hoped it would—

But now?

All those negative things he'd said were also true—but that was the dark side. There must be a bright side to the coin.

"Well," I said, "it's still the 'Air Age.' On the positive side, we almost have everything paid for. And there will always be people
**308**

who want to fly. Maybe not as many, but there will be student pilots as long as babies are born. And there'll always be charter flights—and rides—and a few who'll want to own their own planes. Then there'll be fuel to sell—and service—and hangar rent. We may not have the volume we once had, but neither will we have the expense—and we won't have to work so hard. Since we won't need as many planes, selling the surplus will make a difference financially."

"You're right," he agreed.

Taking a deep breath, he got up and walked to the window and stood, slouching, his hands in his pockets, staring out.

"Remember that charter trip I made to Arkansas?" he asked, turning back to face me.

I nodded.

"I like it down there," he said. "I got my training in two engine aircraft there. It's great for hunting and fishing—but—oh, what the hell!" he said and went out to service the Blue Bird.

A few days later, the wind slackened and traffic, both in and out, picked up. Carl made several flights to deliver parts to the harvest fields, including trips to Kansas City, Wichita, and other cities, for parts unavailable locally. He also made several commercial flights, one of which entailed flying the corpse of a baby to Kansas City. The infant, who had been killed in an automobile accident, was to be flown from there to Indiana.

# Business—As Usual

As I circled the Ace fifteen-hundred feet over Hanover, I kept a watchful eye on the planes on my wingtips.

At Carl's signal, I pulled the wheel back sharply. Depressing the left rudder, I entered into a tight spin over the downtown center while Carl peeled off to the left and George to the right to begin a series of wingovers. When I pulled out of the spin, they had maneuvered their planes to fall in behind me so that we were once more flying in formation. We circled twice more, then peeled off, one by one, to land in the pasture previously selected by Carl.

Although the maneuvers were not complicated, and placed no stress on the light aircraft, they provided entertainment for the crowd and drew passengers to the improvised landing strip.

We'd flown to Hanover after clearing our early morning trainees, arriving while the parade was in progress. Though simple, the routine, worked out by Carl over time, was successful as an attention-getter. It added aerial entertainment and served as our entrance.

When Carl asked George McAnany if he'd like to fly with us, he had been thrilled to take Jim's place.

Dad had flown in with Carl and had been dropped off at the pasture prior to the parade. By the time we landed, a crowd was already converging at the site and Dad had already sold enough ride tickets to keep Carl busy for quite some time. While he took off with his first passenger, George and I joined Dad, visiting and answering questions.

From the time we did our first, three years ago, we'd been in demand for events such as Pioneer Days, rodeos, and other celebrations. Today's occasion was Hanover's "Days Of '49."

The day was hot and sultry; the sun beat down mercilessly and the dust, stirred up by the trampling feet of the crowd, burned our throats and eyes. Although the field was otherwise suitable, the southwest wind made crosswind take-offs and landings necessary.

"I hope the wind doesn't get any stronger," I said as Dad and I paused in the shade of the wings of the L-2 for a sip from the water bottles tucked away in a bucket of ice. "Carl will be beat when evening comes."

A jar of lemonade and sandwiches put together by Mrs. Jones were cooling in the ice chest in the L-2. At noon, Carl took time out for a brief rest and a sandwich.

As the afternoon dragged by, the hot sun beat down mercilessly. The wind; however, continued to be moderate, the crowd enthusiastic.

We landed back at the airport at dusk.

"Are you sure you want to continue with these?" I asked, concerned, as Carl climbed out of the Blue Bird and limped slowly toward the office, his body bent from a long hot day in the cramped cockpit.

"I'll be all right after a cool bath and a good night's rest," he said, dropping into his chair. "I'm glad we don't have to go back tomorrow though. One day in this heat is enough."

When we counted our earnings for the day, it had turned out to be one of our most profitable.

"How many fairs do we have lined up?" he asked the next morning.

"Two fairs and a Pioneer Day," I replied.

Even though the runway surfaces were in flyable condition most of the time, we had never, in almost four years in business, seen activity at the airport so slow. A few planes flew in and out—both recreational and business—but it was nothing compared to previous years. Even charter flights had slowed down, and the number of students had fallen off to the point that we now scheduled appointments pretty much to suit our needs.

In mid-August, Carl flew three Marysville business men to Lake McConaughy for a couple days fishing.

Since Carl was Airport Manager, someone had to be at the airport at all times, so I was left in charge.

"IT PAYS TO GET THE BEST IN EDUCATION" read the heading to the quarter-page advertisement in *The Marysville Advocate*. The article continued, "The Marysville High School building, erected 1939, accredited as Class A, is rated one of the best in the state."

I laid the paper aside. I was bored and looking forward to Carl's return. I'd had a few solo students out, but business flights, both coming and going, were at a minimum.

The most interesting visitor was Dennis McClendon, of Decatur, Illinois, national director of the Flying Farmers. McClendon had stopped in to refuel on his way to the National Flying Farmers convention in Fort Collins, Colorado. Over 365 planes and 1,065 flyers were expected to attend the convention this year, he said.

I was shocked when, a few days later, I picked up the paper and my eyes fell on a news item: Starr Nelson, America's oldest flying farmer and a legend in Kansas flying circles, had suffered a heart attack and died while at the convention. He was eighty-four years old. According to the story, Starr had started flying at age seventy-eight and had logged more than 1,000 hours.

A few days later, more bad news dominated the headlines: While participating in The Thompson Trophy Race, held on September fifth, Bill Odom's P-51 had gone out of control on the second lap and crashed into a house near the airport. Odom, along with a woman and child on the ground, was killed.

The same newspaper reported that Britain had taken the lead in the development of jet airliners from the United States. "The utilization of American-built craft has been challenged by the successful maiden flight of the British-built De Haviland Comet—the world's first jet-powered airliner," the article read.

Flying conditions had been fairly decent during Carl's absence, but shortly after his return, it began to rain. Since the grass sod had not yet set, muddy runways were, again, a major problem. Our commercial trainees could handle it, but in order to catch up on schedule, Carl flew a couple of fledgling students to Beatrice, where they could fly off hard-topped runways.

Our three commercial pilot trainees were nearing completion of the course and were flying day and night to meet the requirements necessary for the flight check. Experience in cross country and night flying, as well as proficiency in flight maneuvers and a well-grounded knowledge of navigation, meteorology, etc., were necessary before qualifying to take passengers for hire.

When Jim returned home, after completing the liaison pilot course in September, there wasn't enough activity at the airport to keep him busy. Rather than sit around and twiddle his thumbs after he checked the planes over, he took a job with Stanton Hardware.

# Deer Hunting

"**L**et's go deer hunting!" Carl said.

"But we can't both leave the airport."

"Sure we can. Flying is almost at a standstill. We'll leave Wallace in charge."

Wallace, my brother, was a commercial student and would soon complete his training. He would be happy to take on the airport manager job for a week.

Carl, Dad, I, and three local businessmen left Marysville on October 11 and drove to Colorado. This would be my first deer hunting experience.

We drove two cars loaded down with guns, tents, folding cots and blankets, and a food supply put together by Dad and Lillian—five fried chickens, potato salad, a large ham, five pounds of bacon, five pounds of cheese, eight loaves of bread, six pounds of coffee, a sack of potatoes, a dozen cans each of soup, beans, spaghetti, meat, and vegetables, plus utensils, cups, and paper plates.

Mayor Kenny Henderson drove his car, accompanied by Ken Erit, while Dad, Bud Koppes, and I rode with Carl, our car optimistically pulling a trailer in which to bring back the deer.

Carl seemed to be unusually thoughtful the entire trip.

"How would you like to move to Arkansas and live off the land?" he asked one morning. We were sitting behind a crop of rocks with a view of the valley below, waiting to sight a deer.

"*What?*" I exclaimed, stunned by the question.

"Shhhh. Not so loud," he said. "I just asked how you'd like to move to Arkansas."

"You mean give up our flying business?"

He nodded.

"You're serious?"

"Yep."

I had to think about that. I knew he'd had something on his mind and, although he'd mentioned Arkansas before, I hadn't taken him seriously. Talk about drastic moves! Flying had been our life for four years; more than that for Carl. It was hard to imagine doing anything else.

Before I could reply, a big buck appeared, not thirty feet away.

"Shoot!" Carl said.

All thoughts of Arkansas disappeared a few minutes later. I had bagged my first deer!

Edna with Deer

# A Decision

I n the excitement, nothing more was said about Arkansas until we returned to Marysville. On his way out the door one morning, Carl pulled a scrap of paper from his pocket and tossed it on my desk. It was a United Farm Agency advertisement.

"Order their brochure," he said, and left the office.

*So, he* is *serious,* I thought.

I ordered the brochure.

As was usually the case, when Carl made up his mind, things moved fast.

The brochure arrived a week later. We spent several evenings studying it.

"I kind of like the looks of this," he said, pointing at a listing with an agent in Hardy, Arkansas.

"Are you sure this is what you want to do?" I asked. "What if we move and you don't like it?"

"What's not to like?" he said. "There's a lot of game—all kinds of game, in fact—and the fishing can't be beat. We've already talked about where this flying business is going. We're signing up fewer and fewer students. We could probably sweat it out, but why? I think we've earned a little R and R."

"But how will we earn a living?"

"We'll live off the land," he replied. "In addition to the wild game and fish, we'll buy a few cattle and some chickens, grow a garden—take it easy for a change."

I thought about that as I made the call for an appointment.

A week later, we drove to Arkansas.

We met the agent, Web Long, and his wife, Juanita, acting secretary, at his office. They were a lovely couple, exuding friendliness.

"Another family business," I said as we shook hands.

"I don't think they could do without us," Juanita smiled.

And, just like that, I knew I'd met a life-long friend.

Long had sold the property we'd inquired about, but said he had another place he thought we'd like even better.

Up and down hills and around more curves than I could count, we drove through some of the most beautiful country I'd ever seen, finally breaking from the heavy woods into a clearing where sat a small frame house and an out-of-this-world view of the Ozark hills.

"What do you think?" Carl asked that night as we prepared for bed in a rustic, though comfortable motel. "Do you think you'd like to live there?"

"It *is* beautiful," I said, "but are you sure you want to give up on the airport?"

"Yeah. I'm afraid I'm all flown out, Honey," he said, his expression rueful.

The next afternoon, papers signed, transaction in progress, we headed back to Marysville and began to pack.

The week after Thanksgiving, we returned to Hardy to finalize the purchase of 640 acres of land.

On December first, Carl handed in his resignation as airport manager. The mayor tried to talk him out of it, of course, but Carl was adamant.

Mrs. Jones stayed with us to the end. Because of her arthritis, she wasn't much help with packing, but she served our meals, did our laundry, and, despite the mess made in packing, kept the house picked up as best she could.

She was firm in her decision not to live with her daughter so, after careful investigation, Rose talked her into entering the new nursing home. She would have friends her age there, and care would be available should she need it.

# Goodbye

The transition was going smoothly, but there was one more thing I needed to do before leaving Marysville.

My grandmother had recently celebrated her eighty-sixth birthday, and my mother had written to say that she was failing. Grandma, who had raised me, meant more to me than anyone except Carl. I felt I had to see her one more time before moving even further away.

Carl opted not to go. He would stay and continue to get everything in order before we left.

I took off in the Ace on a bright, sunny morning for the flight to Liberal. Flying into a headwind, I arrived shortly after noon.

As I flew the downwind leg of the flight pattern at the old Liberal Air Base—now the Liberal Municipal Airport—the gigantic empty hangars sprawled ludicrously on acres of concrete below.

I wished Carl had come with me. Had it been only five years since this vast expanse of runways, taxiways, and aprons—this monument to other days—had buzzed with the activity of B-24 Liberators? It seemed so long ago—another world. The small planes, now flying in and out, looked like flies buzzing over a flat cake.

*What a waste*, I thought.

Liberal had changed so rapidly when the air base came to town— mushrooming from a sleepy prairie town into a buzzing war town within weeks. I thought of the excitement as the town grew, becoming populated—over-populated—first with construction workers and their families, then with airmen who lived both on and off base. Finally, we had watched in awe as the gigantic B-24 Liberator bomber planes flew in.

I offered up a prayer that those days would never return—that the air base would continue to be what it was now—a monument to the past. It had served its purpose then and, although the space was excessive, it now served another purpose.

I landed, and as I taxied past the monstrous empty hangars, I spied a lone B-24 surrounded by a rank overgrowth of grass and weeds, its presence guarding the base of which it once was Lord.

Even before the war ended these planes, outliving their usefulness, were being replaced by an even more impressive machine— the B-29 Superfortress—newer, faster, longer range, and boasting more sophisticated equipment.

The aviation industry, under the driving, prodding, necessity of war, had designed, invented, and produced new war planes with giant strides which had carried forward into the post-war era.

Thinking about it, I was glad that I'd been a part—though ever so small a part—of such an exciting era.

Despite my delay, my mother and stepfather were there to meet me. Even though Mama and I had never been close, she seemed overjoyed to see me.

"Grandma doesn't get around much anymore," Mama said as we drove to Kismet. "I doubt if she'll be with us much longer." Tears filled my eyes.

When we arrived at Mama's house, it was like being in a different world; a world I'd never been a part of; nor did I want to be now. But spending time with Grandma, for even a short time, meant everything to me.

I slept in the twin bed in her room, and we spent every waking minute talking about the years I had spent with her as a child. For me, they were happy years. Talking about them, I often elicited a smile.

"Remember the time when I was five, Grandma, that we drove to Waynoka, Oklahoma to visit Granddaddy's relatives?" I asked, hoping to unveil a secret from the past.

She nodded. "That was a long time ago, child," she said.

"I remember it though. Who was the old man Granddaddy spent so much time with?"

"Old man?"

"Yes. He was confined to his bed; Granddaddy spent most of our time there with him."

"I don't remember."

We talked about roaming the prairie and picking wild flowers and looking for arrow heads. Remembering, Grandma smiled.

And then it was time to say goodbye.

"See you later, Grandma," I said, kissing her on the brow.

As I walked to the car, I burst into sobs. It had been good to spend time with my grandmother—but I was sad. This might well be the last time I would see her.

As planned, I took off at noon for the return trip home. As I flew eastward, events of the past two days flooded my mind.

Though Kansas is seldom considered beautiful by outsiders, I have always appreciated the magnificence of this state. I sensed a glamour, an excitement, not often seen by strangers. I loved the golden wheat fields, the prairie, the rolling Flint Hills; the cliffs, canyons, and dry riverbeds; the ever-changing scenery which stretched out below as I flew from the extreme south-western corner of the state to Marysville far to the northeast.

I never looked out across the plains—the prairie, now marked with narrow ribbons of black-topped highways—without visualizing the mystery and the changing drama of days gone by—the Indian tribes, the buffalo, the wagon trains plodding westward, cattle herds, and cowboys.

Huge tumbleweeds, tossing south across the plain below, indicated that the wind had become stronger. I adjusted my compass reading to keep the Ace on course. Checking my position on the map, I saw that my ground speed was slower. If the wind direction and velocity remained constant, I would arrive at the Marysville airport about thirty minutes later than I'd calculated.

As a life-long Kansan, I was accustomed to change. I smiled, thinking of a favorite expression during the war: "You don't like the weather? Just wait a few minutes. It'll change!"

I've always found cross country flying boring. There isn't much to do. While Carl prefers higher altitudes, I enjoy flying at a lower level where there is more to see. Though the landscape is pretty from a higher altitude, you're too far away to enjoy the detail or anything of significance on the ground.

Now, flying at 500 feet, I admired a herd of Hereford cattle, spread out below, grazing the prairie grasses. Off to the left, four coyotes trotted single file down a narrow ravine. Partially concealed by dense wild plum bushes, they looked like large friendly dogs rather than predators searching for the rabbits and birds seeking refuge in the ravine.

Further on, buzzards circled an almost picked-clean carcass of a cow while crows and smaller birds fluttered about in the perimeter. Occasionally, a brave one darted in to grab a morsel. How had the cow died? I wondered. Perhaps giving birth? Coyotes, wolves, and bobcats seldom attacked a large, healthy animal. It could have broken a leg leaping the ravine. Then it would have been easy prey.

The weather had been relatively mild, the eastern Kansas countryside still fairly green for December. Small fields, orchards, and flowing streams began to appear below. Soon, I would be home.

My thoughts turned to what lay ahead. Arkansas was beautiful, but I hated to leave Kansas.

We had debated as to whether or not to take a plane with us but decided it would be an unneeded expense since the nearest airport (West Plains) was almost fifty miles from our ranch.

We weren't expecting to do much flying anyway.

We had already sold all but two planes—the 170 and the Ace.

Offered for sale, they'd gone quickly. I breathed a sigh of relief when George McAnany bought our faithful old L-2 which had patiently waited out the war in Dad's garage and had been our standby through the years. It had brought me here the first time I'd seen Marysville. I'd gotten my private pilot license in the L-2; it had landed me in one piece in a raging storm, brought us safely through coyote hunts and gales and landed us unharmed when we overshot daylight hours.

As Marysville hove into sight I smiled to myself, my mind turning to the first time I viewed this scene when, as a bride, I'd flown here with Carl in the L-2 over five years ago. To think of all that had happened since then was mind-boggling. I had grown to love this town. It had welcomed me with open arms. To be honest, it had been my first real home. This change would be as drastic as was starting our flying service four years ago.

As I entered the flight pattern, I thought of those early days—the struggle to get "our airport" and flying service started—

How exciting it had been!

My eyes fell on the big hangar, its aluminum siding gleaming in the setting sun. In my mind's eye, I could see Carl and Dad hammering away, building our first shelter for the L-2 and the post-war planes we hoped to acquire. Sitting snuggly adjacent to the hangar was the "henhouse" office in which I'd spent so many hours tussling with government forms; and there, sitting on the flight line alone—as it had then—was the L-2.

The old windsock on the eave of the hangar came to life as I cut the throttle and headed into the wind for a landing. This would probably be the last time. I brushed a tear from my eye.

As I touched down, I wondered what it would be like "living off the land."

# Postscripts

# The Flying Ungerers
# Jim and Frederick

After completing his Liaison Pilot Training in September, Jim returned to Marysville. Since activity was still falling off at the airport, there was very little for him to do, so he took a job with Stanton Hardware. After Carl resigned in December, Jim was appointed Airport Manager, a position he held while still working at Stanton Hardware, and continued after he opened his own business—an office supply store, in 1958.

Jim and Nelda had four children: Jim, Jeff, Marna, and Jon. Jon is the only offspring of the "Flying Ungerers" still living in Marysville.

Frederick, the fourth "Flying Ungerer," operated his Welding and Repair Shop until moving to Wichita to work for Cessna Aircraft Corporation. He and Viola had four children: Frederick, Jr., Max, Doris, and Vicky.

Jim and Nelda Ungerer: Jim Receives his Liaison Pilot Wings

# Living Off the Land

I n 1949, my husband, Carl, and I decided to move to Arkansas, take life easy, and "live off the land." We had been operating a flying service in Marysville, Kansas, since the end of the war, and before that Carl had flown B-24s and B-29s for the Air Corps. I was a photographer.

About as close as either of us had come to farming was Carl weeding his dad's annual spring garden when he was a boy. He figured, however, that anyone intelligent enough to fly bombers and operate airports surely had enough sense to learn how to farm.

We ordered a United Farm Agency catalog, contacted an agent in Hardy, Arkansas, made an appointment to look at some property, and headed south.

Why did we choose this area? Because of the abundance of wild game; Carl loved to hunt and fish.

At the agent's office, we looked at brochures and discussed available properties. We chose one that, according to Carl, sounded exactly like what we were looking for, then we headed for the country – or, to be more exact, the hills.

## Home sweet home

After driving several miles over a rough gravel road, we turned onto a narrow rocky lane. After "hitting bottom" a few times, we rounded a curve and pulled up in front of a small white house sitting on the crest of a hill.

Even in winter, the view was spectacular. Like a painting, the lane continued its winding course down the hill and disappeared into the forest. Beyond, ridge upon ridge of tree-covered mountains blended into the azure-blue sky.

The house, divided equally into four square rooms, was a definite "fixer-upper." There was no electricity and no well. Outside the back door was a cistern, a work shed with stairs leading to a cellar, and an outhouse – all in need of repair.

A large garden plot, a small chicken house, and a large red barn with a fenced-in corral sat to the west of the house. The lane to the east led past a small orchard and on to the "bottomland" divided by a clear-water creek.

Though the setting was nice, I thought the place was a little too run-down and remote. After looking everything over, however, Carl said, "It's exactly what we're looking for."

It didn't take a rocket scientist to figure out that the selling point was the abundance of fish in Spring River, just down the hill, and the hundreds of acres of forest, rife with game.

Back in town, we completed the paperwork, then headed back to Marysville, where we traded the car for a Chevy pickup and began to pack. A month later we moved into our new home.

## Making the most of the land

Once settled in, we visited the county extension office. The county agent gave us a stack of pamphlets and assured us that living off the land was indeed possible. (Doing so while taking life easy, we learned, was another matter.)

A farmer could produce all the food necessary for a family of four for a total expenditure of only $20 per month, the agent said. This would go for flour, sugar, coffee and salt. (The cost would be less if the farmer grew his own grain and ground it into flour, kept bees for honey, and substituted herbal teas for coffee.)

Carl signed up for weekly classes on livestock care, crop cultivation, gardening and more, conducted by the extension service, and we returned home to spend the next two days studying the pamphlets.

Our initial livestock purchase was a starter herd of Hereford cattle, a Duroc brood sow, and a dozen Leghorn hens and a rooster. We also bought three horses – a work team and a riding horse we named Trigger. However, Carl wound up riding one of the workhorses most of the time because he could never catch Trigger when he needed a horse to ride.

With spring just around the corner, we tackled the garden, which was overgrown with weeds. A neighbor kindly contributed a load of chicken manure to fertilize the soil, and after the garden had been plowed, fertilized, disked, harrowed and rid of rocks that surfaced during the process, we drove stakes into the ground and strung cord from one end of the garden plot to the other to make nice straight rows.

According to our neighbor, the "natives" always planted English peas on February 8. While we were at it, we also planted radishes, onions and lettuce. The weather was warm for February and, to our delight, in less than a week, tiny seedlings emerged from the ground. In the weeks that followed, we also planted tomatoes, cucumbers, green beans and corn.

Carl built an irrigation system to pump water from Spring River, and our garden thrived.

Until he had time to build a filter and clean out the cistern, we carried water to the house from a spring that also provided an abundance of delicious watercress for the table.

## Producing our own food

Next we purchased 100 baby chicks to raise for fryers, and a Guernsey cow named Elsie.

Observing local custom, we planted vegetables again in July, and yet again in September.

We also planted raspberry vines, strawberries and rhubarb. The orchard provided all the apples we could eat, and from the wild we gathered blackberries, mushrooms, watercress, black walnuts, persimmons and a delicious, nutritious green called poke sallet.

Our flock of hens supplied more eggs than we could eat, and Elsie provided us with milk, cream, cottage cheese, yogurt and cheese. I learned to make butter by shaking sour cream in a half-gallon jar until it separated into butter and buttermilk.

Butchering the animals was our most daunting task, but we

somehow managed to accomplish it, and we learned to follow instructions accurately to cure hams and bacon.

Though I approached the canning process skeptically, it wasn't as difficult as I'd expected. Before summer was over, the cellar was stocked with pint and quart jars of vegetables and fruits, as well as jams, jellies and preserves.

Before frost, we stored winter radishes, turnips, beets and carrots between layers of hay in an underground pit, and we pulled the tomato vines, laden with green tomatoes, and stored them in the cellar. (Our Christmas dinner included sliced tomatoes, ripened on the vine.)

Although chores were demanding, we found time to hunt and fish, supplementing the beef, pork and chicken we raised with quail, rabbit, squirrel, deer, trout and bass.

Not long before moving to Arkansas, we'd purchased a new electric range, refrigerator, freezer and washer. However, with no electricity, my beautiful appliances stood idle in a bedroom corner for more than a year while I washed clothes on a scrub board, preserved our food in an antiquated icebox, and prepared our meals on a wood-burning range.

One thing I never learned to do was build a proper fire. Carl often came into the house at noon to find no meal on the table, and me, frustrated and in tears, struggling to get a fire going.

The day The North Arkansas Electric Cooperative crews came through, clearing trees to install poles and string wire, was a memorable occasion. Within weeks we had electricity, and life became easier and much less complicated.

I had never doubted Carl's ability to master the art of farming, but, as I told a friend, "If I can do it, anyone can!"

We learned a lot that first year. The county agent had been right. It was possible not only to live off the land, but to live well. We learned we were more resourceful than we'd ever dreamed and, though not easy, with a little ingenuity and a lot of hard work, life could be very rewarding.

# Marysville Municipal Airport Today

The Marysville Municipal Airport in 2018 is considered one of the finest, as well as one of the busiest, small airports in northeast Kansas.

The airport now boasts a 4,200 by 60-foot northwest/southeast lighted asphalt runway, paralleled by a full-length taxi strip. Lighting improvements include precision approach path indicator lights and instrument approach lights in both directions, a new beacon on a 40-foot-tall pole, and a lighted wind cone which tells pilots the wind's direction at night.

A lighted 50-by-50 foot helipad is present for the convenience of *Lifestar* and other helicopter pilots. The airport also boasts AWOS-III—an automated airport weather monitoring system. There are now eleven hangars and nine planes are currently based there.

With help to the city from both the state and federal governments in the past decade, several million dollars has been invested in the facility. It now accommodates small jets and serves the area's business community, medical providers, flight ambulance services, recreational pilots, military planes and helicopters, and occasional operations from Fort Riley. It is also used heavily by agriculture spray planes for both spraying and air seeding.

There is no on-site manager at the airport. It is managed by the Marysville city clerk. Flight instruction is provided to those wanting to learn to fly by a local instructor.

Landoll Corporation, which has 800 employees and is one of the leading industrial transportation manufacturers in the United States, is responsible for a large portion of the traffic, both in and out, as company executives, farmers, and other customers fly in for business dealings with the company. The company is a recognized leader in innovative design, world-class manufacturing, and marketing of quality products and services for the agriculture, transportation, material handling, OEM and government industries. Over the years, Don Landoll, founder and sole owner of the corporation, has contributed financially to improvements to the airport. He has also played a significant role in the local community and surrounding areas since 1963. The corporation houses four aircraft at the airport, and Mr. Landoll himself flies a TBM850 Socata.

Current information about the airport was provided by Landoll Corporation.

# Chapter Notes

"Air Base" is a version of the chapter printed in *Fragile Hopes, Transient Dreams* (publisher, date).

A version of "I Learned About Flying From That" appeared in the "I Learned About Flying From That" column in the December 1950 issue of *FLYING* magazine.

"Living Off the Land" was published in the May/June 2011 issue of *Grit Magazine*.

Photos not otherwise credited are from the family and/or courtesy of the *Marysville Advocate* and the former *Marshall County News*.

# Acknowledgments

DECEMBER 9, 2018

My deepest appreciation to all those who contributed in so many ways to the successful publication of *Headwinds*. The following are not listed in order of importance. Each and every one was equally important in bringing *Headwinds* to market.

First, my thanks to my editor, Roy Beckemeyer, a writer himself who, despite his busy schedule, was instrumental in getting *Headwinds* put together and off to market. I encourage you to read his latest book of poems: *Stage Whispers.*

I will be forever grateful to Byron and Eulala Guise, publishers of *The Marysville Advocate*, for their love, encouragement and support during the years we created and operated Marysville's first airport. *Headwinds* would not have been possible were it not for their many articles, columns, and photos. May they rest in peace.

I am also obliged to the publishers of *The Marshall County News* for their support "back then." And for the many articles, columns, and photos that make up this book. Sadly, the newspaper is no longer being published.

Thank you as well to Sarah Kissenger, present owner and publisher of *The Marysville Advocate*, for the publicity she has given us and her support and assistance in obtaining needed information.

Thanks also to Jim, Jeff, Marna, and Jon Ungerer, children of Jim, one of the "Flying Ungerers," who so kindly provided information, photos, and support vital to the book.

Peg Nichols, friend and a terrific writer herself, for her critiques, advice and support during the development of *Headwinds*. Thanks for the great title, Peg! (The wind was so prevalent; I wonder if it shouldn't be listed as a character)? You wrote a superb blurb!

Don Landoll, founder, owner and chairman of Landoll Corporation, and his "top man," Coby Sedlacek who provided information and photos of the present-day Marysville Municipal Airport for the addendum to *Headwinds*.

Desiree Ultican, who not only worked diligently; bringing 70-year-old photos back to life, but also designed the cover.

Dianna Booth Byrd, who has been at my side, provided the love and support as I faced the challenge of bringing the story to life.

# About the Author

**Edna Bell-Pearson's stories, articles, essays, and poems** have appeared in hundreds of magazines, newspapers, literary journals, and anthologies world-wide. She has published six books. She is most noted for ***Fragile Hopes, Transient Dreams and Other Stories***, a Southwest Kansas saga, which was chosen during Kansas sesquicentennial year, as one of "150 Best Kansas Books."

## BELL-PEARSON'S BOOKS:

*Fragile Hopes, Transient Dreams and Other Stories* - A Family Saga
(Chosen as one of 150 Kansas Best Books)

*Cul de Sac* – The life and times of retirees living on a Cul de Sac in Paradise Village

*Caribbean Sunrise* – A Romantic/Suspense Novella

*7½ 1 BIG STEPS – Stories From the Yucatan Peninsula*

*Charlie* – A Novel

*James and Jack* – A Young Adult Novel

# www.bell-pearson.com

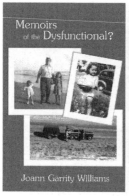

# WWW.MEADOWLARK-BOOKS.COM

Specializing in Books by Authors from the Heartland since 2014

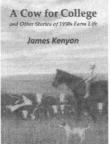

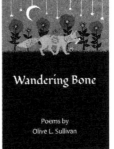

**Memoirs by Meadowlark Books**

*A Cow for College and Other Stories of 1950s Farm Life*
By James Kenyon


*Memoirs of the Dysfunctional?*
By Joann Garrity Williams


*Headwinds, a Memoir*
By Edna Bell-Pearson


Coming 2019
*And I Cried, Too: Confronting Evil in a Small Town*
By Mike Hartnett


Coming 2020
*The Land that I Love: Rural America and Four Miles per Hour*
By Lisa D. Stewart

Made in the USA
Columbia, SC
29 January 2021

31940900R00191